International Security in Practice

How do once bitter enemies move beyond entrenched rivalry at the diplomatic level? In one of the first attempts to apply practice theory to the study of International Relations, Vincent Pouliot builds on Pierre Bourdieu's sociology to devise a theory of practice of security communities and applies it to post-Cold War security relations between NATO and Russia. Based on dozens of interviews and a thorough analysis of recent history, Pouliot demonstrates that diplomacy has become a normal, though not a self-evident, practice between the two former enemies. He argues that this limited pacification is due to the intense symbolic power struggles that have plagued the relationship ever since NATO began its process of enlargement at the geographical and functional levels. So long as Russia and NATO do not cast each other in the roles that they actually play together, security community development is bound to remain limited.

VINCENT POULIOT is Assistant Professor in the Department of Political Science at McGill University. His PhD, on which this book is based, was awarded the 2009 Vincent Lemieux Prize by the Canadian Political Science Association.

Cambridge Studies in International Relations: 113

International Security in Practice

Cambridge Studies in International Relations is a joint initiative of Cambridge University Press and the British International Studies Association (BISA). The series will include a wide range of material, from undergraduate textbooks and surveys to research-based monographs and collaborative volumes. The aim of the series is to publish the best new scholarship in International Studies from Europe, North America and the rest of the world.

Cambridge Studies in International Relations

Series list continues after index

International Security in Practice

The Politics of NATO–Russia Diplomacy

VINCENT POULIOT

CAMBRIDGE UNIVERSITY PRESS

CAMBRIDGE UNIVERSITY PRESS
Cambridge, New York, Melbourne, Madrid, Cape Town, Singapore,
São Paulo, Delhi, Dubai, Tokyo

Cambridge University Press
The Edinburgh Building, Cambridge CB2 8RU, UK

Published in the United States of America by Cambridge University Press, New York

www.cambridge.org
Information on this title: www.cambridge.org/9780521122030

First published 2010

Printed in the United Kingdom at the University Press, Cambridge

A catalogue record for this publication is available from the British Library

Library of Congress Cataloguing in Publication data
Pouliot, Vincent, 1979–
    International security in practice : the politics of NATO–Russia diplomacy / Vincent
    Pouliot.
      p.   cm. – (Cambridge studies in international relations ; 113)
    ISBN 978-0-521-19916-2 (hardback)
    1. Security, International.   2. North Atlantic Treaty Organization–Russia
    (Federation)   3. Russia (Federation)–Foreign relations.   I. Title.   II. Series.
    JZ5930.P68 2010
    327.4701821–dc22   2009043235

ISBN 978-0-521-19916-2 Hardback
ISBN 978-0-521-12203-0 Paperback

Diplomacy is letting someone else have your way.
Lester B. Pearson, Nobel Peace Prize (1957)

Contents

Figures and tables

Preface

I have long been convinced that the practice of diplomacy is just as necessary to International Relations (IR) theory as the latter is to the former. While I am far from the first to put forward such an argument, in this book I try to substantiate it with a new perspective on international politics largely inspired by Pierre Bourdieu's sociology. As powerful as theory may be to explain the origins and structure of contemporary practices, abstract models and concepts generally are unable, in and of themselves, to account for the practical logics that make everyday action possible and meaningful. Hence my recourse to *practice theory*, an oxymoron that aptly captures the particular bent of this book.

One generation after the end of the Cold War, continuing tensions in security relations between the North Atlantic Treaty Organization (NATO) and Russia constitute something of a tragedy in international politics. Despite some progress, both sides have missed a rare opportunity to genuinely pacify and finally move beyond self–fulfilling security dilemmas. Things obviously did not have to go that way; if this book can help explain what went wrong and why in the post-Cold War Russian-Atlantic relationship, it will have achieved more than I can hope. In a pragmatic spirit, my analysis starts with the world as its actors have (erratically) shaped it. I am not normatively attached to current forms of interstate diplomacy and I do hope that better alternatives are in the making. In the meantime, however, I believe that IR scholarship should try to illuminate, in a rigorous and thorough fashion, the political and social dynamics that too often produce self-defeating outcomes on the international stage. The task I set myself in this book is thus primarily analytical. Its critical implications are in showing, first, how things could have been otherwise in NATO–Russia diplomacy and, second, what prevented both sides from taking a direction more favorable to peace.

An impressive number of people have helped with the completion of this book. It started as a PhD dissertation at the University of Toronto, where I was blessed with the mentorship, supervision and now friendship of Emanuel Adler. Emanuel will have a deep and lasting influence on my thinking and I learned a great deal from his constant stimulation and intellectual exchange. As well as being a first-rate mind, he is also a very kind and supportive human being who will inspire my own professorship for long years to come. I am also grateful to David Welch and Stefano Guzzini, the other two dissertation committee members, who provided very useful advice along the way.

During my PhD years and later, a number of scholars were kind enough to read my works and comment on them extensively, demonstrating in and through practice that debate and critique are the real engines of social scientific refinement. Among them I am especially indebted to Alexander Wendt, who generously encouraged me and shared his thoughts with me on my theoretical works very early on; to Michael Williams, who was a tremendous source of intellectual and personal inspiration in using Bourdieu in the study of international security; as well as to Iver Neumann, who enthusiastically communicated his passion for social theory and Russian politics at a later stage of writing. Other members of the academic community who generously helped along the way include, with apologies to those inadvertently omitted: Amar Athwal, Steven Bernstein, Janice Bially Mattern, Christian Büger, Jeffrey Checkel, James Der Derian, Raymond Duvall, Henry Farrell, Karin Fierke, William Flanik, Frank Gadinger, Catherine Goetze, Patricia Greve, Lene Hansen, Matthew Hoffman, Ted Hopf, Jef Huysmans, Patrick Jackson, Markus Kornprobst, Érick Lachapelle, Niels Lachmann, Anna Leander, Halvard Leira (and other NUPI staff), Catherine Lu, Gale Mattox, Frédéric Mérand, Jennifer Mitzen, Daniel Nexon, T. V. Paul, Liliana Pop, Edward Schatz, William Schlickenmaier, Nisha Shah, Ole Jacob Sending, Jean-Philippe Thérien, Trine Villumsen, Antje Wiener and Ruben Zaiotti. Many thanks to each of them for their valued contribution to my thinking.

John Haslam, Carrie Parkinson and the rest of the team at Cambridge University Press provided timely guidance in the final stages of production. I am also grateful to my research assistants Virginia DiGaetano and Séverine Koen, who not only helped with copyediting but also pushed me to clarify important parts of my argument. In addition,

I want to thank the editors and publishers of the *Journal of Peace Research* (Sage), *International Organization* (Cambridge University Press) and *International Studies Quarterly* (Wiley Blackwell) for allowing me to reuse and build upon already published materials. Chapter 1 contains a summary of my "Pacification Without Collective Identification: Russia and the Transatlantic Security Community in the Post-Cold War Era," *Journal of Peace Research* 44(5): 603–20; Chapter 2 is a revised and expanded version of "The Logic of Practicality: A Theory of Practice of Security Communities," *International Organization* 62(2): 257–88; and Chapter 3 draws on and further develops "'Sobjectivism': Toward a Constructivist Methodology," *International Studies Quarterly* 51(2): 359–84.

A number of institutions provided invaluable practical support, in particular by making possible the many trips abroad that my methodology required. Many thanks to the Trudeau Foundation (including Lloyd Axworthy), the Social Sciences and Humanities Research Council of Canada (SSHRC), the Fonds québécois pour la recherche sur la société et la culture (FQRSC) and the University of Toronto's School of Graduate Studies, Centre for International Studies and Department of Political Science. I also want to thank Jocelyne Mathieu and Tanya Mogilevskaya who helped organize my stay in Moscow through the Université Laval's Centre Moscou–Québec. I finally want to acknowledge my many interviewees who spared some of their precious time to meet with me and made the whole project much more interesting.

My deepest debt of gratitude goes to my partner Magdaline Boutros, who staunchly stayed on my side throughout the PhD's hardships and beyond. I discussed many of the ideas below with her first, and she turned out to be at once my toughest critic and my strongest supporter. My most sincere thanks for all the happiness – past, present and future.

I dedicate the book to my parents, Lorraine and Claude, whose delicate care and stimulating upbringing lie behind much of what follows.

Abbreviations

ABM	Anti-Ballistic Missile (treaty)
BBC	British Broadcasting Corporation
CFE	Conventional Forces in Europe (treaty)
CIS	Commonwealth of Independent States
CSCE	Conference on Security and Cooperation in Europe
CSTO	Collective Security Treaty Organization
EAPC	Euro-Atlantic Partnership Council
EU	European Union
G8	Group of Eight
IFOR	Implementation Force
IR	International Relations
ISAF	International Security Assistance Force
KFOR	Kosovo Force
NAC	North Atlantic Council
NACC	North Atlantic Cooperation Council
NATO	North Atlantic Treaty Organization
NRC	NATO–Russia Council
OSCE	Organization for Security and Cooperation in Europe
PfP	Partnership for Peace
PJC	Permanent Joint Council
SACEUR	Supreme Allied Commander Europe
SCO	Shanghai Cooperation Organization
SFOR	Stabilization Force
SHAPE	Supreme Headquarters Allied Powers Europe
SORT	Strategic Offensive Reductions Treaty
START	Strategic Arms Reductions Treaty
UN	United Nations

UNPROFOR	United Nations Protection Force
US	United States of America
USSR	Union of Soviet Socialist Republics
WTO	World Trade Organization

1 | Introduction

What if we adopted a different perspective on international security – one that stresses the practical logics of day-to-day diplomacy? More specifically, what if we conceived of interstate peace less as an abstract category than as a particular way to engage with the world of diplomacy? On the ground of international politics, how do daily interactions between representatives whose states are at peace differ from those of rival states? What makes a given international practice more or less commonsensical in certain contexts but not in others? How are pervasive power relations and domination patterns expressed, in and through practice, on the international stage? In brief, what can we learn by adding to our theories and social scientific interpretations the practical perspectives of those agents involved in the quotidian unfolding of international security?

In this book I argue that, in practice, interstate peace rests on self-evident diplomacy. When security practitioners engage in the non-violent resolution of disputes as if it were the axiomatic way to go, they come to debate *with* diplomacy but not *about* its opportunity. Diplomacy becomes commonsensical – the practice from which all further interactions take place. Building on Pierre Bourdieu's sociology, I show that this peaceful commonsense is made possible by the contingent alignment between the practitioners' dispositions (the stock of background knowledge accumulated from experience) and their positions in the field of international security (defined by evolving rules of the game and stocks of valued resources). When diplomats on both sides of an interstate relationship behave in tune with how the structure and terms of the relationship are understood to work, then the non-violent settlement of disputes may become self-evident, paving the way to peace in and through practice. Where a mismatch between positions and dispositions exists, however,

chances are that the development of a peaceful order will be undermined by more or less intense symbolic power struggles over the
very terms of interaction.

This book demonstrates that the politics of NATO–Russia diplomacy appertain to the second of these scenarios. I argue that in
the post-Cold War era, the non-violent settlement of disputes has
become a normal yet not self-evident practice between the two
former enemies, largely due to a growing disconnection between
the dispositions that players embody and their positions in the contemporary game of international security. The dominant player,
NATO, possesses large stocks of resources that are highly valued in
the contemporary field of international security; as a result Alliance
officials think *from* their superior position to Russia and act accordingly. In Moscow, however, pervasive Great Power dispositions lead
security practitioners to construe their country's position as much
higher in the international security hierarchy than other players in
the field, especially NATO, are inclined to recognize. As a result
of this mismatch, which after Bourdieu I call hysteresis, the contemporary Russian–Atlantic relationship is primarily characterized
by fierce symbolic power struggles that thwart security community
development.

Although real, pacification between NATO and Russia remains
limited. On the one hand, compared to the Cold War era and
the continually looming specter of mutually assured destruction, contemporary Russian–Atlantic relations have significantly
pacified. The possibility of a military confrontation has receded
considerably and the many heated disputes that have plagued the
relationship over the last twenty years have consistently been solved
peacefully. On the other hand, NATO–Russia diplomacy has been
and remains rather uneasy: bones of contention abound, startling
differences in international outlook keep surfacing, and legacies of
mistrust endure. Overall, Moscow and the Alliance have come to
solve their many disputes through power struggles that, as intense
as they may be, do not hinge anymore on the possibility of using
military force against one another. Despite persisting tensions and
struggles, NATO–Russia power politics seem to have uneasily
migrated from the realm of war, however cold, to that of normalized diplomacy.

Security community development and the NATO–Russia puzzle[1]

One of the oldest and most fruitful theoretical lenses through which to study international peace is the concept of security community. As Karl Deutsch *et al.* conceptualized fifty years ago, a security community is an interstate group of peoples among whom there is a "real assurance that the members of that community will not fight each other physically, but will settle their disputes in some other way."[2] With the constructivist turn in International Relations (IR) theory, Emanuel Adler and Michael Barnett revisited the concept to argue, in opposition to the view that the international system is invariably based on rivalry and self-help because of anarchy, that states can establish a variety of intersubjective forms of order, one of which is a security community. By their definition, a security community is "a transnational region comprised of sovereign states whose people maintain dependable expectations of peaceful change," where peaceful change means "neither the expectation of nor the preparation for organized violence as a means to settle interstate disputes."[3] Contrary to a widespread view, then, security communities are *not* characterized by the absence of disputes, but rather by the fact that disputes are systematically solved peacefully.[4]

According to the standard constructivist account, the main mechanism of security community development is collective identity formation – "a cognitive process in which the Self–Other distinction becomes blurred and at the limit transcended altogether."[5] As the redefinition of Self and Other creates a common in-group identity, this sense of community or "we-ness" leads to the shared belief "that common social problems must and can be resolved by processes of 'peaceful change.'"[6] Mutual identification plays a constitutive role by redefining states' interests and instilling a pacific disposition. We-ness, the cement of a security community, becomes part of states' self-understandings and practices, thus producing dependable expectations of peaceful change. Deutsch *et al.* theorized that we-ness

---

[1] This section draws on Pouliot (2007).
[2] Deutsch *et al.* (1957, 5).   [3] Adler and Barnett (1998, 30 and 34).
[4] See Pouliot (2006).   [5] Wendt (1999, 229).   [6] Deutsch *et al.* (1957, 5).

fosters dependable expectations of peaceful change among countries because transnational interactions instill a sense of community that leads statesmen to solve their disputes "without resort to large-scale physical force."[7] Likewise, for Adler and Barnett mutual identification is a "necessary condition of dependable expectations of peaceful change."[8] As such, for students of security communities, collective identification is the key source of common interests in fostering international cooperation and eventually pacification.

Yet this account of security community development faces serious limitations in the case of post-Cold War Russian–Atlantic security relations. On the one hand, the post-Cold War track record of peaceful settlement of disputes between NATO and Russia seems to provide evidence of a security community: even profoundly vexing conflicts, such as the Kosovo crisis, Ukraine's Orange Revolution or the Georgia War, did not lead to a military standoff between the two former enemies. That fierce disputes such as these could be consistently solved "by means short of war," as Deutsch *et al.* would have it, is testimony to peaceful change – the essence of security community. In addition, contemporary Russian–Atlantic relations score at low to medium levels on all five indicators of security community devised by Adler and Barnett.[9] In effect, NATO and Russia have: (1) established numerous multilateral channels; (2) significantly decreased border defense; (3) partly adapted military planning away from mutual confrontation; (4) similarly defined several security threats; and (5) generally held, although with some inconsistencies, a discourse of community.[10] Although it has made a comeback in the wake of the American project of ballistic missile defense, nuclear deterrence has also receded from the security landscape.[11] Overall, then, it is quite plausible that a trend toward a rudimentary Russian–Atlantic security community has developed over the first post-Cold War generation.

[7] Deutsch *et al.* (1957, 5).   [8] Adler and Barnett (1998, 39).
[9] Adler and Barnett (1998, 55–6).
[10] Pouliot (2007) expands on each of these indicators.
[11] In 1994, Bill Clinton and Boris Yeltsin pledged to re-target all their nuclear forces away from each other's territories. As two Russian experts confirm, "deliberate conventional or nuclear war between Russia and the European Union or the NATO states is unthinkable"; Arbatov and Dvorkin (2006, 32). On more recent developments in nuclear relations, see Pouliot (n.d.).

Paradoxically, however, this process is not accompanied with what Deutsch and Adler and Barnett theorize as the key mechanism of security community development: we-ness or collective identification. In effect, survey data indicate that mutual representations between Russia and the NATO member states are quite lukewarm twenty years after the end of the Cold War.[12] Qualitative studies also indicate that the two entities still construe each other as political "Others." Ted Hopf contends that the West constitutes the main "External Other" in Russian foreign policymaking, whereas Iver Neumann observes that Russia has historically been and remains to this day Europe's "Eastern Other."[13] This NATO–Russia puzzle suggests that the constructivist hypothesis by which security community development rests on collective identification is in need of theoretical refinement. Peoples and state representatives do not have to think of themselves as the same to develop dependable expectations of peaceful change. In fact, the notion that stable interstate peace has to rest on some form of prior consensus about a collective identity seems mistaken, as the transatlantic rift over Iraq recalled.[14] Communities, whatever their nature, continually experience disputes, including about their own identities. The symbolic power politics of peace are irreducibly part of security community processes. Interstate peace does not imply perpetual agreement about collective identity; instead, it emerges out of shared practices in the management of disagreements.

In taking a "practice turn" in the study of security communities, in this book I make the wager that *it is not only who we are that drives what we do; it is also what we do that determines who we are.* By starting with the concrete ways in which state representatives handle disputes in and through practice, I reverse the traditional causal arrow of social action – from ideas to practice – and emphasize how practices also shape the world and its meaning. With Adler, I start from the premise that security communities are first and foremost "communities of practice."[15] This leads me to focus less on how people *represent* one another than on what practitioners actually *do* when they interact on the diplomatic floor. To use Bourdieu's formula, I want

---

[12] See, e.g., PIPA (2002); Zimmerman (2002); White, Light and McAllister (2005); Allison (2006); Colton (2008); and the EU's yearly Eurobarometer.
[13] Hopf (2002); Neumann (1999).
[14] Pouliot (2006).   [15] Wenger (1998); Adler (2005).

to look into interstate pacification as a *modus operandi* instead of an *opus operatum*. In order to do this, I develop a theoretical and methodological framework to conceptualize and empirically reconstruct the logic of practicality in NATO–Russia diplomacy.

Plan of the book

This book intends to demonstrate that in order to understand interstate pacification, our theories need to be attentive to the logic of practicality on the ground of diplomacy. In the first part of the book, I develop a theoretical and methodological framework specifically geared toward the restoration of the practical logics of peace. In the second part, I delve into the politics of NATO–Russia diplomacy and account for the limited development of a security community with the growing symbolic power struggles over the rules of the international security game.

Chapter 2 develops a theory of practice of security communities. I begin by showing that most theories of social action focus on what people think *about* instead of what they think *from*. I then explain how taking a practice turn redresses this representational bias. Building on Bourdieu's sociology, I theorize the logic of practicality and argue that any and all practices are informed by a substrate of inarticulate know-how. Finally, I apply this insight to the issue of international peace and contend that security communities exist in and through practice when security practitioners resort to diplomacy – the non-violent settlement of disputes – as a self-evident, everyday practice to solve disagreements. Drawing on Bourdieu's concepts of doxa and hysteresis, I devise a theoretical apparatus to explain the power dynamics that render such a peaceful commonsense possible or, alternatively, undermine it.

Chapter 3 lays out a sobjective methodology that is specifically tailored to the recovery of the logic of practicality in world politics. My main contention is that social scientific inquiries need to develop not only objectified (or experience-distant) but also subjective (experience-near) knowledge in order to produce incisive narratives about international life. I start with a short discussion of the epistemological and ontological requirements of the constructivist style of reasoning. I then infer the need for a methodology that is inductive, interpretive and historical. A sobjective methodology follows a three-step logic from the recovery of subjective meanings to their objectification, thanks to contextualization and historicization. I inventory a number of methods that can be put to work toward that end, paying special attention to the challenges of studying practices and their non-representational dimension. After a brief discussion of standards of validity, I explain the methodological underpinnings of my case study and offer a detailed picture of how the research proceeded.

Turning to the case study, Chapter 4 reconstructs the logic of practicality at the NATO–Russia Council (NRC). Building on sixty-nine interviews conducted in 2006 with officials in Moscow, Brussels, Washington, Berlin, London and Ottawa, I look at diplomatic dealings from the point of view of their practitioners. In order to operationalize my theory of practice of security communities, I abductively devise a set of three empirical indicators of the embodiment of diplomacy: the disappearance of the possibility of using force, the normalization of disputes and daily cooperation on the ground. The evidence that I present is mixed: while diplomacy was the normal practice in NATO–Russia relations in 2006, it stopped short of self-evidence. I also discover that at the NRC table there are two masters but no apprentice. As a result, fierce symbolic power struggles characterize Russian–Atlantic politics at the practical level.

Chapters 5 and 6 seek to trace back in time the sources of symbolic upheaval or hysteresis in NATO–Russia diplomacy in the post-Cold War era. My main focus is on NATO–Russia dealings over the double enlargement (geographical and functional) – certainly the main bone of contention over the last fifteen years. My analytical narrative hinges on the evolving match or mismatch between players' dispositions and their respective positions in the game of international security. I first show that in the immediate aftermath of the Cold War, NATO promoted the internal mode of pursuing security while Russia seemed happy to play the junior partner. Yet NATO's 1994 decision to enlarge both in functions and membership abruptly put an end to this pattern of domination, largely because, for the Russians, the Alliance's practices undermined the new rules of the international security game. The resurgence of the Great Power habitus in Moscow created intense hysteresis effects that were compounded in the wake of the Kosovo crisis. Despite a temporary hiatus in the immediate aftermath of September 11, 2001, which led to another short-lived honeymoon in Russian–Atlantic relations, the Great Power habitus further consolidated in Moscow as NATO's double enlargement continued into the new millennium. I conclude that the Georgia War of summer 2008 vividly illustrated the sharp decline in the Alliance's authority over Russia. Overall, the politics of NATO–Russia diplomacy consist of shifting phases of alignment and misalignment between dispositions and positions – an evolution that explains the limited security community development in the post-Cold War era.

Finally, the seventh and concluding chapter takes stock of the contributions that this study seeks to make to IR scholarship, as well as to the analysis of the post-Cold War Russian–Atlantic relationship. First, I return to my theory of practice of security communities and highlight how it expands and rejuvenates the study of international security and interstate peace more specifically. Second, I infer from my theoretical framework two key policy recommendations that might contribute to easing contemporary symbolic power struggles between NATO and Russia. Finally, I briefly analyze how practice theory shares common ground with existing IR theories, while also opening new avenues for dialogue and cross-fertilization. Ultimately a better grasp of the logic of practicality in international politics promises innovative solutions to pressing problems, both practical and theoretical.

PART I

Restoring the practical logic of peace

2 | *The logic of practicality: a theory of practice of security communities*

Most theories of social action focus on what agents think *about* at the expense of what they think *from*. In IR, rational choice theorists primarily emphasize representations and reflexive knowledge in explaining political action. In the rationalist equation (desire + belief = action), ideas factor in an individual calculation informed by intentionality. Agents deliberately reflect on the most efficient means to achieve their ends. For their part, several constructivists theorize that norms and collective identities reflexively inform action. Intersubjective representations of reality, morality or individuality determine socially embedded cognition and action. In a related fashion, Habermasian constructivists concentrate on collective deliberation and truth-seeking as a form of communicative action. Overall, the three logics of social action that have the most currency in contemporary IR theory – the logics of consequences, appropriateness and arguing[1] – suffer from a similar bias toward representational knowledge. Conscious representations are emphasized to the detriment of background knowledge – the inarticulate know-how from which reflexive and intentional deliberation becomes possible.

In and of itself, this focus on representational knowledge is not necessarily a problem: the logics of consequences, appropriateness and arguing cover a wide array of social action, as recent studies about socialization in Europe have demonstrated.[2] The problem rests with the many practices that neither rational choice nor rule-based and communicative action theories can explain properly. Take the case of diplomacy, perhaps the most fundamental practice in international politics. For most IR theorists, diplomacy is primarily about strategic action, instrumental rationality and cost-benefit calculations. Yet this scholarly understanding is at odds with that of practitioners,

---

[1] March and Olsen (1998); Risse (2000).   [2] See Checkel (2005).

who rather emphasize the very practical and inarticulate nature of diplomacy. A former diplomat turned professor argues that diplomacy is "not a matter of mathematical calculation; it is not an exact science; it remains a matter of human skills and judgments."[3] In fact, seasoned diplomats are at pains to explain their craft in abstract, social scientific terms: Harold Nicolson contends that "common sense" is the essence of diplomacy, while Ernest Satow defines it as "the application of intelligence and tact to the conduct of official relations between the governments of independent states."[4] Clearly, commonsense, intelligence and tact cannot be learned in books through formal schemes; nor are they strictly the result of conscious deliberation or reflection. The diplomatic skills identified by practitioners, and that constitute the social fabric of international politics, are background dispositions acquired in and through practice.[5]

This chapter starts from the premise that in everything that people do, in world politics as in any other social field, there is always a practical substrate that does not derive from conscious deliberation or thoughtful reflection – instrumental, rule-based, communicative or otherwise. An essential dimension of practice is the result of inarticulate, practical knowledge that makes what is to be done appear self-evident or commonsensical.[6] Citing Ludwig Wittgenstein, Charles Taylor illustrates this fundamental point:

Some outsider, unfamiliar with the way we do things, might misunderstand what to us are perfectly clear and simple directions. You want to get to town? Just follow the arrows. But suppose that what seemed the natural way of following the arrow to him or her was to go in the direction of the feathers, not of the point? We can imagine a scenario: there are no arrows in the outsider's culture, but there is a kind of ray gun whose discharge fans out like the feathers on our arrows.[7]

Rules do not come with their own instruction manual, concludes Taylor; most of the time people figure out their application unthinkingly, based on their practical experience in the world.

---

[3] Watson (1991, 52).   [4] Nicolson (1963, 43); Satow (1979, 3).
[5] Neumann (2002; 2005a; 2007).
[6] Practices are patterned social activities that embody shared meanings; see Adler and Pouliot (n.d.). As Barry Barnes notes, contrary to habits, practices can be done correctly or incorrectly (Barnes 2001).
[7] Taylor (1993, 45).

I call this inarticulate sense that allows agents to perform social activities the logic of practicality, a fundamental feature of social life that is often overlooked by social scientists. By emphasizing this logic, I join a larger trend advocating a "practice turn" in social theory.[8] To simplify a bit, practice theorists seek "to do justice to the practical nature of action by rooting human activity in a non-representational stratum."[9] Against the representational bias that pervades most theories of social action, practice theory brings background knowledge to the foreground of analysis. In IR, a few pioneering scholars are already part of this theoretical movement. Neumann urges students of world politics to move away from the "armchair analysis" of discourse to study social action as enacted in and on the world.[10] Hopf suggests that social identities (and foreign policies) thrive on a "logic of habit" that generates unreflexive action.[11] Adler uses the concept of "community of practice" to theorize the background knowledge that cements constellations of agents across borders.[12] Michael Williams takes inspiration from Bourdieu to reconceptualize security practices as cultural strategies in the international field.[13] Jennifer Mitzen emphasizes routine and unthinking action in the international drive for ontological security.[14]

Building on these works, in this chapter I seek to bolster the practice turn in IR theory by offering an in-depth discussion of the logic of practicality.[15] The first section levels a theoretical critique at dominant strands of social and IR theory, arguing that both rationalism and constructivism suffer from a representational bias whose epistemological roots run deep into modernity. The second section explains how other disciplines including philosophy, psychology and sociology provide important clues as to how to conceptualize the logic of practicality in world politics. In the third part of the chapter, I define practical knowledge and distinguish it from representational knowledge. Using Bourdieu's conceptual apparatus, I assert the ontological priority of the logic of practicality in relation to the mutually constitutive

---

[8] Schatzki, Knorr Cetina and Von Savigny (2001).
[9] Schatzki (2005, 177).   [10] Neumann (2002).   [11] Hopf (2002).
[12] Adler (2005).   [13] Williams (2007).   [14] Mitzen (2006).
[15] Though inspired by Bourdieu's "logic of practice," the notion of practicality is meant to specifically theorize the non-representational basis of practices. In Bourdieu's more ambitious framework, the logic of practice covers both representational and non-representational action (see Bourdieu 1990a).

dynamics between agency and structure. Overall, the relationship between practicality, consequences, appropriateness and arguing is one of complementarity. The fourth section seeks to illustrate this point with the case of security communities. I argue that peace exists in and through practice when security officials' practical sense makes diplomacy the self-evident way of solving interstate disputes. Finally, the concluding section addresses the peculiar methodological challenges raised by the study of the logic of practicality in world politics.

The representational bias

Most contemporary theories of social action are unable to account for the non-representational bedrock on which practices rest. The logics of consequences, appropriateness and arguing all tend to focus on what agents think *about* (reflexive and conscious knowledge) at the expense of what they think *from* (the background of know-how that informs practice in an inarticulate fashion). This representational bias, which pervades both modern and postmodern social theory, finds its epistemological roots in the evolution of Western thinking since the Enlightenment and the scientific revolution. In an illuminating book, Stephen Toulmin laments that the epistemic revolution of modernity gave birth to an imbalance between universal rationality and contextual reasonableness. Local knowledge that makes sense in particular contexts is dismissed in favor of generalizable and abstract precepts; so much so that nowadays "the human values of Reasonableness are expected to justify themselves in the Court of Rationality."[16] Against this powerful tide, Toulmin advocates everyday experience as the necessary complement to "desituated" and "disembedded" logic.

The epistemic shift that has led Western thinkers away from practical knowledge over the last few centuries can be illustrated with the practice of map-making.[17] During the Middle Ages, "maps" consisted of rectilinear routes from an origin to a destination, comprising the different steps to go through (places to eat, to shelter, to pray and so on) and walking distances in days between them. In other words, medieval maps were performative itineraries that reproduced the knowledge learned in and through practice. Starting in the fifteenth

[16] Toulmin (2001, 2).   [17] De Certeau (1990, 177–9).

and sixteenth centuries, however, maps began to evolve into the geographical representations from above that still exist today. Of course,
this epistemic transformation took place over centuries. For a while,
maps conveyed both practical and representational knowledge: in pre-
modern maps, for instance, "ships drawn on the sea convey the maritime expedition that made representations of the coast possible."[18]
But progressively the god-like posture of modern science, which looks
at the world from above, triumphed over practical knowledge. As
"totalizing representations," contemporary maps do not convey the
practical operations that made them possible. The entire modern scientific enterprise can be interpreted as a similar movement away from
practical knowledge and toward formal and abstract representations
of the world.

The representational bias in modern thinking is reinforced by the
logic of scientific practice and its institutional environment. In trying to see the world from a detached perspective, social scientists
put themselves "in a state of social weightlessness."[19] Looking at the
world from above and usually backward in time implies that one
is not directly involved in social action and does not feel the same
proximity and urgency as agents do. In contrast to practitioners,
who act in and on the world, social scientists spend careers and lives
thinking about ideas, deliberating about theories and representing
knowledge. As a result, they are enticed "to construe the world as a
spectacle, as a set of significations to be interpreted rather than as
concrete problems to be solved practically."[20] The epistemological
consequences of such a contemplative eye are tremendous: what scientists see from their ivory tower is often miles away from the practical logics enacted on the ground. For instance, what may appear to
be the result of rational calculus in (academic) hindsight may just as
well have derived from practical hunches under time pressure. This
"ethnocentrism of the scientist"[21] leads to substituting the practical
relation to the world for the observer's (theoretical) relation to practice – or, to use Bourdieu's formula, "to take the model of reality for
the reality of the model."[22]

---

[18] De Certeau (1990, 178).
[19] Bourdieu (2003, 28). This and further translations from French are mine.
[20] Wacquant (1992, 39).   [21] Bourdieu and Wacquant (1992, 69).
[22] Bourdieu (1987, 62). See also Bourdieu (1990b); and Pouliot (2008) for an
epistemological discussion in IR.

To return to diplomacy, Henry Kissinger, whose career spanned the divide between the academic and the policy worlds, concurs that "there is a vast difference between the perspective of an analyst and that of a statesman":

The analyst can choose which problem he wishes to study, whereas the statesman's problems are imposed on him. The analyst can allot whatever time is necessary to come to a clear conclusion; the overwhelming challenge to the statesman is the pressure of time ... The analyst has available to him all the facts ... The statesman must act on assessments that cannot be proved at the time that he is making them.[23]

As a result, diplomacy is an art, not a science.[24] It is a practice enacted in and on the world, in real time and with actual consequences for the practitioner. As such, the practicality of diplomacy cannot be fully captured by detached, representational observation. At issue is not whether diplomats carefully ponder their options – they clearly do – but whether IR scholars appropriately take into account the considerably different context in which they do so (for instance, thinking forward as opposed to backward). Diplomacy certainly contains a strategic ingredient; but where does Thomas Schelling's "focal point"[25] come from, for instance, if not from an inarticulate and socially shared practical sense?

From this perspective, the epitome of the representational bias is rational choice theory and its tendency to deduce from the enacted practice (*opus operatum*) its mode of operating (*modus operandi*).[26]

---

[23] Kissinger (1994, 27).

[24] Kissinger (1973, 2 and 326). There is no doubt that, in so arguing, Kissinger is also positioning himself as the holder of better knowledge than his fellow IR scholars. Beyond its analytical value, the distinction between the art and the science of politics is obviously part of a larger symbolic struggle over authoritative knowledge in the field of IR. As will become clear in Chapter 3, I believe that both practical and theoretical knowledge are necessary and mutually enlightening.

[25] Schelling (1980).

[26] Because it argues that the cost-benefit model "is a legitimate approximation of real processes," empiricist rational choice is the primary target here (Tsebelis 1990, 38). However, instrumentalist rational choice, premised on the notion that models need not be realistic so long as they explain social outcomes accurately, also falls victim to the representational bias in that it overlooks the process of practice (which is modeled regardless of what happens at the level of action) to focus on its outcome (as congruent with

The problem is deeper than the well-known tautology of revealed preferences. By mistaking the outcome of practice for its process, rational choice "project[s] into the minds of agents a (scholastic) vision of their practice that, paradoxically, it could only uncover because it methodically set aside the experience agents have of it."[27] While social scientists have all the necessary time to rationalize action *post hoc*, agents are confronted with practical problems that they must urgently solve. One cannot reduce practice to the execution of a theoretical model. For one thing, social action is not necessarily preceded by a premeditated design. A practice can be oriented toward a goal without being consciously informed by it. For another, in the heat of practice, hunches take precedence over rational calculations. In picturing practitioners in the image of the theorist, rational choice theory produces "a sort of monster with the head of the thinker thinking his practice in reflexive and logical fashion mounted on the body of a man of action engaged in action."[28] In IR, the literature on the rational design of international institutions best exemplifies this representational bias.[29] It is correct that states seek to mold international institutions to further their goals; but it does not follow that this design is instrumentally rational. The outcome of political struggles over institutions and the process of struggling over institutions follow two different logics – observational vs. practical. What has been done (output) cannot fully account for what is being done (process). Imputing to practitioners a theoretical perspective that is made possible by looking at social action backward and from above comes with great analytical costs.

In IR, the representational bias is not the preserve of rational choice theory, however: dominant constructivist interpretations of rule-based behavior also fall victim to it. In James March and Johan Olsen's seminal formulation, the logic of appropriateness deals with norm- and rule-based action conceived "as a matching of a situation to the demands of a position."[30] This definition, however, encompasses two

what the model expects). In other words, instrumentalist rational choice suffers from a bias toward representation at the level of observation, whereas empiricist rational choice is biased toward representations at the level of action.

[27] Wacquant (1992, 8).   [28] Bourdieu and Wacquant (1992, 123).
[29] See Koremenos, Lipson and Snidal (2001).
[30] March and Olsen (1989, 23).

distinct modes of social action.[31] On the one hand, the logic of appropriateness deals with rules that are so profoundly internalized that they become taken for granted. On the other hand, the logic of appropriateness is a reflexive process whereby agents need to figure out what behavior is appropriate to a situation.[32] Ole Jacob Sending calls these two possible interpretations "motivationally internalist" vs. "motivationally externalist,"[33] a distinction that hinges on whether agents reflect before putting a norm into practice. I argue that a vast majority of constructivist works fall in the latter camp, according to which norm-based actions stem from a process of reflexive cognition based either on instrumental calculations, reasoned persuasion or the psychology of compliance. Even those few constructivists who theorize appropriate action as non-reflexive assimilate it to the output of a structural logic of social action or to a habit resulting from a process of reflexive internalization. Problematically, nowhere in these interpretations is there room for properly theorizing the logic of practicality (see Table 2.1).

Three main strands of constructivist research construe appropriateness as a motivationally externalist logic of social action.[34] A first possibility is to introduce "thin" instrumental rationality in the context of a community or a norm-rich environment. Margaret Keck and Kathryn Sikkink's "boomerang model" is one of the best-known frameworks of this genre: state elites' compliance with transnational norms first comes through strategic calculations under normative pressure; only at a later stage do preferences change.[35] Frank Schimmelfennig's notion of rhetorical action – "the strategic use of norm-based arguments"[36] – follows a similar logic of limited strategic

---

[31] Risse (2000, 6).

[32] March and Olsen lean toward this second interpretation when they write that in order to enact appropriate behavior, actors pose questions such as "Who am I?" or "What kind of situation is this?" (March and Olsen 1989, 23).

[33] Sending (2002).

[34] Arguably, a fourth externalist strand is rule-based constructivism, which also seems to presume a reflexive dimension to rule-following. As Nicholas Onuf writes: "As agents begin to *realize* that they should act as they always have, and not just because they always have acted that way, the convention gains strength as a rule" (Onuf 1998, 67; emphasis added). By contrast, I suggest below that rules become doxa, and thence gain strength, precisely when they are forgotten as rules.

[35] Keck and Sikkink (1998).   [36] Schimmelfennig (2001, 62).

Table 2.1 *Constructivist interpretations of the logic of appropriateness*

Logic of appropriateness	(1) Externalism	(a) Thin rationality within normative environments
		(b) Communicative action/ persuasion
		(c) Psychological mechanisms of compliance
	(2) Internalism	(a) Structural logic of action
		(b) Habituation through reflexive internalization

action constrained by constitutive communitarian norms and rules. A second possibility is to conceive of appropriateness as a logic that relies on reasoned persuasion. Building on Jürgen Habermas's theory of communicative action, some constructivists theorize that the "logic of arguing" leads actors to collectively deliberate "whether norms of appropriate behavior can be justified, and which norms apply under given circumstances."[37] Other constructivists build on the notion of "social learning" to explain the workings of argumentative persuasion in social context.[38] Finally, a third externalist interpretation of appropriateness emphasizes cognitive processes that take place at the level of the human mind. Relying on psychological notions such as acceptability heuristic, omission bias and images, Vaughn Shannon argues that "[a]ctors must feel justified to violate a norm to satisfy themselves and the need for a positive self-image, by interpreting the norm and the situation in a way that makes them feel exempt."[39]

Meanwhile, a few constructivists take the internalist route and emphasize the non-deliberative nature of the logic of appropriateness. Yet I contend that even these works fail to capture the practicality of social life because they construe appropriateness either as

---

[37] Risse (2000, 7). Note that Thomas Risse tends to emphasize the representational dimension of Habermas's social theory (i.e. collective truth-seeking) at the expense of what the Frankfurt theorist calls *Lebenswelt* or lifeworld.
[38] Checkel (2001).   [39] Shannon (2000, 300). See also Johnston (2001).

a structural logic devoid of agency or as a form of habituation that is reflexive in its earlier stages. To begin with the former, some constructivists claim that the internalist logic of appropriateness is plagued with a "structural bias" that renders it "untenable as a theory of *individual* action."[40] In this account, the essence of agency rests with choice and the capacity to deliberate among options before acting: "If the [logic of appropriateness] is to be individualistic in structure, the individual actor must be left with a reasonable degree of choice (or agency)."[41] But this restrictive notion of agency seems unwarranted within the structurationist ontology that characterizes constructivism. Agency is not simply about "defying" structures by making choices independently of them. It is a matter of instantiating structures in and through practice.[42] Without practice intersubjective realities would falter; thus agency or the enactment of practice is what makes social reality possible in the first place. In introducing contingency, agency need not be reflexive; and inarticulateness does not logically imply structural determination.

Taking a different tack, a number of constructivists equate the logic of appropriateness to the internalization of taken-for-granted norms. For instance, Jeffrey Checkel seeks to understand how norm compliance moves from "conscious instrumental calculation" to

[40] Sending (2002, 445).
[41] Sending (2002, 451). As Sending continues: "It is thus a central feature of structuration theory, which is a key building block of constructivist theory, that the actor is always in a position to evaluate, reflect upon and *choose* regarding what rules to follow and how to act" (Sending 2002, 458). On a closer look, however, there is nothing in Anthony Giddens's definition that restricts agency to choice: "Agency concerns events of which the individual is the perpetrator" (Giddens 1984, 9).
[42] Patrick Jackson locates agency in:

the double failure of social structures to cohere on their own. First, particular constellations of processes are never inevitable, but represent *ongoing accomplishments of practice*. The "fit" of particular legitimating practices with one another has less to do with intrinsic properties of the practices themselves, and more to do with active processes of tying practices together to form relatively coherent wholes. Second, cultural resources for action are always *ambiguous*, and do not simply present themselves as clearly defined templates for action. Instead, cultural resources provide opportunities, but actualising those opportunities demands practical, political and discursive work to "lock down" the meaning of the resource and derive implications from it.   (Jackson 2004, 286).

"taken-for-grantedness." In what he calls "type II socialization," agents switch "from following a logic of consequences to a logic of appropriateness."[43] A similar view can be found in Alexander Wendt's discussion of internalization, from "First Degree" to "Third." This process essentially consists of certain practices getting "pushed into the shared cognitive background, becoming taken for granted rather than objects of calculation."[44] Norms begin as explicit "ought to" prescriptions but progressively fade from consciousness and become taken for granted. Significantly, this internalist interpretation remains embroiled in the representational bias that plagues externalism: the taken-for-granted knowledge that informs appropriateness necessarily begins as representational and conscious.

In distinguishing the "logic of habit" from that of appropriateness, Hopf comes closest to accounting for practical knowledge in IR. As he perceptively argues: "Significant features distinguish habitual action from normative compliance. Generally, norms have the form 'in circumstance X, you should do Y,' whereas habits have a general form more like 'in circumstance X, action Y follows.' "[45] This all-important distinction, upon which this chapter builds, represents a significant step toward a practice turn in IR theory. That said, I want to fix three main limitations in Hopf's framework. First, it remains partly embroiled in an internalization scheme not so distant from Checkel's or Wendt's. In using the language of norm selection vs. norm compliance, Hopf implies that the internalist logic of habit follows from the externalist logic of appropriateness. By contrast, this chapter theorizes practical knowledge as unreflexive and inarticulate through and through. Second, while both logics of habit and practicality build on past experiences, the latter does so contingently while the former is strictly iterative.[46] While habit is fundamentally repetitive, practicality is partly improvisatory because it results from the intersection of a particular set of dispositions and a social configuration. Third, Hopf insists that his is only a *methodological* distinction between the logic of habit and the logic of appropriateness, which entices researchers to look for evidence of norm compliance in the unsaid instead of explicit

[43] Checkel (2005, 804).   [44] Wendt (1999, 310–11).
[45] Hopf (2002, 12). See also Weldes (1999) on the social construction of "commonsense."
[46] See Hopf (n.d).

invocations.[47] Though an important piece of methodological advice, this point falls short of granting practicality the full ontological status that it deserves in social theory.

At the level of observation, in IR the representational bias also shows up in a lack of attention to the structural conditions under which practices of meaning-making are enacted. Intersubjective knowledge and discourse are produced out of social and political struggles that exert very real and practical constraints on intertextuality and other interpretive processes. As I argue in the concluding chapter, the positional dimension of the social construction of knowledge has yet to be fully taken into account by IR constructivists, including those located closer to postmodernism. In fact, by its very epistemological standpoint, postmodernism tends to epitomize the representational bias: detached from, and sometimes even willingly indifferent to, the social urgency of practices, it runs the risk of intellectualizing discourse to the point of distorting its practical logic and meaning. Against this tendency, a number of poststructuralists fruitfully move closer to Michel Foucault's conceptualization of discourse as practice.[48] Discourse must always be studied in combination with political structures in order to understand the positional constraints on practices. Taking a practice turn promises to help overcome the representational bias in IR theory, whether rationalist, constructivist or postmodernist.

Practice turns

Still a recent development in IR, the practice turn has also been promoted in a number of other disciplines. The philosophical interest in practical knowledge dates back at least to Aristotle who, in his discussion of practical reasoning (that is, reasoning oriented toward action), highlighted the importance of *topoi* or the "seat of argument."[49] These commonplaces are tacit in nature: one discusses or acts *with* them but not *about* them. According to Gilbert Ryle, however, this Aristotelian insight was later overshadowed by his disciples' fascination with representational knowledge. With René Descartes, centuries later, the representational bias entrenched itself within Western philosophical

---

[47] Hopf (2002, 11 fn. 44).   [48] E.g. Ashley (1987); Neumann (2002).
[49] In IR, see Kratochwil (1989).

thought, a situation that lasts to this day.[50] In an illuminating critique of this philosophical evolution, Toulmin equates the philosophical tendency to favor the universal to the detriment of the contextual with "the behavior of an intellectual ostrich."[51] This view is inspired by the later Wittgenstein, arguably the most prominent figure in opposing the representational bias in philosophy.[52] Most famously, Wittgenstein denounced his colleagues for studying language as a theoretical system of signs and representations whereas it is primarily a practice whose meanings are determined not *in abstracto* but in and through its context and use. In his Wittgensteinian interpretation of rule-following, Taylor aptly summarizes the case for practice theory in philosophy and more largely in social science:

To situate our understanding in practices is to see it as implicit in our activity, and hence as going well beyond what we manage to frame representations of. We do frame representations: we explicitly formulate what our world is like, what we aim at, what we are doing. But much of our intelligent action in the world, sensitive as it usually is to our situation and goals, is carried on unformulated. It flows from an understanding which is largely inarticulate ... Rather than representations being the primary locus of understanding, they are similarly islands in the sea of our unformulated practical grasp on the world.[53]

Three other disciples of Wittgenstein – Ryle, Michael Polanyi and John Searle – have also been instrumental in advocating a practice turn in philosophy. The first convincingly derides the doctrine of the "ghost in the machine" that pervades Western philosophy, according to which a chef has to recite his recipes to himself before cooking.[54] On the contrary, Ryle argues, "[e]fficient practice precedes the theory of it."[55] His distinction between "knowing-that" and "knowing-how" remains fundamental to the practice turn. In the same way, Polanyi asserts that one may know *how* to use a machine without knowing *that* doing so requires the operation of such and such mechanisms.[56] This

---

[50] Ryle (1984).   [51] Toulmin (2001, 168).
[52] Wittgenstein (1958). Among other philosophers who argued in a similar direction, the American pragmatists (e.g. John Dewey, Charles Peirce) as well as Martin Heidegger and Maurice Merleau-Ponty are particularly prominent.
[53] Taylor (1993, 50).   [54] Ryle (1984, 15–16, 29).
[55] Ryle (1984, 30).   [56] Polanyi (1983, 19).

know-how Polanyi calls "tacit knowing," which consists of attending *from* something (e.g. the machine's internal mechanisms) *to* something else (e.g. using the machine).[57] Tacit knowing primarily rests on bodily experience and practice: it is knowledge *within* the practice instead of *behind* the practice. This is obviously not to say that the brain plays no role in tacit knowing. A professor of chemistry, Polanyi recalls that "mathematical theory can be learned only by practicing its application: its true knowledge lies in our ability to use it."[58] One may know the theorems by heart but their application must be learned in and through practice as a form of tacit knowing. A similar insight informs Searle's notion of Background. As he explains, "the general thesis of the Background ... is that all of our intentional states, all of our particular beliefs, hopes, fears, and so on, only function in the way they do – that is, they only determine their conditions of satisfaction – against a Background of know-how that enables me to cope with the world."[59] This pre-intentional knowledge is non-representational and pre-reflexive: it is only activated in and through practice.

The philosophical metaphysics of the practice turn find solid empirical support in the latest strands of psychological research. In his Nobel Prize lecture in 2002, Daniel Kahneman argues that there are "two generic modes of cognitive function: an intuitive mode in which judgments and decisions are made automatically and rapidly, and a controlled mode, which is deliberate and slower."[60] These two modes of cognition coexist and complement each other. But intuitive judgments are not mere perceptions although both are equally fast: contrary to the latter, the former "deal with concepts" and "can be evoked by language."[61] Psychologists usually refer to these two ways of knowing as "System 1" and "System 2."[62] The theoretical revolution here regards automatic cognition: with the exception of the Freudian tradition, psychology has traditionally paid most of its attention to conscious cognition. More recently, thanks to several experiments, psychologists have found "evidence from everyday life of the existence of an automatic, intuitive mode of information processing that operates by different rules from that of a rational mode."[63] From that perspective, cognition falls into two ideal-typical categories, as Table 2.2 shows.

[57] Polanyi (1983, 10).   [58] Polanyi (1983, 17).   [59] Searle (1998, 108).
[60] Kahneman (2002, 449).   [61] Kahneman (2002, 451).
[62] Stanovich and West (2000).   [63] Epstein (1994, 710).

Table 2.2 *Two ways of knowing in psychological theory*

Experiential way of knowing (System 1)	Rational way of knowing (System 2)
1. Holistic	1. Analytic
2. What feels good	2. What is sensible
3. Associative	3. Logical
4. Behavior mediated by hunches from past experiences; automatic	4. Behavior mediated by conscious appraisal of events; controlled
5. Encodes reality in concrete images, metaphors, and narratives	5. Encodes reality in abstract symbols, words, and numbers
6. More rapid processing: oriented toward immediate action	6. Slower processing: oriented toward delayed action
7. Slower to change: changes with repetitive or intense experience	7. Changes more rapidly: changes with speed of thought
8. Context-specific processing	8. Cross-context processing
9. Experienced passively and preconsciously; tacit thought processes	9. Experienced actively and consciously; explicit thought processes
10. Self-evidently valid	10. Requires justification via logic and evidence

Note: Adapted from Epstein (1994, 711); and Stanovich and West (2000, 659).

Though interactive, System 1 and System 2 in Table 2.2 present different characteristics. A form of cognitive unconscious, System 1 is "a fundamentally adaptive system that automatically, effortlessly, and intuitively organizes experience and directs behavior."[64] Empirical data suggest that this is the natural mode of operation and that it is a lot more efficient than conscious cognition. A pioneer in this strand of psychological theory, Arthur Reber builds on decades of empirical studies to establish the pervasiveness of "implicit learning" in cognitive processes, that is, "the acquisition of knowledge that takes place largely independently of conscious attempts to learn and largely in the absence of explicit knowledge about what was acquired."[65] Importantly, Reber insists, acting on the basis of such tacit knowledge does not make individuals irrational. Their practices, which

[64] Epstein (1994, 710).   [65] Reber (1993, 5).

are informed by past experiences and exposure to environmental demands, should rather be conceived as "arational,"[66] that is, based on non-representational knowledge and thought processes.

Philosophical and psychological arguments in favor of a practice turn have spilled over to social sciences. For instance, Roy D'Andrade's "cognitive anthropology" intends, among other things, to counter the representational bias in social theory. As he argues, "social scientists sometimes ascribe *rules* to the actor when it is only the actor's *behavior* that is being described. In many cases in which behavior is described as following rules, there may be in fact no *rules* inside the actor."[67] In sociology, Eviatar Zerubavel emphasizes the social aspects of cognition as well as the tacit dimension of socialization, for instance in the process of learning a language.[68] In becoming part of collectives, human beings learn how to think socially, a skill that rests on inarticulate knowledge first and foremost. A similar premise gave birth to Harold Garfinkel's ethnomethodology and to Giddens's structuration theory.[69]

More recently, a few prominent scholars have advocated taking a practice turn in social theory.[70] Among the theoretical innovations advanced is the premise that social action stems from practical logics that are fundamentally non-representational. These inarticulate meanings cannot readily be verbalized or explicated by the agents themselves because "practice does not account for its own production and reproduction."[71] In sociology, this theoretical strand has been best developed by Bourdieu, whose works have the rare advantage of being systematically applied to various empirical investigations. In IR, a handful of scholars have already demonstrated how Bourdieu's sociology could enrich our understanding of security,[72] power,[73] integration[74] or political economy.[75] This chapter adds to this burgeoning

---

[66] Reber (1993, 13).   [67] D'Andrade (1995, 144).

[68] Zerubavel (1997, 16).   [69] Garfinkel (1967); Giddens (1984).

[70] Schatzki, Knorr Cetina and Von Savigny (2001).

[71] Barnes (2001, 19).

[72] Bigo (1996); Gheciu (2005); Huysmans (2002); Villumsen (2008); Williams (2007).

[73] Ashley (1987); Guzzini (2000).

[74] Adler-Nissen (2008); Kauppi (2005); Pop (2007); Madsen (2007).

[75] Dezalay and Garth (2002); Fourcade (2006); Leander (2001). For wider discussions of Bourdieu in IR, see Mérand and Pouliot (2008) and Jackson, Peter (2008).

literature by focusing on Bourdieu's attempt to reach the inarticulate in social life – the huge body of background knowledge that every social being carries and uses constantly, if unconsciously, in daily practices. Many practices appear self-evident without our having to reflect on them; how can that be? Bourdieu's conceptual triad of habitus, field and practical sense offers a useful apparatus to theorize the logic of practicality.

The logic of practicality

Practice theory seeks to save practical know-how from the "nocturnal abyss" of social activities in order to put it at the center of social scientific inquiries.[76] The objective, ultimately, is to bring the background to the foreground. By countering the representational bias, practice theory opens a whole new domain of inquiry too often excluded from modern theories of social action: the logic of practicality. This section defines what practical knowledge consists of and then establishes the ontological priority of the logic of practicality over the logics of consequences, appropriateness and arguing. Throughout this theoretical discussion, I use Bourdieu's theory of practice as the linchpin of my argument for a practice turn in IR.

Practical knowledge

An interesting starting point to understand the logic of practicality is James Scott's *Seeing Like a State*, a rare study, in political science, that takes practical knowledge seriously. To explain the failure of certain states' grand schemes for social engineering, Scott argues that state projects of societal legibility and simplification usually fail because they ignore what the Greeks used to call *mètis*, "a rudimentary kind of knowledge that can be acquired only by practice and that all but defies being communicated in written or oral form apart from actual practice."[77] This practical knowledge is absolutely necessary for the implementation of any policy because it is on it, and not on bureaucratic models, that people's everyday lives thrive. Contrary to the abstract schemes produced by technocrats and social scientists, *mètis* presents three main characteristics. First, it is local and situated.

---

[76] De Certeau (1990, xxxv).   [77] Scott (1998, 315).

Mètis is knowledge-in-context and derives from concrete applications. Second, *mètis* is plastic and decentralized: there is no core doctrine since it is continually changing with the practices it informs. Third, *mètis* knowledge is extremely difficult to convey apart from putting it in practice. In Scott's words, "[m]*ètis* knowledge is often so implicit and automatic that its bearer is at a loss to explain it."[78] It resists being translated into the deductive and abstract models required by states' social engineering initiatives.

Whether called *mètis*, tacit knowing, background or an experiential way of knowing, this stock of inarticulate know-how learned in and through practice that makes conscious deliberation and action possible can conveniently be called practical knowledge. Table 2.3 captures, for heuristic purposes, the main differences between practical and representational knowledge (this distinction is obviously blurred in practice). While representational knowledge is conscious, verbalizable and intentional, practical knowledge is tacit, inarticulate and automatic. The former type of knowledge is acquired through formal schemes, whereas the latter is learned experientially, in and through practice, and remains bound up in it. Representational knowledge is rational and abstract; practical knowledge is reasonable and contextual. Thus the inferences drawn from each type are respectively explicit and justified vs. implicit and self-evident. Representational knowledge factors in reflexive cognition (in situation X, you should do Y – whether for instrumental or normative reasons), whereas practical knowledge remains unsaid (in situation X, Y follows).[79] In fact, it is precisely because it is unthinking that the background is forgotten as knowledge. It is located *within* practices instead of behind them. Practical knowledge is inarticulate because it appears self-evident to its bearer: "This is simply what I do," as Wittgenstein quipped.[80] Thus, a defining feature of the practices informed by the background is that their rules are not thought but simply enacted. Inarticulate, concrete and local, practical knowledge is learned from experience and can hardly be expressed apart from practice. It is "thought-less": that is, without thought – what popular parlance calls commonsense, experience, intuition, knack, skill or practical mastery.

[78] Scott (1998, 329).   [79] Hopf (2002, 12).
[80] Wittgenstein (1958, § 217).

Table 2.3 *Two ideal types of knowledge*

	Representational knowledge (knowing-that)	Practical knowledge (knowing-how)
Cognitive status	Conscious, verbalizable, intentional	Tacit, inarticulate, automatic
Mode of learning	Acquired through formal schemes; reflexive	Learned experientially, in and through practice; unsaid
Relation to practice	"Behind" the practice; knowledge precedes practice	Bound up in the practice; knowledge is in the execution
Nature of inferences	Explicit and prone to justification	Implicit and self-evident
Direction of fit	Mind-to-world (observing)	World-to-mind (doing)
Type of reasoning	"In situation X, you should do Y" (instrumental or normative reasons)	"In situation X, Y follows" (unthinking)
Popular categories	Scheme, theory, model, calculation, reasoning	Commonsense, experience, intuition, knack, skill

Another useful way to grasp the distinction between representational and practical knowledge is what Searle (after John Austin and G. E. M. Anscombe) calls the "direction of fit" between the mind and the world.[81] As Searle explains, when a man goes to the grocery store and buys items on his shopping list, the direction of fit is from world to the mind: the man alters the world to fit his mind (here materialized in the list). But imagine now that a detective investigates what groceries this man buys and notes them on a list as they are being placed in the cart. Now the direction of fit is reversed, from the mind (the detective's list) to the world. The list is trying to match the world as it is being acted upon. A similar difference arises between practical knowledge, which is oriented toward action (world-to-mind direction of fit), and representational knowledge, which seeks to capture in

[81] Searle (1998, 100–2).

words or other representations practices enacted in and on the world (mind-to-world direction of fit). Doing and observing, in sum, are two distinct ways of relating to the world.

Although practical knowledge is generally taken for granted or unreflexive, not all taken-for-granted knowledge is practical. In Hopf's logic of habit, for instance, taken-for-granted knowledge was once reflected upon before becoming internalized; whereas practical knowledge is learned tacitly. But just how could a minimally complex practice be learned without ever being explicitly taught? Building on decades of experiments, psychologist Reber asserts the "primacy of the implicit": "other things being equal, implicit learning is the default mode for the acquisition of complex information about the environment."[82] Babies learning the complex syntactic rules of their mother tongue are a good example of such non-representational competence-building. In Ryle's example, even the game of chess need not be explicitly taught for a boy to be able to play by the rules:

> By watching the moves made by others and by noticing which of his own moves were conceded and which were rejected, he could pick up the art of playing correctly while still quite unable to propound the regulations in terms of which "correct" and "incorrect" are defined ... We learn *how* by practice, schooled indeed by criticism and example, but often quite unaided by any lessons in the theory.[83]

The point is not that practices rest exclusively on implicit learning, but that there is always some part of implicit learning in any practice. Though often imperceptible, implicit learning is the rule not the exception.

In world politics, for instance, state elites come to master the international rules of sovereignty and non-intervention in part through implicit learning. Most of them were never trained in the formal schemes of international law. Statespersons simply replicate, in and through practice, the way things are done in international society (or else they may face social or political sanctions). As such, it is no wonder that realpolitik practices form the dominant commonsense among international practitioners.[84] On the international stage, most of the

---

[82] Reber (1993, 25).   [83] Ryle (1984, 41).
[84] Ashley (1987); George (1993).

complex workings of diplomatic practice rest on a stock of practical knowledge that is tacitly learned. Reviewing dozens of classics on diplomacy, G. R. Berridge observes that there is "an overwhelmingly strong sentiment that *practical knowledge* could be acquired only at the elbow of a master, that is to say, by apprenticeship."[85] This inarticulate mode of learning is a useful complement to the dominant model of norm internalization and socialization advocated by several IR constructivists.

Habitus, field and practical sense

As a "knowledge that does not know itself,"[86] practical knowledge does not lend itself easily to scientific inquiry. In this endeavor, Bourdieu's theory of practice appears especially helpful because his conceptual triad of habitus, field and practical sense has been empirically operationalized time and again – it works in practice. To begin with, habitus is a "system of durable, transposable dispositions, which integrates past experiences and functions at every moment as a matrix of perception, appreciation and action, making possible the accomplishment of infinitely differentiated tasks."[87] Four main dimensions of the concept need to be highlighted. First, habitus is historical. The dispositions that comprise it are the sediment of individual and collective trajectories. It turns history (and intersubjectivity) into second nature; as a result the past is actualized into the present. In Bourdieu's theory of practice, people do what they do because "this is how things are" according to the collective and individual experiences embodied in their habitus. These dispositions are acquired through socialization, exposure, imitation and symbolic power relationships. Though "ever-changing" as history unfolds, the habitus instills path dependence in social action, for revisions take place on the basis of prior dispositions.[88]

Second, habitus is practical. It is learned by doing, from direct experience in and on the world: "The core modus operandi that defines practice is transmitted through practice, in practice, without acceding to the discursive level."[89] This is not to say that individuals do

---

[85] Berridge (2004, 6).   [86] De Certeau (1990, 110).
[87] Bourdieu (2000, 261).   [88] Bourdieu (2003, 231).
[89] Bourdieu (2000, 285).

not form representations; but they do so on the basis of the habitus's inarticulate dispositions. Without reflection or deliberation, habitus tends to generate commonsensical or reasonable practices whose principle agents may find difficult to explain. In that sense, it is a form of "learned ignorance" (*docte ignorance*).[90] Borrowing from Merleau-Ponty, Bourdieu contends that habitus is inarticulate because it is comprised of "corporeal knowledge" (*connaissance par corps*), a practical mastery of the world that profoundly differs from representational knowledge. Whether one rides a bicycle or plays a flute, these practices express an unspoken, bodily knowledge that is learned and deployed corporeally: "Our body is not just the executant of the goals we frame or just the locus of the causal factors which shape our representations. Our understanding itself is embodied."[91] Being a female or a male, to take a general example, is a bodily form of knowledge that informs most of our practices without conscious reflection about it. People behave in a gendered manner often without any explicit teaching; their masculine or feminine behavior is not something they can readily express in words. In world politics, meetings between statespersons similarly involve the bodily knowledge of habitus as a "sense of one's place" and of the other's place.[92] As Bourdieu explains: "What is 'learned by body' is not something that one has, like knowledge that can be brandished, but something that one is."[93] In this sense, practice theory de-emphasizes what is going on in people's heads – what they *think* – to focus instead on what they *do*. This is not to say that the mind plays no role in social action: the point rather is that more often than not, mental processes are so inarticulate that the brain should be treated as just one part of the body among others.[94]

Third, habitus is relational: its dispositions are embodied traces of intersubjective interactions. In tune with the view that agents are the products of social relations,[95] Bourdieu calls this process the

---

[90] Bourdieu (2000, 308).   [91] Taylor (1993, 50).

[92] Williams (2007, 28–31).   [93] Bourdieu (1990a, 73).

[94] One example of a non-reflexive practice that nevertheless goes through the brain is verb conjugation. When one conjugates a verb in one's mother tongue, one usually applies grammatical rules without thinking: practical mastery is based on background knowledge derived from experience. This is starkly different from conjugating verbs in a foreign language, an action that cannot be undertaken without reference to formal and explicit representations such as conjugation tables.

[95] Jackson and Nexon (1999).

internalization of externality. Though located at the subjective level, habitus constitutes the intersection of structure and agency. Thus what look like individual dispositions are in fact profoundly social. Social psychologist Lev Vygotsky similarly supports the view that "[a]ny higher mental function [is] external because it was social at some point before becoming an internal, truly mental function."[96] More recently, an increasing body of psychological theory postulates "the dynamic mutual constitution of culture and the psyche."[97] As a kind of socialized subjectivity, the concept of habitus paves the way to a relational ontology of practice.

Fourth, and finally, habitus is dispositional. Far from automatically or deterministically leading to a specific practice, habitus instead inclines or disposes actors to do certain things. It generates propensities and tendencies. One could compare habitus to legal custom: both work on the basis of a small number of schemes that generate a limited number of possible responses or "regulated improvisations."[98] Habitus is not habit, for the former is fundamentally generative while the latter is strictly iterative. Habitus is an "art of inventing" that introduces contingency into social action: the same disposition could potentially lead to different practices depending on the social context. That said, habitus also negates complete free will or fully fledged creativity: agents improvise within the bounds of historically constituted practical knowledge. Habitus is a grammar that provides a basis for the generation of practices; but it does so only in relation to a social configuration, or field.

The concept of field is the second key notion in Bourdieu's theory of practice. Simply put, a field is a social configuration structured along three main dimensions: relations of power, objects of struggle and taken-for-granted rules. First, fields are comprised of unequal positions, where some agents are dominant and others are dominated. It is the control of a variety of historically constructed forms of capital, from economic through social to symbolic, that defines the structure of power relations in the field and the positions that result. Specific to a field, capital refers to any type of resources that are recognized as such in a given social context, thus allowing a player to play the game more or less successfully. For instance, one may own huge stocks of

---

[96] Quoted in Marti (1996, 67).
[97] Fiske *et al.* (1998, 915).   [98] Bourdieu (2000, 301).

economic capital in the form of money, yet in the academic field that will only take one so far. It is rather the accumulation of a specific form of cultural capital, notably publications and professional titles, that can move the agent toward the top of this unique configurational hierarchy. In Bourdieu's words, "capital is accumulated labour": "It is what makes the games of society ... something other than simple games of chance offering at every moment the possibility of a miracle."[99] Since positions in the field are defined by the distribution of capital, the concept paves the way to relational and positional analysis.

Second, fields are defined by the stakes at hand, that is, the issues around which agents converge. Fields are relatively autonomous because they are characterized by certain struggles that have been socially and historically constituted. All participants agree on what it is they are seeking – political authority, artistic prestige, economic profit, academic reputation and so on. Thus the field is a kind of social game, with the specificity that it is a game "in itself" and not "for itself": "one does not embark on the game by a conscious act, one is born into the game, with the game."[100] In addition to this innate investment in the game, which Bourdieu calls *illusio*, agents also struggle over the value and forms of capital, leading both to evolve over time and space. Hence the third characteristic of fields is that they are structured by taken-for-granted rules. This doxa is comprised of "all that is accepted as obvious, in particular the classifying schemes which determine what deserves attention and what does not."[101] Positions in the field are determined by the possession of certain resources whose value is defined by doxa. Generally, dominant players have a vested interest in preserving the doxic rules of the game (including the conversion rate between forms of capital) by turning them into social things – institutions, norms, procedures, etc. In this endeavor, symbolic capital – those resources that allow one to change or maintain the rules of the game and to endow these rules with a doxic aura of naturalness and legitimacy – becomes a "meta-capital," because it potentially presides over the definition of other capital conversion rates.[102]

---

[99] Bourdieu (1986, 241).   [100] Bourdieu (1990a, 67).
[101] Bourdieu (1980, 83).   [102] Bourdieu and Wacquant (1992, 114).

From the interplay between habitus and field results practical sense, "a socially constituted 'sense of the game.' "[103] As the intersection of embodied dispositions and structured positions, practical sense makes certain practices appear reasonable and axiomatic, that is, in tune with commonsense. Of course, agents are not all equally endowed with this social skill. In order to have a feel for the game, agents need to have embodied specific dispositions (habitus) in the past and face a social context (field) that triggers them. It is through the actualization of the past in the present that agents know what is to be done in the future, often without conscious reflection or reference to explicit and codified knowledge. In this sense, practical sense is fundamentally dialectic – a synthesis between the social stuff within people and that within social contexts.[104] Thanks to practical sense, agents do what they *could* instead of what they *should*. Practice is "the done thing ... because one cannot do otherwise."[105] Contrary to normative compliance in the logic of appropriateness, practical sense unthinkingly aims at the commonsensical, given a peculiar set of dispositions and positions.

The practical sense is inarticulate not only because it feeds on the unreflexive dispositions of habitus, but also because it hinges on what I call positional agency. Positional agency refers to those practices that derive from their performers' location in a field's hierarchical structure. To paraphrase the famous dictum, where you sit is what you *do*. Generally speaking, people go on with their lives using the tools and resources that are ready at hand and enact practices based on their resource endowments and the opportunity constraints they face. Put differently, they think *from* the resources in their possession (i.e. their position in the field). In the same way that players are taken by their game, agents are "invested" by the field, including its capital value delineations. As such, they make use of what is available around them to get their way. In practice, social action often derives from the materials that are immediately available in the social configuration; means regularly matter more than ends. The practical sense is an inarticulate feel for the game at both dispositional and positional levels.

The notion of practical sense offers a promising way to tease out the mutually constitutive dynamics between agency and structure. Social

---

[103] Bourdieu and Wacquant (1992, 120–1).
[104] Bourdieu (1981, 305–8).   [105] Bourdieu (1990a, 18).

action derived from the feel for the game follows neither a structural nor an individualistic logic, but a relational dialectic of "the internalization of exteriority and the externalization of interiority."[106] Habitus is embodied at the subjective level but it is comprised of intersubjective dispositions. The field is a bundle of structured relations within which agents are variously positioned. Put together, habitus and field trigger practice in a non-representational way, as an intuition that more or less fits a social pattern. Given a social configuration and agents' trajectories, action X follows somewhat unreflexively from situation Y. Suspended in between structure and agency, practical sense is a "prereflective, infraconscious mastery that agents acquire of their social world by way of durable immersion within it."[107] This view is akin to what Erving Goffman calls the "sense of one's place" – the seemingly natural feeling people usually have about how to behave in a given social situation. It is the practical sense and not interests, norms or truth-seeking that allows people to thoughtlessly comport themselves in tune with commonsense.[108] In Bourdieu's sociology, then, social action is neither structural nor agentic, but relational.

By implication, the logic of practicality is ontologically prior to the other three logics of social action mentioned above. To put it simply, it is thanks to their practical sense that agents feel whether a given social context calls for instrumental rationality, norm compliance or communicative action. The intersection of a particular set of embodied dispositions (constituted by a historical trajectory of subjectivized intersubjectivity) and a specific field of positions (comprised of power relations, objects of struggle and taken-for-granted rules) is the engine of social action – be it rational, rule-based, communicative or habitual. For instance, while it may make sense to be instrumentally rational when planning investments in the economic field, it is quite nonsensical (and socially reprehensible) to constantly calculate means and ends with family and friends. In certain social contexts, but not others, instrumental rationality is the "arational" way to go thanks to the logic of practicality. Practicality is ontologically prior to instrumental rationality because the latter is not a priori inscribed in human

---

[106] Bourdieu (2000, 256).   [107] Wacquant (1992, 19).

[108] Goffman (1959). As I explain below, however, the practical sense is not infallible as dispositions can be out of touch with positions (what Bourdieu calls the "Don Quixote effect" or hysteresis).

beings' minds but historically constituted in habitus and fields. Of course, people continuously think, talk, deliberate, make judgments, have expectations, etc. in what is overall a very active reflexive life. Yet it is the logic of practicality, as the contingent intersection of structure and agency, that makes this reflexivity and intentionality possible in the first place.

The same logic applies to rule-governed behavior: in that case, the practical sense reads from context and embodied dispositions the need for socially appropriate or norm-based action. This inarticulate feeling differs from the externalist interpretation of the logic of appropriateness by which agents reflexively match the demands of a situation with their identity in order to decide on the course to be taken. To return to the example above, one would not instrumentally calculate costs and benefits within family because this is not appropriate. But one need not reflect to "know" this because it is an unspoken disposition learned in and through practice. Even when the logic of appropriateness requires reflexivity, prior to intentional deliberation the agent must feel from practical sense that rule-based reasoning is the way to go given habitus and the field. In other words, contrary to norm compliance, the logic of practicality is not based on a "should" but instead on a "could": "The practical sense is what allows one to behave appropriately without posing or executing a 'should.' "[109] There is no explicit ought-to because "practice does not imply – or rather excludes – mastery of the logic that is expressed within it."[110] When one feels from practical sense that the way to go is to comply with a norm, one may be able to verbalize what that norm is, but one probably cannot explain why one figured one had to follow a norm in the first place. Although it is inarticulate, the logic of practicality is ontologically prior: as the dynamic intersection of structure and agency, it determines which further logic of social action applies, given positions and dispositions.

Another important implication is that the relationship among the four logics of social action is one of complementarity instead of mutual exclusion. The ontological priority of the logic of practicality means that it informs any and all conscious and reflexive action, whether it stems from the logic of consequences, appropriateness or arguing.

---

[109] Bourdieu (2003, 201).   [110] Bourdieu (1990a, 11).

For instance, Adler notes that "the capacity for rational thought and behavior is above all a background capacity."[111] The same could be said of normative compliance and communicative action. Contrary to practicality, these three logics of social action share a similar focus on representations: instrumental rationality is premised on calculated interests; appropriateness derives from normative judgment; and communicative action is informed by explicit notions of truth and deliberation. In practice, however, the four logics are necessarily interwoven because any reflexive action stems from the practical sense. When contemporary statespeople are involved in a deterrence situation, for instance, their practical sense may lead them to calculate the costs and benefits of their policy options. In the field of military strategy, comparing means and ends is inscribed in agents' dispositions as well as in the rules of the game. When the same statespeople face close allies in a disagreement about core values, their practical sense may guide them to abide by shared norms. Within NATO, for instance, cold calculations do not always make sense in view of the embodied shared identity and history of the community. When, finally, these statespeople seek to reach an agreement on new international norms of intervention, they may feel from their practical sense that reasoned dialogue is the way to reach a compromise. In sum, which logic of reflexive social action is to apply typically depends on an unreflexive practical mastery of the world. Such is also the case with interstate peace.

Outline of a theory of practice of security communities

Both Deutsch's and Adler and Barnett's frameworks on security communities tend to focus on the study of representational knowledge. In Deutsch's scheme, a crucial test of "integration" consists of the "subjective" representations that elites share about themselves: "Did influential people in all parts of the wider area believe that a firm sense of community existed throughout its territories?"[112] The focus here is on what people think about each other, that is, how they represent each other. Similarly, Adler and Barnett's revamped framework asserts that collective identity – the blurring of the Self–Other

[111] Adler (2002, 103).   [112] Deutsch *et al.* (1957, 32).

distinction – is a "necessary condition of dependable expectations of peaceful change."[113] Mutually encompassing representations are theorized as the constitutive foundation of peace. No doubt these representations are important for the social construction of peaceful realities: Deutsch's subjective beliefs factor in rational decisionmaking, while Adler and Barnett's collective identity informs socially appropriate behavior. Admittedly, the logics of consequences, appropriateness and arguing all play an important role in security communities.

Yet there is more to peace than representations. To begin with, one could argue that identity is not entirely reflexive and articulate. In fact, a number of studies in IR have shown its practical and everyday dimension.[114] Inside the research program on security communities, however, identity has traditionally been theorized as a representation, a discourse or a narrative.[115] Veronica Kitchen argues, for instance, that "identity is reflexive and intersubjective. That is, in this particular case, it exists only as long as states consciously see themselves as having the Atlantic identity."[116] Given her interest in argumentation as a process of identity change, a focus on the explicitly invoked obviously makes sense. My point is not that mutual representations do not matter, but simply that they may not play the principal role in explaining peace.

Moreover, it is quite limiting to treat identity as primordial to practices. Because of the representational bias, IR constructivists typically envision the following theoretical sequence: identity constitutes interests, which drive action. Discussing identity change in the transatlantic security community, Kitchen observes that "the question of 'who we are together' defines the question of what we do together."[117] But what happens if we reverse the theoretical order and conceive of practice as the determinant of identity? From a practice perspective it is equally true that what we do together defines the question of who we are. As Etienne Wenger argues: "The experience of identity in practice is a way of being in the world. It is not equivalent to a self-image; it is not, in its essence, discursive or reflective ... Who we are lies in the way we live day to day, not just in what we think or say about ourselves."[118] All in all, taking a practice

---

[113] Adler and Barnett (1998, 38).   [114] E.g. Neumann (2005a); Hopf (2002).
[115] E.g. Mattern (2005).   [116] Kitchen (2009, 100).
[117] Kitchen (2009, 97).   [118] Wenger (1998, 151).

turn throws light on the constitutive nature of practices, including identity and security community.

From this perspective, peace is a very practical relation to the world, characterized, among other things, by non-violent dealings. While it is primarily mutual representations that strike the eye of the social scientist, on the ground the practicality of peace entails several non-representational dimensions. Security communities thrive on a practical *modus operandi* that has a different logic than its objectified *opus operatum*. Take, for instance, the key role played by trust, correctly theorized by Adler and Barnett as the second constitutive foundation of security communities. Trust, defined as "believing despite uncertainty,"[119] is a good example of an inarticulate feeling derived from practical sense. Based on personal and collective history (habitus) and faced with a particular social context (field), security practitioners "feel" (practical sense) that they could believe despite uncertainty – that is, they trust their security community counterparts. As a background feeling, trust does not derive from instrumental calculations, norm compliance or reasoned consensus: it is informed by the logic of practicality. The reasons why an agent trusts another are not readily verbalizable; they derive from tacit experience and an embodied history of social relations. Trust is practical sense. Given its central role in interstate peace, and for that matter in almost any aspect of world politics and social relations, the logic of practicality needs to be integrated into the security communities framework and into IR theory in general.

Self-evident diplomacy

How does peace exist in and through practice? The first conceptual challenge is to identify the constitutive practice of security communities. I define a constitutive practice as a social action endowed with intersubjective meanings that are shared by a given community and that cement its practitioners.[120] In the IR literature, Adler suggests that "peace is the practice of a security community."[121] But this

---

[119] Adler and Barnett (1998, 46).   [120] See Wenger (1998).

[121] Adler (2005, 17). In a more recent article, Adler suggests that security communities "spread by the co-evolution of background knowledge and subjectivities of *self-restraint*" (Adler 2008, 197). See also the Norbert Elias-inspired notion of "habitus of restraint" in Bjola and Kornprobst (2007).

formulation needs to be refined because peace is better categorized as a social fact (such as money) than as a practice (such as purchasing groceries). In the everyday life of the current interstate system, security communities are all about the practice of diplomacy, defined as "[t]he conduct of relations between states and other entities with standing in world politics by official agents and by peaceful means."[122] As a dialogue of states "by means short of war,"[123] the diplomatic practice constitutes peace in the current Westphalian system. Critics may find this claim tautological. Yet it is no more tautological than saying that H_2O constitutes water: atoms constitute molecules in the natural realm in a way analogous to how practices constitute social facts in the social world. Without atoms there cannot be molecules; without practice there cannot be any social reality. The semblance of tautology here stems from the very logic of constitutive analysis.[124] One would hardly dispute that the discovery of the atomic structure of water was no tautology but an all-important step forward for humankind. The same arguably goes for the search for the constitutive practices of the social fact of interstate peace.

Of course, the simple occurrence of the diplomatic practice does not mean that peace is waiting around the corner. Diplomacy may be observed in highly turbulent relationships and *in*security communities, from the contemporary Middle East to the East–West rivalry during the Cold War. No doubt diplomacy is not the preserve of security communities. The key distinction lies in the self-evidence of the practice. Inside a mature security community, diplomacy is the only thinkable way to solve disputes, to the exclusion of others (including violent practices). As peace settles in, diplomacy becomes second

---

[122] Bull (1995, 156). Limited to the current international order, this historically contingent observation does not rule out that peace may be constituted by different practices in political orders other than the current interstate system, nor is it a normative stance in favor of the international status quo. My focus on state-to-state peace certainly does not exhaust diplomacy in twenty-first-century global politics.

[123] Watson (1991, 11). In this book I do not thickly describe the diplomatic practice and its evolution over time because my main focus is not on the practice per se but on the political processes that make it self-evident in certain contexts and not in others. For rich accounts of the diplomatic practice, see Cross (2006); Der Derian (1987); Hamilton and Langhorne (1995); Jönsson and Hall (2005); Neumann (2005a; 2007); Sharp and Wiseman (2007); and Watson (1991).

[124] Wendt (1998).

nature. The theory of practice of security communities argues that peace exists in and through practice when security officials' practical sense makes diplomacy the self-evident way of solving interstate disputes. Diplomacy is the constitutive practice of security communities insofar, and only insofar, as it is the axiomatic or "natural" practice, to the exclusion of violent ones. When diplomacy is doxa, states do not live under the shadow of war anymore: diplomacy is the commonsensical way to go.

The theory of practice of security communities leads to a positive notion of peace, defined as an international relationship in which security practitioners think *from*, instead of about, diplomacy. Peace is more than simply non-war; it is self-evident diplomacy. Conversely, an insecurity community is characterized by the fact that resorting to diplomacy to solve disputes is only one possibility among others, including violent practices. In between these two political constellations, one finds what Ole Wæver (after Hakan Wiberg) calls a "non-war community,"[125] which entails normal though not self-evident diplomacy. Figure 2.1 illustrates how different degrees of diplomacy embodiment lead to a variety of interstate relations in and through practice. In mature peaceful interstate relations, the non-violent settlement of disputes forms the background against which all further interactions take place. Officials continue to think about a variety of policies, either instrumentally or normatively; but they take for granted that all possible options for solving mutual disputes start from the diplomatic practice. They think *from* diplomacy and not *about* its opportunity. The scenario of violence (or threats thereof) recedes from their horizon of possibility, which is narrowed down to a set of diplomatic possibilities. This is peace in and through practice.

By way of illustration, take the case of the transatlantic security community.[126] Innumerable pundits have announced its demise in the wake of the US-led invasion of Iraq. Most famously, Robert Kagan argued that "on major strategic and international questions today, Americans are from Mars and Europeans are from Venus: They agree on little and understand one another less and less."[127] Thanks in part to all this expert talk, the transatlantic rift in security cultures and

---

[125] Wæver (1998).   [126] See Pouliot (2006).   [127] Kagan (2003, 3).

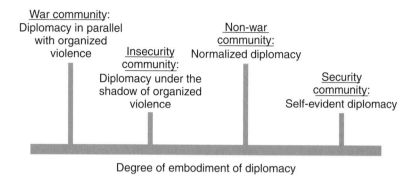

Figure 2.1 Diplomacy in interstate relations

identities may become a new intersubjective reality. That said, while the Iraq crisis revealed important differences in international outlook between certain NATO members, it has made equally obvious that even deep disagreements over sensitive issues of defense cannot distract allies from what they have come to routinely do together – diplomacy: that is, the peaceful resolution of mutual disputes. That a security community such as NATO is inhabited by disagreements and identity struggles should hardly come as a surprise: politics and conflict never recede, not even from tightly knit circles of friends. But so long as diplomacy remains the axiomatic or self-evident practice in mutual dealings, one has to conclude that the security community is alive and well. Recent strains between transatlantic countries, all solved peacefully if at times painfully, empirically demonstrate just that. In practice, even disagreements over the most sensitive issues of security and defense have not prompted anything like a veiled threat of possible violent retaliation among community members. Insofar as the non-violent settlement of disputes remains the self-evident practice among security officials, or, better put, insofar as practitioners think *from* diplomacy instead of *about* it, then the transatlantic security community is a social reality to be reckoned with.

When this axiomatically peaceful logic of practicality settles in, it takes on a dimension of habit or routine. Without instrumental calculations, reflexive rule-following or communicative action about the opportunity of settling disputes non-violently, the security officials' practical sense leads them to go on diplomatically. Although routine is an important part of practicality, however, practical sense cannot be reduced to habit. Routinized diplomacy is more than habitual repetition because practical sense results from the necessarily contingent intersection of a set of dispositions (habitus) and positions (field). For instance, Frédéric Mérand shows that the diplomatic practices behind the design of the European Security and Defense Policy followed neither a rational nor a structural pattern, but a haphazard, creative and combinatorial one. Dozens of interviews with practitioners indicate that to build tools, they try materials that work and discard others that do not, following their inspiration to change the shape of the object incrementally. Eventually, security officials end up with something completely different from what they had planned (a "bricolage").[128] Another study of the European diplomatic corps concludes that its autonomy does not so much depends on the institutions and explicit rules of the game that formally define and constrain it. Instead, the room for maneuver rests with what diplomats *do* with these constraints in and through practice.[129] Even when routinized as in security communities, then, the diplomatic practice retains a crucial element of contingency. To paraphrase Ryle, practitioners attend *from* diplomacy *to* the contingent matters at hand.

Hysteresis, (dis)positions and order in security communities

The crucial question awaits: how do we get there? What are the sociopolitical processes that turn diplomacy into the self-evident way of solving interstate disputes? The conventional constructivist take on the matter would center on norm internalization. Following this, the peaceful settlement of disputes begins as an explicit norm with which security elites at first comply out of instrumental rationality. With iteration, the practice becomes internalized as legitimate or taken-for-granted. In this connection, Checkel envisions three "modes of rationality" whereby deep socialization occurs: instrumental (strategic calculation), bounded (role-playing) and communicative (normative suasion).[130] Though useful, this internalization framework suffers from two main shortcomings. First, it remains

---

[128] Mérand (2008, 134).   [129] Cross (2006).   [130] Checkel (2005).

embroiled in the representational bias: taken-for-granted knowledge necessarily began as explicit representations upon which agents once reflected intentionally. Practice theory, by contrast, emphasizes tacit learning, a cognitive mechanism that accounts for the transmission of practices without explicit teaching or reflexive compliance. For example, the concept of communities of practice allows for the theorization of "learning as social participation."[131] Collective learning occurs in and through practice, within communities of doers.

Second, the norm internalization framework is sociologically thin: the social context that makes the logic of practicality possible is barely theorized. Especially lacking is a theorization of the power relations that constitute self-evident practices such as diplomacy within security communities. Contrary to widespread liberal views, peace is more than the result of the "arrangement of differences" or a "win-win compromise." Peace originates from the imposition of meanings through power relations, as barely perceptible as they may be. As Foucault argues: "What makes power hold good, what makes it accepted, is simply the fact that it doesn't only weigh on us as a force that says no, but that it traverses and produces things, it induces pleasure, forms knowledge, produces discourse."[132] Just like any social fact, peace or security communities never simply happen to be there: they are necessarily the result of past struggles among agents to define reality. As Barnett and Adler observe, "the ability to create the underlying rules of the game, to define what constitutes acceptable play, and to be able to get other actors to commit to these rules because they are now part of their self-understandings is perhaps the most subtle and effective form of power."[133] Peace is a form of doxa and it is infused with all the symbolic violence that comes with the order of things. Indeed, symbolic power – the imposition of meanings (including legitimacy) through social relations – turns a zero-sum struggle for defining reality and morality into something that has all the attributes of a win-win relationship: interstate peace.

---

[131] Wenger (1998, 4).
[132] Foucault (1980, 119). In IR, see Barnett and Duvall (2005); and Guzzini (2005).
[133] Barnett and Adler (1998, 424).

Security communities are peaceful patterns of order in interstate relations.[134] At the micro level, this pattern rests on diplomatic practical sense. At the macro-level, it is doxa that consolidates self-evident diplomacy into intersubjective, taken-for-granted structures. The micro–macro mechanism that links up the two levels is the power-laden aligning of positions and dispositions. A given practice becomes doxic – or, put differently, a pattern of social order settles in – when there exists what Bourdieu calls a "homology" between positions in the field and dispositions in habitus. In other words, when agents' habitus mirrors the configurational hierarchy of which they are part, the practical sense becomes a self-regulating mechanism whereby inclinations become in perfect tune with the structure of positions and the rules of the game. This is the inarticulate side of Goffman's sense of one's place. Under conditions of homology, necessity makes virtue, so to speak. The (objectively) impossible is (subjectively) unthinkable and the (objectively) plausible is (subjectively) inevitable.[135] This "orchestra without a conductor" is at the very root of social order and domination: a habitus that is homologous to the field's structure basically reproduces it as part of the order of things. As Bourdieu notes: "It is the pre-reflexive fit between the objective and the embodied structures ... that explains the ease (which in the end really is amazing) with which, throughout history but for a few crisis situations, dominant agents impose their domination."[136]

The use of the gerund form – the *aligning* of positions and dispositions – is meant to introduce agency and political struggles in the fight for domination of the field. Dispositions do not simply happen to fit with positions (a functionalist argument) but are actively and often painstakingly fitted by the dominant agents.[137] The order of things is established through the iterated practices performed by capital-endowed players: in effect, their doing something in a certain way makes the implicit but powerful claim that "this is how things are."[138] Power is exerted at the level of inarticulate knowledge: meanings are imposed in and through practice. This "practical mimesis," as Bourdieu notes, differs from imitation, which requires "a conscious

---

[134] Mattern (2001; 2005); Williams (2001); and Pouliot and Lachmann (2004).
[135] Bourdieu (2003, 332–3).   [136] Bourdieu (2003, 256–7).
[137] Jackson (2006a).   [138] See Swidler (2001, 87).

effort."[139] The archetype of a power relation in and through practice is apprenticeship, in which the master's competence is felt by the apprentice as a relation of immediate adherence to the very nature of things. As Polanyi put it:

> To learn by example is to submit to authority. You follow your master because you trust his manner of doing things even when you cannot analyse and account in detail for its effectiveness. By watching the master and emulating his efforts in the presence of his example, the apprentice unconsciously picks up the rules of the art, including those which are not explicitly known to the master himself. These hidden rules can be assimilated only by a person who surrenders himself to that extent uncritically to the imitation of another.[140]

The key resource in aligning positions and dispositions is symbolic power, which, by legitimizing the order of things, "somatizes" domination. As a result, patterns of order (i.e. self-evident practices) cloak themselves as doxa – "the relationship of immediate adherence that is established in practice between a habitus and the field to which it is attuned, the pre-verbal taking-for-granted of the world that flows from practical sense."[141]

When habitus is perfectly attuned to the field's distribution of positions and rules of the game, dominant players become masters whose higher position in the game and control over its rules are self-reinforcing assets. In effect, a habitus homologous to the field's structure is the ultimate vehicle of domination because the weaker players, disposed to take a social configuration for granted as part of the natural order of things, become complicit in maintaining the domination pattern. Despite the clear disadvantage conferred by their position in the distribution of capital and especially by the rules of the game, dominated players partake in their domination as they willingly (though usually not reflexively) play the game of their own exploitation. In this context, domination becomes invisible to the dominated: it is self-evident, as part of the natural order of things. This is what Bourdieu calls "misrecognition" – "the fact of recognizing a violence which is wielded precisely inasmuch as one does not perceive

---

[139] Bourdieu (1990a, 73).
[140] Quoted in Lynch (1997, 339).
[141] Bourdieu (1990a, 68); see Bourdieu (2001a).

it as such."[142] Misrecognition renders domination invisible as part of the (legitimate) order of things: misrecognized power is *re*cognized as authoritative but *mis*cognized as the source of domination. Under a perfect alignment between positions and dispositions, order is just as strong as it is invisible.

Conversely, when the homology between history-made things (field) and history-made bodies (habitus) is broken, the domination pattern weakens. Bourdieu calls the possible disconnection between positions and dispositions "hysteresis," a concept derived from the Greek *hysterein* (to be behind) that refers, in physics, to the lag that may occur between the cause and its effects on the behavior of a particle subject to a physical force. Comparing a social field with a magnetic field (where the magnet is the stake at hand), Bourdieu defines hysteresis as "cases in which dispositions function out of phase and practices are objectively ill-adapted to the present conditions because they are objectively adjusted to conditions that no longer obtain."[143] In any type of social configuration, one always finds agents who exhibit awkward practices and who behave out of place.[144] These "Don Quixote effects" are captured by the notion of hysteresis. When their practical sense (i.e. the interplay between habitus and field) is socially ill-adapted to a concrete situation, quixotic agents do not behave in tune with commonsense. Given one's historical exposure to struggles in other fields, for instance, one may be inclined to mistake one's own place in a social configuration. In Bourdieu's words: "Habitus is a principle of invention which, generated by history, is somewhat dragged away

---

[142] Bourdieu and Wacquant (1992, 168).

[143] Bourdieu (1990a, 62). For an intriguing modelization of hysteresis in economics, see Katzner (1999).

[144] In international politics, Williams uses a trivial yet telling example of hysteresis when General Alexander Lebed from Russia visited President Clinton in the 1990s, a meeting that prompted negative reactions inside the White House. As Williams comments:

> What was "shocking" was that Lebed clearly did not appear to be the "kind of man" that he was supposed to be, that in significant ways it appeared he did not "belong." That he didn't know where to stand, and could not "look you in the eye," reflects a series of judgements emerging out of the habitus of the American official and the field of accepted practice in which it operates. This is then directly and evaluatively applied in an appreciation of Lebed's personal and political stature via an evaluation of his own bodily *hexis*.   (Williams 2007, 30).

from history: since dispositions are *durable*, they spark all sorts of hysteresis effects (of lag, gap, discrepancy)."[145] When the subjectivized imprint of habitus is not homologous to intersubjective rules of the game and positions in the field, this disconnection weakens social order and domination patterns and opens the door to social change.

In Bourdieu's theory, therefore, domination rests not only with the possession of valuable resources (capital) as mediated by the rules of the game. While power is a social distance defined along structural and relational properties, it also hinges on the ways that these are reflected within agents' bodies. In other words, a power relation is necessarily "sobjective" – both objectified and subjective (see Chapter 3). As Bourdieu contends, conceiving power in symbolic terms "does remind us that social science is not a social physics; that the acts of cognition that are implied in misrecognition and recognition are part of social reality and that the socially constituted subjectivity that produces them belongs to objective reality."[146] One cannot understand domination patterns unless one inquires into the embodied dispositions of the players involved, both dominant and dominated. First, while capital accumulation defines the objectified structure of the field in positional terms, the very definition and value of capital is the object of constant struggle among agents. The issue, thus, is not only what power agents *have* but also what power *is* in practice.[147] Second, domination can only work if it is (mis)recognized as such in and through social relations. For this to happen, there must be a homology between history-made bodies (habitus) and history-made things (field). As Bourdieu sums up: "One only preaches to the converted."[148]

Interestingly, this dispositional view generates a different understanding of social causality than usual. For instance, Ryle recalls that it is not correct to say that the glass broke because a stone hit it. Instead, we should say that the glass broke when the stone hit it because it is breakable. In other words, we cannot say that one specific event has had a determinant effect on behaviors in and of itself; instead, it is dispositions that, being susceptible to such a determinant effect, give the event its historical efficacy.[149] In terms of social practice, Searle

[145] Bourdieu (1990a, 135).
[146] Bourdieu (1990a 122); see also (Bourdieu 1989).
[147] I owe this formulation to Stefano Guzzini.
[148] Bourdieu (2001a, 186).   [149] Quoted in Bourdieu (2003, 214).

similarly notes that "we should not say that the experienced baseball player runs to first base because he wants to follow the rules of baseball, but we should say that because the rules require that he run to first base, he acquires a set of background habits, skills, dispositions that are such that when he hits the ball, he runs to first base."[150] It is habitus that makes social patterns possible, not free-floating structures. In order to capture this crucial dimension of social life, one must recover the logic of practicality.

All in all, applying Bourdieu to security communities leads to two key theoretical innovations upon which this book's case study builds. First, it defines self-evident diplomacy as the constitutive practice of security community. When a practice is so fully part of everyday routine that it is commonsensically enacted, it forms the background knowledge against which all social interaction takes place. When this embodiment takes place among states' officials, diplomacy becomes the shared background against which they interact. They think *from* diplomacy not *about* its opportunity. As a result, peaceful change can be dependably expected; the orchestra can play without a conductor. Second, the doxic nature of diplomacy inside security communities is part of patterns of domination that rest on matching dispositions and positions. Wielding power in and through practice endows diplomacy with a doxic aura of self-evidence and naturalness. Under such a political pattern, the practicality or self-evidence of diplomacy makes the social fact of international peace possible.

Conclusion

The logic of practicality is meant to be an epistemic bridge between practical and theoretical relations to the world. In fact, the very notion is an oxymoron: practice is logical to the point that being logical ceases to be practical, as Bourdieu quips.[151] This raises thorny issues at the methodological level.

---

[150] Searle (1995, 144). As Searle further notes, a dispositional conceptualization of causality and power is in fact akin to Charles Darwin's evolution theory, which basically turned conventional wisdom on its head. Instead of: "The fish has the shape that it does in order to survive in water," Darwin professed: "The fish that have that shape (thanks to their genes in reaction to environment) are more likely to survive than fish that do not."

[151] Bourdieu (1987, 97–8).

The representational bias that plagues modern social theory arguably originates from the fact that norms, ideas or identities usually lend themselves to empirical scrutiny more easily than background knowledge does. Representations such as norms are part of discourse and debates; they are often explicitly invoked and the objects of open contestation. Background knowledge, by contrast, is unsaid and unthought. Agents almost never explicitly mention it even though it is part of each and every one of their practices. Practical knowledge is everywhere but always concealed in practices. Consequently, it must be interpreted from contexts and practices as well as through agents' dispositions and subjective meanings. Even so, gaining knowledge about background knowledge is often like asking fish, if they could speak, to describe the water in which they swim.[152]

In his critique of practice theory, Stephen Turner calls this predicament the "Mauss problem."[153] In order to decipher the meanings of a practice, the practice must be both alien *and* native to the interpreter's own system of meanings. On the one hand, if the meanings of a practice are too deeply embodied by the interpreter, chances are they will remain invisible as second nature. If, on the other hand, the meanings of a practice are completely alien to the interpreter, then they may not be properly understood within their context. The Mauss problem is a genuine methodological challenge for practice theorists as well as for interpretivists. The next chapter takes it up by devising a sobjective methodology in tune with practice theory.

---

[152] Rubin and Rubin (1995, 20).
[153] Turner (1994, 19–24) after French sociologist Marcel Mauss.

3 | A "sobjective" methodology for the study of practicality

This chapter seeks to map out the main lines of a methodology specifically geared toward a constructivist approach centered on practices. In keeping with the argument put forward in Chapter 2, my objective is to overcome the representational bias by systematically restoring the practical logics of international politics and social life in general. The "sobjective" label intends to convey the central idea that constructivist inquiries need to develop not only objectified, but also subjective knowledge about social and international life. As Bourdieu famously explains, both forms of knowledge "are equally indispensable to a science of the social world that cannot be reduced either to a social phenomenology or to a social physics."[1] The methodology outlined below offers practical guidance as to how to achieve such a sobjective-with-an-o social science.

Methodology is, according to one prominent observer, "the major missing link in constructivist theory and research."[2] Another leading scholar concurs that "the time is ripe for further debate about best practices for those working with discourse and texts."[3] Indeed, constructivists have yet to devise a distinct *modus operandi* designed to study the social construction of meaningful realities. This is not to deny the commonly held view that "constructivist analysis is compatible with many research methods currently used in social science and political science"[4]; indeed, I would argue that constructivism does *not* require the development of brand new methods. That said, the approach would certainly benefit from engaging more systematically and coherently with pressing methodological issues. In addition, the consolidation of constructivist methodology would facilitate dialogue with other IR theoretical approaches by making its standards of validity more explicit and amenable to non-constructivist ways of doing research.

[1] Bourdieu (1990a, 25). [2] Adler (2002,109).
[3] Checkel (2004, 239). [4] Finnemore and Sikkink (2001, 392).

As such, this chapter seeks to foster methodological conversations across the spectrum of IR approaches, particularly by allowing for the comparative assessment of constructivist works and more mainstream research. By showing how scholars with arguably unbridgeable ontological and epistemological differences can still share some methods and use a similar language, I aim to ground abstract debates and avoid all-too-common dialogues of the deaf. There is no pretense here that positivism and interpretivism can ultimately be reconciled – they most probably cannot. Nevertheless, there is much to be gained from learning how to make constructivist and mainstream works speak to each other on fundamental issues of validity, falsifiability and generalizability. Although *conversions* are unlikely, academic *conversations* across metatheoretical divides often are at the source of promising new ways of thinking.

Following others, I distinguish between research *methods*, which consist of concrete tools of inquiry, and *methodology* – an encompassing term referring "to those basic assumptions about the world we study, which are prior to the specific techniques adopted by the scholar undertaking research."[5] Put differently, while the same methods may be shared by various methodologies, a methodology comprises a set of epistemological and ontological requirements that formulates its own scientific standards and truth conditions. Research methods, in other words, should be aligned with the researcher's style of reasoning – ontology *and* epistemology.[6] I do not mean to dispute that methodological choices need to be problem-driven – that research questions should come first and methods second. But on a deeper level, the horizon of thinkable (or what is deemed interesting or relevant) research questions is circumscribed by one's style of reasoning.

The chapter contains five sections. In the first section I discuss the peculiarities of the constructivist style of reasoning as I conceive of it. The second section argues that constructivist methodology needs to be inductive, interpretive and historical in order to develop not only objectified but also subjective knowledge about social and international life. In the third section I outline a three-step methodology that moves from the recovery of practical logics to their contextualization and objectification. The fourth section engages with mainstream methodology and specifies where constructivism stands on scientific

---

[5] Fierke (2004, 36).   [6] See Hall (2003).

standards such as validity, falsifiability, and generalizability. Finally, I conclude the chapter with a discussion about the book's case study and its methodological underpinnings.

Two qualifiers about the purpose of the chapter are in order. First, I do *not* claim to develop *the* constructivist methodology but *a* constructivist methodology. The goal is certainly not to force anyone into a methodological straitjacket but simply to offer one view about how to "go on" with constructivist research; there is no doubt that methodological pluralism remains a valuable state of affairs in IR. Second, in the following pages I neither claim to survey the entire constructivist literature of the last decade nor do I intend to reinvent the constructivist wheel, so to speak. I take inspiration from existing works and seek to systematize, under the sobjectivist umbrella, a variety of methodological insights that remain scattered to this day. Ultimately, my objective is to foster debate about best research practices, not only among constructivists but within IR scholarship more generally.

The constructivist style of reasoning

The central claim of this first part is that constructivism constitutes a "style of reasoning" of its own in social science, a claim that has crucial methodological implications. Following Guzzini, I conceive of constructivism as a "metatheoretical commitment" based on three tenets: first, knowledge is socially constructed (an epistemological claim); second, social reality is constructed (an ontological claim); and third, knowledge and reality are mutually constitutive (a reflexive claim).[7] Accordingly, the social construction of knowledge and the construction of social reality are two sides of the same coin.

The notion of "style of reasoning" was developed by philosopher of science Ian Hacking in the early 1980s.[8] Reminiscent of Thomas Kuhn's "paradigms," Hacking's concept underscores the fact that throughout history there have been "new modes of reasoning that have specific beginnings and trajectories of development."[9] However, contrary to Kuhn, Hacking is preoccupied not by the incommensurability of styles of reasoning – that different paradigms are not

---

[7] Guzzini (2000; 2005); see Adler (2002).
[8] Hacking (1982; reprinted in Hacking 2002a, 159–77).
[9] Hacking (2002a, 162).

mutually expressible – but rather by their capability to define new worlds as well as the very meanings of truth and falsehood. For Hacking, styles of reasoning are historically constituted epistemes. Some have disappeared over time: alchemy and witchcraft, dominant during the Middle Ages, or Renaissance medicine are examples of vanished styles of reasoning that are almost impenetrable to the twenty-first-century mind. In the natural sciences, Hacking documents the historical emergence of the "laboratory style" ("which does not observe the workings of nature but intervenes in them") and, later, of the "probabilistic style" (which envisions "a world in which everything is cloaked in probabilities").[10]

A style of reasoning is defined by "a new domain of objects to study" (an ontology), a new kind of "truth conditions" (an epistemology), as well as "its own criteria of proof and demonstration" (a methodology).[11] First, "[e]very style of reasoning is associated with an ontological debate about a new type of object."[12] For instance, today's scientific realists argue that unobservable theoretical entities in the laboratory style really exist; empiricists deny this. Second, styles of reasoning "introduce new ways of being a candidate for truth or for falsehood."[13] To return to the example of statistics, Hacking argues that this style contains within itself all the epistemological standards for "self-authentification." The objective truth of a sentence depends on reasoning in a manner that recognizes such truth; hence the relative stability of scientific styles of reasoning, which internally define their standards of validity.

Third, a style of reasoning rests on a number of techniques and methods that produce a specific type of evidence. Methodology settles "what it is to be objective (truths of certain sorts are what we obtain by conducting certain sorts of investigations, answering to certain standards)."[14] People in laboratories do not use the same research techniques as statisticians to arrive at truth. Consequently, the validity of their findings is assessed in fundamentally different ways. This is the crucial lesson taken from Hacking's philosophy of science: any style of reasoning entails a particular methodology, which is itself comprised of a set of methods that are specifically geared toward tackling

---

[10] Hacking (2002b, 3).   [11] Hacking (2002b, 4).
[12] Hacking (2002a, 189).   [13] Hacking (2002a, 190).
[14] Hacking (2002a, 181).

a particular kind of object (ontology) and arriving at a characteristic notion of truth (epistemology).

Hacking does not venture very far in identifying styles of reasoning in social sciences; this is not, after all, his domain of philosophical inquiry. In keeping with the insight that each new style "brings with it new sentences, things that we quite literally never said before,"[15] one can imagine a few social scientific styles of reasoning. Though it has fallen into disrepute, structural functionalism and its talk of systems, equilibria and structures can be considered an autonomous style with its own structural ontology and functionalist epistemology. In contemporary political science and IR, the dominant style of reasoning remains rationalism or rational choice. This style possesses its own language (e.g. cost-benefit calculations, expected utility), its own ontology (a world comprised of pre-given, calculating individuals), as well as its own epistemology (positivism). It has been argued that the main contender for the rationalist style of reasoning in current IR scholarship is constructivism.[16] No doubt constructivism too has its own dialect, full of social constructions, norms, and identities. Admittedly, however, there is no common front in terms of ontology and epistemology. While a few scientific realists advocate a naturalistic version of constructivism in tune with positivism, others exhibit strong postmodernist leanings. In between these two extremes can be found the great majority of constructivists whose ontology/epistemology can conveniently be labeled "postfoundationalist."[17]

A slash divides ontology and epistemology because more and more constructivists argue that "the nature of being (*ontology*) cannot be separated from ways of knowing (*epistemology*)."[18] Developing knowledge about ontology is an activity firmly grounded in epistemology, and vice versa. Indeed, Jackson's view is in tune with Guzzini's aforementioned three tenets of constructivism when he notes that "a monist position avoids the thing/thought dichotomy altogether, concentrating instead on those practical (worldly) activities that *give rise* to *both*

---

[15] Hacking (2002a, 190).   [16] Katzenstein, Keohane and Krasner (1998).

[17] Pouliot (2004). Postfoundationalism is a metatheoretical commitment to the notion that, in the absence of ontological foundations of knowledge, the best way forward for social science is to build on the social facts that are already reified by agents. Thanks to Daniel Nexon who suggested the term "postfoundationalism."

[18] Fierke (2005, 7).

'things' *and* 'thoughts.'"[19] First, constructivism holds that knowledge and meaning in general are socially constructed. This epistemological claim is far-reaching for it also includes scientific knowledge. Second, constructivism posits that social reality is constructed instead of exogenously given. Our world is intersubjectively real because others agree it is. Third, constructivism stresses "the reflexive relationship between the social construction of knowledge and the construction of social reality."[20] In other words, many constructivists postulate that knowledge and reality are mutually constitutive, mostly through linguistic feedbacks such as looping effects and self-fulfilling prophecies. There is no meaningful reality prior to knowledge and vice versa.

In sum, postfoundationalist constructivism is just as much a science of knowing as it is a science of being.[21] Neither ontology nor epistemology should have priority over the other, for they are two sides of the same coin. Importantly, to say that reality and knowledge are mutually constitutive is *not* to give in to Idealism. As Friedrich Kratochwil explains, "hardly anyone – even among the most ardent constructivists or pragmatists – doubts that the 'world' exists 'independent' from our minds. The question is rather whether we can recognise it in a pure and direct fashion, i.e., without any 'description,' or whether what we recognise is always already organised and formed by certain categorical and theoretical elements."[22] For constructivists, the phenomenal world cannot be known outside the socially constructed meanings that we attach to it: one simply cannot know the world apart from *meaning*ful realities. Thus the world (ontology) and knowledge (epistemology) are mutually constitutive processes.

Contrary to scientific realism, which gives precedence to ontology over epistemology, postfoundationalism remains agnostic as to what is "really real" and what is not. There are three related reasons for such agnosticism which, when taken together, suggest that postfoundationalism is a more coherent metatheory for constructivism than is scientific realism. First, assuming an a priori reality in the manner of Wendt's "rump materialism" carries political consequences that essentially contradict constructivist tenets: material conditions need to be politically construed as limitations instead of

---

[19] Jackson, Patrick (2008, 133).   [20] Guzzini (2005, 499).
[21] I thank David Welch for this language.
[22] Kratochwil (2000, 91).

scientifically assumed.[23] Indeed, assuming the existence of a world prior to knowledge leads to reifying one's commonsensical and/or scientific representations as natural and universal. Second, claiming with realists that what our models depict is "really real" or "out there" amounts to scientific hubris. History shows that scientific concepts are just that – concepts, not reality – and that others will supersede them as new theories surface. Third, the positivist notion that science should aim at defining big-R reality – grasping its essence, so to speak – runs counter to the critical disposition that constructivism endorses by its very logic. Again with Hacking, to say that X is socially constructed aims to show that X is neither "natural" nor "inevitable."[24] Instead of seeking to establish the definitive and universal ontology of reality, constructivism must problematize what is held to be real in diverse political contexts by looking into the constitutive effects of knowledge.

A principled refusal to assume reality prior to knowledge means that, for postfoundationalist constructivism, there are no such things as ontological foundations of knowledge. A correspondence theory of truth is therefore impossible. Yet postfoundationalism certainly does not embrace epistemological relativism either. Inside a style of reasoning, there exist criteria for validity that are not transcendental but intersubjective, an issue to which I will return in the fourth section of this chapter. In this postfoundationalist context, the way forward consists of building on the social facts[25] that are naturalized by social agents. Already reified by agents, social facts provide constructivists with "epistemic foundations"[26] that allow them to develop knowledge about social life while remaining agnostic about reality. The focus is on what it is that *social agents*, as opposed to analysts, take to be real. In this epistemological sense, social facts are "the essence of constructivism."[27] They are reified knowledge that makes social worlds come into being. Ultimately, to know whether a social fact is "really real" makes no analytical difference; the point is to observe whether agents take it to be real and to draw the social and political implications that follow. In so doing, postfoundationalism charts

---

[23] Zehfuss (2002).   [24] Hacking (1999, 6).
[25] Social facts are "those facts that are produced by virtue of all the relevant actors agreeing that they exist" (Ruggie 1998, 12). The concept is Émile Durkheim's and the classic example used by Searle is money (Searle 1995).
[26] Adler (2005).   [27] Pouliot (2004).

a middle course between scientific realism (which rests on allegedly natural foundations) and antifoundationalism (which denies the possibility of foundations for knowledge altogether).

Methodological implications

Three main methodological implications follow from characterizing the constructivist style of reasoning as postfoundationalist social science. First, induction is the primary mode of knowing because social facts constitute the essence of constructivism. Research must begin with what it is that social agents, as opposed to analysts, believe to be real. Second, interpretation constitutes the central methodological task, as constructivism takes knowledge very seriously. To use Clifford Geertz's famous words, it is first and foremost a science "in search of meaning."[28] Third, the constructivist style of reasoning is inherently historical for it "sees the world as a project under construction, as *becoming* rather than *being*."[29] The mutual constitution of knowledge and reality therefore necessitates a process-centered approach.

An inductive methodology

Inductive analysis – a research strategy that moves from the local to the general – is the necessary starting point for any constructivist inquiry, as theorization destroys meanings as they exist for social agents. Deductive theorizing, for instance, deliberately imposes scientific categories upon practical ones. Yet constructivism's foundations of knowledge rest not on a set of a priori assumptions but on agents' taken-for-granted realities. In order to recover such meanings, the analyst must avoid superseding them with theoretical constructs. In addition, since the construction of social reality hinges on the social construction of knowledge, analysts also need to refrain, within the realms of possibility, from imposing their own taken-for-granted world onto their object of study. In sociology, Barney Glaser and Anselm Strauss famously dubbed this inductive enterprise "grounded theory":[30]

---

[28] Geertz (1973, 5). [29] Adler (2005, 11).
[30] Glaser and Strauss (1967, 226).

a firsthand immersion in a sphere of life and action – a social world – different from one's own yields important dividends. The field worker who has observed closely in this social world has had, in a profound sense, to live there. He has been sufficiently immersed in this world to know it, and at the same time has retained enough detachment to think theoretically about what he has seen and lived through.

Induction allows constructivists to recover the meanings and workings of the world as it exists for the actual agents of international politics. In so doing it acts as a safeguard against two related fallacies in social science. The first fallacy, well known since Durkheim's exhortation to fight against "prenotions," results from the socially constructed world inside which the analyst happens to live, with all its taken-for-granted realities. Of course, it is impossible to fully evade one's world and its meanings; because of the "Rashomon effect," different researchers never recover exactly the same practical meanings.[31] But that does not mean it is not worth trying to be as faithful and accurate as possible. The second fallacy countered by induction, which is by far the most pernicious, is what I called the representational bias in Chapter 2. Most social scientists have become used to taking the point of view of an external spectator with a view from nowhere. While perhaps inevitable, this god-like posture has profound epistemological consequences, as the theoretical relation to the world is fundamentally different from the practical one. To repeat Bourdieu's aphorism, a practice is logical up to the point where to be logical ceases to be practical.[32] Using induction and immersion, researchers resist imposing a scholastic and alien logic on practices that are fundamentally defined by their practical urgency and embeddedness in a social context.

That said, my plea in favor of induction does not amount to saying that social science should rely exclusively on subjective meanings. *Contra* Alfred Schütz's "postulate of adequacy," a study that narrowly sticks to the meanings held by actors lacks the detachment required for their historicization (where meanings come from and how they came to be) and their contextualization (how meanings relate to others and to patterns of domination). Interpretation also requires objectification.

[31] Heider (1988).   [32] Bourdieu (1987, 97–8).

An interpretive methodology

According to Adler, constructivism rests on "an *epistemology* in which interpretation is an intrinsic part of the social sciences."[33] Constructivism's interpretive methodology seeks to comprehend meanings in order to explain social life. Decades ago, Geertz convincingly exposed why interpretation must be part of any social scientific inquiry: a twitch is not a wink, a difference that hinges on intersubjective meanings and nothing else.[34] Because of this interest in understanding meaningful realities, constructivists just "cannot escape the interpretivist moment."[35] In contrast to other styles of reasoning, however, in constructivism this interpretivist moment is *double*. Interpretation means not only drawing inferences from data, as even diehard positivists do, but also recognizing (and taking advantage of) the fact that "an important part of the subject matter of social science is itself an interpretation – the self-interpretation of the human beings under study."[36] A constructivist social science therefore develops meanings about meanings.

How do these double hermeneutics transform the meanings that are being interpreted? Building on Hans-Georg Gadamer's understanding of interpretation as a "fusion of horizons" or a meaningful dialogue with an "Other," Paul Ricoeur famously describes the process of interpretation as the "objectification" of meanings.[37] A central claim of Ricoeur's interpretivism is that meanings need to be objectified in order to be not only understood but also explained. Building on speech act theory, he argues that moving from discourse to text transforms meanings in four objectifying ways. First, discourse loses its perlocutionary effect (what one does *by* saying) and to some extent its illocution too (what one does *in* saying). What remains is the locutionary dimension of discourse inscribed in the text (the act *of* saying). Second, contrary to discourse, in a text "the author's intention and the meaning of the text cease to coincide."[38] Intentionality loses its salience in favor of intertextuality. Third, a text is free from "ostensive references," that is, the immediate references drawn from the

---

[33] Adler (2005, 12).   [34] Geertz (1973, 6).
[35] Price and Reus-Smit (1998, 271).
[36] Neufeld (1993, 43–4). On the "double hermeneutics," see also Giddens (1984) and Jackson (2006b).
[37] Ricoeur (1977).   [38] Ricoeur (1977, 320).

context shared with the audience. And fourth, whereas discourse is addressed to someone, a text creates its own (and changing) audience. Objectified meanings lose their temporality and locality to become open to timeless, universal interpretation.

The crucial implication of this line of argument is that, through interpretation, subjective meanings become objectified as part of an intersubjective context. To objectify meanings is to inquire into what something means not for a specific agent but in a larger context of intersubjectivity. This is the central feature of the hermeneutic circle: interpretation proceeds by relating the parts in terms of the whole and vice versa.[39] To illustrate this idea, Ricoeur uses the example of a proverb. In order to interpret the meaning of a proverb, one has to put it in the wider context of a culture, a language, and a set of related practices. Proverbs are proverbs because uttering them in a certain context means more than they say. This surplus of meaning is to be found outside the specific words contained in the proverb and outside subjective beliefs such as intentions or expectations. Equally, a culture cannot be appropriately interpreted apart from its particular expressions such as proverbs. In interpretation, the whole and the parts cannot be analyzed separately.

Ricoeur's interpretivism targets more than discourse and language; importantly it deals with practices more generally, understood as patterned social activities endowed with intersubjective meaning (see Chapter 2). As he puts it: "Meaningful action is an object for science only under the condition of a kind of objectification which is equivalent to the fixation of a discourse by writing."[40] Therefore the meaning of a practice is detached from its advent through the four objectifying transformations outlined above. Just like a text, any action becomes amenable not only to Understanding – the subjective interpretation of the reasons and beliefs that inform it – but also to Explaining – the objectifying interpretation of its intersubjective context. Interpretivist constructivism is not exhausted by discourse: practice is its main object of study.

A historical methodology

An inductive and interpretive methodology amounts to something similar to Geertz's "thick description," which consists of "sorting

---

[39] Ricoeur (1977, 328 ff.).   [40] Ricoeur (1977, 322).

out the structures of signification"[41] – both subjective and objectified. Yet meanings are never fixed or static but always part of a dialectical process between knowledge and reality. Meanings constantly evolve over time. As a consequence, constructivism is a profoundly historical science: "rather than using history as a descriptive method, constructivism has history 'built in' as part of theories. Historicity, therefore, shows up as part of the contexts that make possible social reality."[42] In addition, the path dependence and feedback loops that characterize the dialectics of knowledge and reality further reinforce the need to study the social construction of international politics in time. As Paul Pierson recalls, one can stir jam into pudding but one cannot stir it out.[43] Process and sequence matter because social life is fundamentally temporal – that is, practice unfolds in real time at the level of action.

Such a historicized understanding of social life is in tune with constructivism's denaturalizing disposition. Recall that to say that X is socially constructed means that X is neither natural nor inevitable: X is historical. We know X to be socially constructed in part because it has a history of its own and results from social processes that are traceable over time. The historicization of X leads to its denaturalization: X needs not be, for it has not always been (or has not always been as it is). As a result, historicization "neutralizes, at least theoretically, the effects of naturalization and in particular the amnesia of the individual and collective genesis of a given world that presents itself under all the guises of nature."[44]

A historical methodology is concerned with the genesis of its object of study, that is, with the historical processes that make possible the constitution of specific social contexts. Since no social realities are natural, they are the results of political and social processes that are rooted in history. To trace them, the analyst needs to build a narrative – a dynamic account that tells the story of a variety of historical processes as they unfold over time. As Donald Polkinghorne explains: "Narrative explanations are retrospective ... They draw together the various episodes and actions into a story that leads through a sequence of events to an ending."[45] In IR, Ruggie takes inspiration from Max Weber to similarly advocate building "narrative explanatory protocols" that show "why things are historically *so* and not *otherwise*."[46]

---

[41] Geertz (1973, 9).   [42] Adler (2002, 102).   [43] Pierson (2004, 157).
[44] Bourdieu (2003, 262).   [45] Polkinghorne (1988, 170).
[46] Ruggie (1998, 32). See Finnemore (2003) for an application.

Narrative-building is different from causal analysis as understood by positivists. Instead of searching for constant antecedents, the researcher traces contingent practices that have historically made a given social fact possible. The small vs. large N controversy is thus irrelevant; from this perspective, explaining causality is subordinate to understanding meaning. Narrative causality traces the historical evolution of meanings (both subjective *and* intersubjective) in order to explain how they brought about, or made possible, a given social context. Causes are not ontological substances to be isolated "out there" but heuristic focal points used by the researcher to make sense of social life. Explanatory narratives order variegated meanings and practices in time around a number of plots or causal stories. Like counterfactual analysis, causal narratives reason backwards in order to understand why the branching tree of history took one direction instead of others. Inside the constructivist style of reasoning, then, historical analysis and interpretation go hand in hand. And because it implies temporally (and figuratively) standing back from current meanings, historicization leads to further objectification.

To tie the three strings together, a constructivist methodology that is inductive, interpretive and historical is able to develop both subjective knowledge (from the meanings that social agents attribute to their own reality, i.e. the logic of practicality) *and* objectified knowledge (which derives from "standing back" from a given situation by contextualizing and historicizing it). While inductive interpretation is necessary for recovering subjective meanings and practical logics, contextual and historical interpretation is required for their objectification in a larger context of intersubjectivity, social relations, and patterns of domination. This subjective-with-an-o methodology aims at overcoming the epistemological duality of subjectivism and objectivism by restoring the practical logic of social life and casting it under the analytical light of its intersubjective context and history.

Geertz's useful distinction between "experience-near" and "experience-distant" concepts, which he borrows from Heinz Kohut, conclusively drives the main point of sobjective methodology home. Experience-near concepts are developed through phenomenological inquiry with the goal of grasping as accurately as possible a reality that is known by the agents under study. By contrast, an experience-distant concept is constructed by the scientist in order to break with commonsensical experience and provide an outsider viewpoint, different from the ones that are practically engaged in the situation at hand. As Geertz explains: "Confinement to experience-near concepts leaves an ethnographer awash in immediacies, as well as entangled in vernacular. Confinement to experience-distant ones leaves him stranded in abstractions and smothered in jargon."[47] Striking a fine balance between practicality (experience-near concepts) and theory (experience-distant concepts) is the main task of a methodology that is inductive, interpretive and historical. In practical terms, as Geertz continues,

The real question [is how] ought one to deploy [experience-near and experience-distant concepts] so as to produce an interpretation of the way a people lives which is neither imprisoned within their mental horizons, an ethnography of witchcraft as written by a witch, nor systematically deaf to the distinctive tonalities of their existence, an ethnography of witchcraft as written by a geometer.[48]

The third part of the chapter explains how to go on with constructivist research by delving into the methodical practice of sobjective research.

The methodical practice of sobjectivism

Sobjectivism is a three-step methodology that moves along a continuum bordered at one end by experience-near concepts and at the other by experience-distant concepts. One begins with the inductive recovery of agents' realities and practical logics, then objectifies them through the interpretation of intersubjective contexts and thereafter pursues further objectification through historicization. In the spirit of grounded theory and abduction, however, these three steps should *not* be conceived as a unidirectional, linear pathway. As research unfolds, chances are that the analyst will feel the need to move back and forth between practical, contextualized and historicized knowledge. In practice, induction, interpretation and historicization should always be put in a close, abductive dialogue.

---

[47] Geertz (1987, 135).   [48] Geertz (1987, 135).

Recovering subjective meanings and practical logics

The first step consists of recovering as faithfully as possible the meanings that agents attribute to their reality: that is, the logic of practicality. Social action is understood from within, so as to recover the logic of practicality as it unfolds at the level of action. This is the most inductive step of all as it shies away from theorization. As Hopf notes: "Theorizing is a form of interpretation, and it destroys meaning. As soon as we begin to impose categories on evidence, that evidence stops meaning what it meant in its earlier context."[49] From this perspective, he continues, "[the] backbone of an interpretivist epistemology is phenomenology and induction. Phenomenology implies letting the subjects speak [while induction] involves the recording of these identities as atheoretically as possible."[50] By immersing oneself in practical lifeworlds, the knowledge apprehended at this first step needs to be as close as possible to the subjective meanings held by agents so as to develop a form of "cultural competence."[51]

This turn to phenomenology runs counter to dominant strands of IR theory, including constructivism. Over the last fifteen years most constructivists have been primarily concerned with epistemically objective realities such as norms, epistemes, institutions or collective identities. Such a focus is well taken as long as it is supplemented with an equivalent consideration for agent-level ideations. After all, only practices and the subjective dispositions that inform them can make the social construction of epistemically objective realities possible. In Adler's apt formulation, background knowledge "is Janus-faced because, in addition to being intersubjective knowledge embedded in practices, it also includes the subjective representations of intersubjectivity."[52] As a case in point, Neumann's research on the practice of diplomacy poses the under-researched question of what it means to be a diplomat.[53] Through his recollection of meanings from practitioners' point of view, he supplies a sophisticated hermeneutics of diplomacy, a central practice in international politics, and goes a long way toward understanding its practicality.

There are many useful ethnographic methods for the recovery of agents' meanings. One method made famous by Garfinkel is

---

[49] Hopf (2002, 25).   [50] Hopf (2002, 23).   [51] Neumann (2008a).
[52] Adler (2008, 202); see also Adler (1997).
[53] Neumann (2002; 2005a; 2007).

ethnomethodology, which seeks to reach the commonsensical and the taken-for-granted of daily life in order to report as faithfully as possible agents' ways of being in the world.[54] A related ethnographic method is participant observation, which involves the researcher's direct participation inside a social setting in order to understand it from the subjects' point of view. Geertz's analysis of Balinese cock-fights is a famous model of that method, which is very effective for the recovery of practicality. Diane Vaughn supports this point when she writes: "Habitus can be known by observing the enactment of dispositions in practice."[55] In IR, Barnett builds on a posting at the United States Mission to the UN in 1993 and 1994 to supply an illuminating "empathetic reconstruction" of the organization's response (or lack thereof) to the Rwandan genocide.[56]

More often than not, however, participant observation is particularly difficult to perform in international political settings, due to the secrecy and closed doors of negotiations, the size of organizations, and the geographical distribution of actors. In his study of nuclear laboratory facilities in California, for instance, anthropologist Hugh Gusterson quickly realized that he would not be allowed to access the premises and perform participant observation. He was consequently forced to "rethink the notion of fieldwork [he] had acquired as a graduate student so as to subordinate participant observation, conventionally the bedrock of fieldwork, to formal interviewing and to the reading of newspapers and official documents."[57] Such is the tough reality of fieldwork. But as Edward Schatz recalls, ethnography is not reducible to the method of participant observation; it also is a "sensibility ... to glean the meanings that the people under study attribute to their social and political reality."[58] In a much celebrated formulation, Renato Rosaldo boiled down ethnographic research to "deep hanging out."[59] A study such as Scott's *Seeing Like a State*, Schatz continues, definitely rests on a close understanding of practical logics but without direct participant observation in the field. When access to the field is denied, as it was with the case study I develop in this book, Schatz proposes a simple rule of thumb: strive for "the nearest possible vantage point."[60]

[54] Garfinkel (1967).   [55] Vaughn (2008, 70).   [56] Barnett (2002).
[57] Gusterson (1993, 63–4).   [58] Schatz (2009a, 5).
[59] Quoted in Gusterson (2008, 93).   [60] Schatz (2009b, 307).

The in-depth or qualitative interview is particularly apt at reconstructing the practitioners' point of view. Steinar Kvale defines interviews as "attempts to understand the world from the subjects' point of view, to unfold the meaning of people's experiences, to uncover their lived world to scientific explanations."[61] Qualitative interviews are specifically devised to reconstruct the practitioners' point of view prior to further objectification through interpretation and historicization. According to Herbert and Irene Rubin, the "philosophy" of interviews is to "[find] out what others think and know, and avoid dominating your interviewees by imposing your world on theirs."[62] The inductive generation of situated, insider knowledge is the key principle behind interviews. As conversations generative of subjective meanings, qualitative interviews provide researchers with an efficient means to penetrate more or less alien lifeworlds. Of course, the goal is not to mine for the truth but to hear life stories. In order to genuinely communicate, the interviewee and the researcher must come to share a similar language and a commonsensical world: "The researcher has to figure out the special new vocabulary and the taken-for-granted understandings within the setting ... Part of becoming a qualitative interviewer is learning to recognise and then explore words that have rich connotative or symbolic meanings for the people being studied."[63]

As I argued in Chapter 2, the practical sense is not something that is readily available for verbalization. So if background knowledge is typically tacit, how can interviews offer any insight into the logic of practicality? In other words, how can a conversation throw light on inarticulate meanings? Clearly, habitus, being mostly unconscious, cannot be reconstructed through direct questions about it. I propose two main ways to help recover practical knowledge indirectly through qualitative interviewing. First, focus less on what interviewees talk *about* than what they talk *from* – the stock of assumptions that ought to be presumed in order to say what is being said. Most often, insider stories are particularly interesting for the myriad of small things they eschew, which typically belong to the realm of background knowledge. As a sensitive outsider, the ethnographically minded interviewer is particularly well equipped to capture these tacit

---

[61] Kvale (1996, 1).   [62] Rubin and Rubin (1995, 5).
[63] Rubin and Rubin (1995, 8 and 21).

assumptions and overcome the "Mauss problem" (see Chapter 2). For instance, Gusterson finds that his interviews "generated articulations not only of fiercely public ideologies, but also of the private, the whispered, the half crystallized on the edge of consciousness."[64] There exist several techniques to devise an interview questionnaire so as to indirectly target and recover inarticulate knowledge. For instance, one could submit hypothetical scenarios to interviewees and ask how they would react were they to be put in such a situation (see Chapter 4). Another useful trick pioneered by Garfinkel is to ask questions that specifically seek to unsettle taken-for-granted knowledge. His classic example is the routine question: "How do you feel?" When asked what that question means, subjects in an ethnomethodological experiment appeared at serious loss: the meaning is so taken for granted that being interrogated about it is puzzling and even destabilizing.[65] Certain questions are simply out of place in terms of practical meanings. Should the interviewee appear disturbed, then chances are that some form of inarticulate knowledge is at work.

Second, ask interviewees to recount other practitioners' practices. As I argued in Chapter 2, asking interviewees to describe their daily lives always runs the risk of imposing a scholastic logic on practices. As Bourdieu notes, "as soon as he reflects on his practice, adopting a quasi-theoretical posture, the agent loses any chance of expressing the truth of his practice, and especially the truth of the practical relation to the practice."[66] Just as chefs do not explain their recipes the same way they cook them, interviews put social agents in the reflexive yet problematic position of observing their own practices. This is obviously not the best way to recover the inarticulate. The corrective that I propose consists of asking interviewees to retell the practices of *others* – that is, the activities that they regularly observe on the part of their fellow practitioners. In this way, the interviewee becomes a kind of participant observer of everyday interactions. What I have in mind here is not so distant from what has been called "hearsay ethnography,"[67] a method which consists of asking insiders to recount the practices and interactions that they can observe in their everyday lives (from which outsiders are excluded).

---

[64] Gusterson (2008, 106).   [65] Garfinkel (1967, 42–3).
[66] Bourdieu (1990a, 91).   [67] Watkins and Swidler (2006).

The analysis of interview transcripts can also be focused on the practical assumptions that make the interviewee's discourse possible. Again, the point is that anytime interviewees discuss *about* something, they have to think *from* something else – islands of background knowledge that can be mapped by the attentive interviewer. To quote Gusterson once more, "the way to understand lab employees was not to ask a series of abstract questions about their ideological beliefs but to elicit life histories that crystallized their commitments in narratives of the events through which they were enacted."[68] Speaking often reveals more than the words uttered.

In sum, qualitative interviews can be performed in such a way that they (imperfectly) make up for the impossibility of participant observation in certain settings. The method is no panacea, yet as a surrogate it does go some distance in recovering practical logics. It is worth recalling that in one of his most famous studies about the poor, Bourdieu himself makes extensive use of interviews in order to reconstruct the world of poverty in French suburbs.[69] Similarly, Loïc Wacquant reconstructs the "pugilistic point of view" mainly through fifty semi-structured interviews with amateur fighters.[70] In their study of knowledge diffusion, Yves Dezalay and Bryant Garth also build on "lengthy personal interviews" with "brokers, courtiers, and learned compradors who are key actors in the import and export of expertises."[71] Their method of "relational biography" follows a key principle of reflexivity, which is to inquire into "who these individuals are and where they come from in order to see the relationship between what they say and their own strategic positions." By being particularly attentive to dispositions and positions, a practice-centric analysis based on qualitative interviews is quite different from traditional discourse analysis.

The method of qualitative interview assumes that relevant agents are alive and willing to discuss their experience with the researcher. This, of course, is not always the case. There are a host of written sources that can also convey subjective meanings without requiring living subjects, including personal diaries, memoirs, correspondence, interview and press conference transcripts, or tapes. The important step in using these documents is to go beyond traditional discourse

---

[68] Gusterson (2008, 98).   [69] Bourdieu *et al.* (1993).
[70] Wacquant (1995).   [71] Dezalay and Garth (2002, 9).

analysis in order to reconstruct the world from the practitioners' point of view. Vaughn's "historical ethnography" – "an attempt to reconstruct structure and culture from archival documents and interviews to see how people in a different time and place made sense of things" – is particularly illuminating.[72] Her application of this method to the case of the Columbia disaster goes a long way toward reconstructing practices that were never observed directly by the researcher. In IR, Jackson proposes "textual ethnography" – "a form of disciplined reading in which one engages in a kind of 'participant observation' of the textual records ... jotting 'field notes' as one reads."[73] Roxanne Doty's study of colonial practices also performs this kind of practice-centered analysis of historical documents with great analytical payoffs.[74]

Generally speaking, the recovery of practical logics from textual sources requires selecting a particular genre that offers a window on enacted practices.[75] For instance, memoirs offer derivative accounts of practices that, as reconstructed as they may be, give a situated (and to an extent objectifiable) viewpoint on performed interactions. Court cases also contain very rich data about unobserved practices. In a slightly different logic, handbooks contain prescriptions about what should be done in a given context. As such, they help infer background knowledge from which practices become possible. Again, these written descriptions or prescriptions may not yield exactly the same interpretations as direct observation on the field. As usual, the interpreter should account for these differences by reflexively analyzing the epistemic relationship between the observer and the social settings under study.

In sum, the recovery of practical logics faces considerable challenges, including the lack of access, the epistemic distance between the subjects and the researcher, the inarticulate nature of background knowledge, and the possibility of self-delusion or voluntary deception. These challenges point to a vital aspect of sobjective methodology: the need for triangulation. Recall that, in the end, interviews are not meant to report personal views, but to reconstruct and aggregate a *lambda* habitus in a given collective. It is therefore necessary to

---

[72] Vaughn (2008, 71).   [73] Jackson (2006b, 273).   [74] Doty (1996).
[75] Many thanks to Iver Neumann and Halvard Leira for sharing their thoughts on the matter.

combine a variety of inductive methods and sources in order to check against the challenges of interpretation. Furthermore, the recovery of subjective meanings should always be supplemented with objectifying methods, both intersubjectively and historically: inductive methods designed for the recovery of subjective meanings are usually not attentive enough to the larger intersubjective and relational context, and the history of practicality. As such, these methods tend to miss crucial social structures such as distributions of power. Experience-near concepts need to be put under the light of experience-distant contextualization.

Putting meanings and practices in context

The second step of the sobjective method seeks to objectify meanings by putting them in their wider intersubjective context. In accordance with the hermeneutic circle, the goal here is to understand specific bits of intersubjectivity in terms of a larger whole. Poststructuralists usually refer to this relationality as "intertextuality" – the fact that any text (or meaning) stands only in reference to others. There cannot be isolated meanings, only webs of them. Webs of meaning are usually interpreted through discourse analysis, a broad methodological category that in fact encompasses a variety of more specific methods. In general terms, by putting meanings in their wider context, discourse analysis takes them out of people's heads to place them inside an intersubjective structure. As Jennifer Milliken explains, discourse analysis rests on three analytical principles.[76] First, discourses are systems of significations that construct social realities. This tenet emphasizes the dialectic between meaning and reality. Second, discourses are productive of the social realities they define. They construct legitimate speakers and authorized practices, as well as common sense. Third, and finally, discourses are articulated through the play of practice. Discursive intersubjective structures falter unless constantly instantiated and re-instantiated through agents' practices.

There exist a number of specific methods of discourse analysis, some more formal than others. "Dialogical analysis," for instance, formalizes the Wittgensteinian notion of "language games."[77] On the less formal side, a popular method in IR is metaphorical analysis.

---

[76] Milliken (1999).   [77] Duffy, Frederking and Tucker (1998).

Metaphors – "conventional ways of conceptualizing one domain in terms of another ... as structuring possibilities for human reasoning and action"[78] – are micro-instances of the hermeneutic circle, as they put one meaning in the context of a larger discourse, culture, and set of practices. In IR, metaphorical analysis helps interpret crucibles of intersubjectivity such as globalization.[79] For Habermasian constructivists who study communicative action, Neta Crawford's method of "informal argument analysis" seems especially well suited.[80] The method contains five steps. The researcher first identifies the arguments that are on the table and then seeks to grasp the *topoi* or commonplaces that inform them. Third, the researcher maps background beliefs. The fourth step consists of tracing the "form and fate" of arguments, especially whether they are replacing dominant beliefs and becoming institutionalized. The fifth stage assesses the causal force of arguments. Crawford suggests a set of "tests" of argumentative causal efficacy such as temporal ordering, congruence between beliefs and behavior, the justification or sanction of deviation and the reframing of interests.

From a poststructuralist perspective, Lene Hansen questions the possibility of discursive causality and opts instead to develop research models centered on intertextuality. Her four models are based on an increasingly large pool of intertextual references, from official discourse narrowly conceived to wider political debates, media, corporate institutions and marginal voices. Hansen efficiently puts to work poststructuralist discourse analysis by outlining a variety of possible research designs that draw attention to central issues of temporal perspective and comparative focus.[81] A similar rigor informs Janice Bially Mattern's mapping of language-power utterances inside security communities in crisis.[82] Karin Fierke's work on Wittgensteinian language games also insightfully highlights the intertextuality of international "grammars."[83]

As the second sobjective step following the inductive acquisition of cultural competence, discourse analysis needs to overcome a thorny methodological dilemma to which there is no clear-cut answer: what

---

[78] Milliken (1999, 235).
[79] Kornprobst, Pouliot, Shah and Zaiotti (2008).
[80] Crawford (2002).   [81] Hansen (2006, 73–92).
[82] Mattern (2005).   [83] Fierke (1998).

are the boundaries of relevant discourses? There are a number of possible delimiting criteria, including time, space, genre and authorship. Some discourse analysts go even further by looking for specific linguistic practices (predicates, metaphors, commonplaces, arguments, etc.). The Copenhagen School, for instance, looks for "securitizing moves" in official discourse.[84] The general point here is that a discourse analysis should, and indeed can, focus on a number of specific elements rather than try to explain everything at once. To be sure, it would be nonsense to abstractly establish uniform criteria for what (and how much) needs to be read. Such criteria should derive from the context: that is, from examining the political and analytical importance of any given discourse. The quality of a discourse analysis partly hinges on its empirical breadth, and achieving this requires the researcher to make explicit, and justify, the reasons behind specific boundaries of intertextuality. Beyond discourse in strict textual form, the analysis of practices as meaningful actions is another way to put meanings in context. After the recovery of practical logics, it is important to put these in a larger context of intersubjectivity and power dynamics. This is where political sociology can improve on intertextual analysis, by locating meanings inside a structure of positions (see Chapter 5 and 6 for examples). In IR, Anna Leander also builds on Bourdieu's social theory to offer much needed guidance on how to methodically contextualize practice, thanks to a variety of "thinking tools."[85] Williams also takes inspiration from Bourdieu to trace cultural strategies in the field of international security, while Neumann studies the evolution of diplomacy from a centralized to a multibased practice.[86] These works share a similar concern for putting practices and their meanings in their intersubjective context. In so doing, they move beyond the search for subjective meanings to an objectified form of interpretation. As in discourse analysis, meanings do not belong to a subject anymore; they become truly intersubjective.

On top of discourse and practice analysis, meanings can be objectified through spatial or topographical analysis. Bourdieu's field theory is an efficient way to map the distribution of different forms of valued capital (see Chapter 2). Alternatively, social network analysis

---

[84] Buzan, Wæver and de Wilde (1998).   [85] Leander (2008).
[86] Williams (2007); Neumann (2002).

provides powerful tools to map the structure of social relations: Emilie Hafner-Burton and Alexander Montgomery, for instance, examine how a state's position in an international organization network shapes its actions.[87] Taking his cue from Charles Tilly's sociology, Nexon maps institutional structures so as to understand how networks and meanings interact.[88] Using a different relational approach, Jackson draws the topography of postwar debates about "the West" by mapping the deployment of cultural resources in the form of rhetorical commonplaces.[89] All these methods seek to objectify meanings by locating them inside a structure. At the end of the day, though, objectifying meanings in their context produces a fairly static form of knowledge. How then is it possible, methodologically, to account for the dialectics of the social construction of knowledge and the construction of social reality?

Setting meanings and practices in motion

The third step of sobjective methodology aims at setting meanings and practices in motion: that is, at further objectifying intersubjectivity by introducing time and history. The objective is more than a study of path dependence. It is also, and in fact primarily, to historicize knowledge and practical logics so as to account for the temporal dimension in the mutual constitution of social reality and knowledge. The logic of practicality is inherently temporal thanks to its intimate connection to action as it happens. Meanings are not reified substances but dynamic processes with a past, a present and a future. Historical analysis reveals these dynamics, especially the political contestation that necessarily surrounds any form of knowledge that makes claims to reality. Since constructivism adheres to a constitutive (as opposed to instrumental) reading of history, a sobjective methodology must explore the historicity of practical sense and the social struggles that make it possible.

Constructivists make use of a variety of methods that allow for diachronic interpretation.[90] On the more formal side, Lars-Erik Cederman's pioneering work on "complex adaptive systems" is based on sophisticated computer simulation that introduces notions such as path

---

[87] Hafner-Burton and Montgomery (2006).   [88] Nexon (2009).
[89] Jackson (2006a).   [90] On historical methods, see Trachtenberg (2006).

dependence and contingency.[91] It then becomes possible to "re-run" the tape of history thousands of time in order to model intersubjective evolution over time. On the poststructuralist side, Jens Bartelson's study of sovereignty is based on Foucault's genealogical method, "a history of logical spaces and their succession in time."[92] As a historicizing method, genealogy is especially efficient in demonstrating ruptures and leaps in the evolution of meanings and practices. The construction of narratives is also widely used by IR constructivists. Erik Ringmar, for instance, builds a historical account of Sweden's changing identities and interests in the seventeenth century on the premise that "[t]he past is no longer fixed and no longer stable, but instead at the mercy of the stories historians tell. The events of the past are nothing in themselves and only something when inserted into the context of a narrative."[93] Historicization, in other words, brings about a new, objectified form of knowledge about the past and the present. Alternatively, other constructivists build dialogical narratives that trace the evolution of debates in history; analyses centered on the Self–Other distinction and its changing boundaries build on such a historical logic.[94]

A more common historicizing method is process-tracing, which "attempts to trace the links between possible causes and observed outcomes."[95] How does X cause Y? The focus is on chains of cause–effect relations: that is, on the causal mechanisms that lead from X to Y. For mainstream social science, the ascendance of process-tracing led to something of a methodological revolution, as the method is informed by a processual (instead of correlational) understanding of causality. As Checkel admits, however, in its positivistic conceptualization process-tracing is incompatible with interpretivism.[96] I propose, however, that process-tracing is amenable to the constructivist style of reasoning with two amendments. First, the scientific realist assumption that mechanisms exist "out there" should be replaced with the postfoundationalist notion that mechanisms are theoretical constructs or heuristic devices which social scientists apply to their observations in order to classify them. Second, the exclusive focus on causation needs to be enlarged to what can be called constitutive mechanisms. Constitutive analysis – the study of how social facts come into being – is the research domain where constructivism is the

[91] Cederman (1997).   [92] Bartelson (1995, 7).   [93] Ringmar (1996, 28).
[94] Neumann (1999).   [95] George and Bennett (2005, 6).   [96] Checkel (2008).

most innovative, if only because it is left unaddressed by contending styles of reasoning such as rationalism. According to Searle, a constitutive relation works by the following formula: X counts as Y in context C. For example: "Bills issued by the Bureau of Engraving and Printing (X) count as money (Y) in the United States (C)."[97] C stands for the evolving context that makes it possible for social facts to be socially constructed. In order to provide a dynamic account of the social processes that lead to C, one must identify constitutive mechanisms – heuristic devices about the social processes that lead to the constitution of Y by X. Theorizing constitutive mechanisms allows for a better understanding of how the historical conditions of possibility of any social facts and/or practical logics are generated, and it also opens the door to cross-case analogies.

But contrary to scientific realism, and *pace* Searle, mechanisms are not "real" or "out there" from a postfoundationalist perspective. Instead, they are mental constructs devised to make sense of our interpretations and which belong to the realm of social scientific knowledge. As I argued above, language (vernacular and scientific) cannot simply mirror reality; one cannot stand behind concepts and words in order to know what is there. As a result, theoretical notions such as mechanisms are part of a socially constructed interpretation that further constructs reality. Narratives, categories, concepts and theories are not *out there* as part of an external reality, but *in there*, inside the web of scientific constructs that is collectively developed in order to make sense of our interpretations. Just like causes, mechanisms are heuristic devices, not substances. They make sense of history but do not drive it.

To sum up this section, the methical practice of sobjectivism entices the analyst to do research moving along an induction–deduction continuum, with an explicit awareness of the gains and tradeoffs associated with each movement. In its first phase, research is conducted as inductively as possible, bearing in mind of course that perfect induction is impossible. The objective is to recover agents' understandings in order to apprehend the insider's perspective on social life. At this point, practical logics are especially well recovered and meanings are interpreted bottom-up. But inductive analysis

[97] Searle (1995, 28).

is often embroiled in commonsense and misses the larger picture of social life – intersubjectively, relationally and historically. In a second step, research moves away from practical logics and subjective meanings in an attempt to objectify it. The goal is to put meanings in their intersubjective context – cultural, intertextual and practical. While this interpretive operation inevitably distorts practical logics, it also offers tremendous gains: meanings do not belong to anyone anymore, but become part of an intersubjective web inside which every text or practice refers and stands in relation to others. The whole of meaning begins to make sense. Third, research introduces time in order to historicize meanings. The theoretical narratives and conceptual categories that are used to make sense of history yield a certain degree of abstraction and even generalization. At that stage of research, practical logics have been rationalized and sometimes even bent out of shape. But such is the price to pay for standing back from commonsense and denaturalizing it. Although objectified knowledge is partly out of sync with agents' worlds, it allows the researcher to learn something other than what agents already know by connecting subjective meanings with context and history. The social construction of reality is carried out under structural and historical constraints that often remain invisible from the practitioners' point of view.

Again, the methodical practice of sobjectivism does not necessitate following the three steps in strict order. Instead, each step should mutually enlighten the others, leading the researcher to move back and forth between them. For instance, while recovering the logic of practicality (step 1) clearly helps put them in context (step 2), it can be just as useful to set meanings and practices in motion (step 3) in order to better understand contemporary practical logics (step 1). Research may benefit a lot from moving back and forth between the level of action and that of observation. In this spirit, sobjective research combines, in an abductive and systematic manner, the recovery of subjective meanings with contextualization and historicization so that practical logics and social structures – intersubjective, relational, historical or otherwise – can enlighten one another.

On validity: engaging mainstream methodology

The objective of a sobjective methodology is not only to systematize and lend coherence to the practice of constructivist research but also

to foster dialogue with other IR perspectives. Arguably, the development of a consistent research *modus operandi* is a necessary step for
constructivists and practice theorists to be able to engage mainstream
IR works. This chapter seeks to clarify constructivism's methodological requirements – induction, interpretation and historicization – in
order to make a comparative assessment with non-constructivist
studies easier. To be sure, there will always remain an element of
incommensurability in interparadigmatic conversations: positivism
and its subject–object distinction, for instance, cannot accommodate
the postfoundationalist premise that reality and knowledge are mutually constitutive. Yet, methodology and the actual practice of research
offer promising ways to move beyond metaphysical debates in IR in
order to attain not synthesis but what Susan Rudolph calls "mutual
epistemic legibility."[98]

Contrasting the meanings that constructivists and mainstream
social scientists attribute to a number of methodological standards
that they share may enhance mutual epistemic legibility. Certainly,
the most important standard is *validity*: what makes a given social
scientific work more valid than others? Many positivists rely on a
correspondence theory of truth according to which the validity of an
explanation derives from matching reality in words. However, this
mirror view of social science is unacceptable from a constructivist
perspective: if reality and the knowledge that constitutes it are both
socially constructed, then it makes no sense to contrast a supposedly
independent reality with scientific knowledge. Instead, several constructivists conceive of validity as an intersubjective category defined
and contested inside a style of reasoning without the arbitration of
Nature or reality. As a result, validity in social sciences is assessed
in a similar way to establishing "truth" and "facts" in a courtroom.
This understanding of validity is at the very heart of interpretivism, as
Ricoeur explains: "Validation is an argumentative discipline comparable to the juridical procedures of legal interpretation. It is a logic of
uncertainty and of qualitative probability."[99] To this, positivists may
be inclined to reply that in a court, "objective facts" ultimately settle
the truth from false accounts.[100] But that is precisely the point: what
counts as an objective fact, and what does not, depends very much

---

[98] Rudolph (2004).   [99] Ricoeur (1977, 330).
[100] Wendt (2006, 215).

upon reasoning along the legalistic style into which lawyers and judges are socialized. Objectivity and validity are not the primordial properties of certain facts or theories: they are socially devised criteria upon which practice communities of social scientists happen to agree.[101]

Positivists also link validity to the issue of *falsification*. In Karl Popper's famous argument, a theoretical statement is valid insofar as it can be shown to be wrong. The assertion "all swans are white," for instance, can be falsified by the discovery of a black swan. But this stylized model idealizes the practice of academic research. In the IR discipline, very few theories (if any) have been discarded in the face of discrepant evidence. This is due to what Willard Quine dubbed the under-determination of theory by facts: "Since theory is involved in deciding what the facts are, there is room for choice when deciding whether the theory at stake is consistent with them."[102] Whether one deals with discourses or with coefficients, interpretation and inference are irreducibly part of social science, rendering Popperian falsification impossible. Nonetheless, many constructivists still believe that a scientific explanation can be shown to be wrong (in relative terms) in the course of academic debate and reinterpretation. The Rashomon effect notwithstanding, constructivist studies are to an extent replicable, insofar as the data that is used for research (interview transcripts, policy documents, official speeches, etc.) can and should be made available for reinterpretation by others. Therefore, it is academic competition, not dialogue with Nature, that helps refine our knowledge about the world: "The fact that scientific producers have as their only clients their most rigorous and vigorous competitors – and hence those most inclined and able to lend to their critique their full strength – is the one Archimedean point upon which scientifically to see reason in scientific reason, to rescue scientific reason from relativistic reduction without having to call in a founding miracle."[103] Informed critical debate is the foundation of scientific knowledge and refinement.

Another traditional way to assess validity is *generalizability*: can the findings travel from one case to another? From a constructivist perspective, the time is ripe to abandon the old dream of discovering nomothetic laws in social sciences: human beings are reflexive and intentional

---

[101] For variants of this pragmatist understanding of validity claims in IR, see among others Kratochwil (2007) and Haas and Haas (2002).
[102] Hollis and Smith (1990, 55).   [103] Bourdieu (2001b, 108).

creatures who do not simply obey external laws. Nonetheless, there exist certain patterns and regularities in social life that many constructivists are keen to analyze. As Richard Price and Christian Reus-Smit correctly point out, "rejecting the pursuit of law-like generalizations does not entail a simultaneous rejection of more contingent generalizations."[104] Such contingent generalizations usually derive from the abstracting power of concepts: by simplifying reality through idealization, concepts such as constitutive mechanisms, for example, allow for analogies across cases. By definition, conceptual analogies are underspecified because they cannot fully put up with contingency. Consequently, the crucial point in drawing contingent generalizations is to be explicit about their boundaries of applicability.

Contrary to positivism, from a constructivist point of view there cannot be such a thing as *the* valid interpretation or theory. Since there is no transcendental way to adjudicate between competing interpretations, validity is never a black-or-white matter; it is all shades of gray. Inside a style of reasoning, validation is a deliberative activity whereby judgments evolve in combination with (though on a different level than) their own criteria. In order to convey the historicity of scientific reason, the best criterion to assess the relative validity of an interpretation is its *incisiveness*: that is, its capacity to "see further" than previous interpretations. As Geertz explains: "A study is an advance if it is more incisive – whatever that may mean – than those that preceded it; but it less stands on their shoulders than, challenged and challenging, runs by their side."[105] He thus makes clear that incisiveness is neither a primordial nor a universal criterion; it is both space- and time-dependent. Indeed, the degree of incisiveness of an interpretation hinges not only on its substance but also on its audience. In this regard, this chapter argues that it is the appropriate combination of experience-near and experience-distant concepts that generates interpretations that not only *make sense* to people, scientists and laypeople alike, but also *add sense* to already held interpretations. It is this supplementary meaning, due to the objectification of practical logics, that leads to an increased degree of incisiveness. An interpretation is all the more incisive (and therefore valid) when it strikes the fine balance between practical and objectified knowledge.

---

[104] Price and Reus-Smit (1998, 275).   [105] Geertz (1973, 25).

Overall, the constructivist style of reasoning and sobjective methodology in particular are animated by a logic of discovery that is
not completely different from the one that drives positivistic methodologies. In Imre Lakatos's famous argument, progressive research
programs are those that lead to the discovery of "novel facts."[106] A
faithful positivist, Lakatos probably had in mind hard facts that lead
to universal Truth. I propose adopting a more circumspect attitude
with regards to scientific discovery. A refined level of incisiveness and
the methodical practice of sobjective research helps discover, quite
simply, a combination of subjective/practical and objectified/theoreti-
cal knowledge that makes more sense of international politics than
previous interpretations. That validity, however, is situated intersubjectively: it is judged by a given community of (scientific) practice in a
particular epoch. Social science is not as universal as eulogists of the
Enlightenment would like it to be, but it is no less worth pursuing to
better understand the pressing matters of world politics. It is precisely
to that world that I now turn.

Case study: methodological underpinnings

How does my sobjective methodology help grasp the logic of practicality inside security communities? As I argued in Chapters 1 and 2,
students of security communities have yet to understand the *modus
operandi* of interstate peace; that is, its practical logic as it unfolds
on the ground of diplomacy. In the second part of this study, I apply
the theoretical and methodological frameworks elaborated in the
two previous chapters to the case of NATO–Russia relations after
the end of the Cold War. Chapter 4 seeks to recover practical logics (the first sobjective step) and begins a micro-analysis of security
practices (step 2). Chapters 5 and 6 further contextualize the meanings and practices of NATO–Russia interactions (step 2) and set them
in motion over the post-Cold War era (step 3). In keeping with my
sobjective research design, chapter 4 leans toward the subjective and
synchronic side of social life, whereas Chapters 5 and 6 belong to
objectification and diachrony. In the spirit of abduction, however,
in Chapters 5 and 6 I put practical logics in dialogue with objectified knowledge. For instance, my discussion of hysteresis effects in

---

[106] Lakatos (1970).

Chapters 5 and 6 should be read as an objectification exercise based in part on dispositions and practical logics.

A key premise of sobjective research and practice theory in general is that in order to understand a different lifeworld, one must "go to the village" so as to immerse oneself directly and interact with those who inhabit this world. Induction and the recovery of practical logics (or background knowledge) is thus the required first step in social scientific research. In an ideal world, my research design would have relied on participant observation in order to recover practical logics at the NRC. Unfortunately, the field of international security retains a unique aura of secrecy that is rarely matched in social life. Diplomacy may have gone public since the days of Metternich, but most decisions related to "high politics" are still taken behind closed (and usually well-guarded) doors. NATO's military committee, for instance, is not ready to welcome a participant observer to its ranks. And yet my first intention was precisely to be able to integrate myself into the NATO organization for a few months and attend the key meetings with Russian diplomats. Since the content of NRC meetings is kept scrupulously secret, however, I quickly realized that this road was not practicable.

As a second-best alternative, I made use of qualitative interviewing. This method is obviously excellent for recovering subjective meanings and reconstructing the world as it exists from the practitioners' point of view. In order to study practicality, I put my ethnographic sensibility to work and sought to distill inarticulate knowledge from between the lines of verbal accounts. As I explained above, I devised my semi-directed questionnaire so as to indirectly explore the background knowledge of NATO–Russia relations. For instance, I would submit various scenarios to interviewees and ask them how they would react to such a situation. From their answers, I could often infer tacit assumptions and practical logics. Second, in my interviews I devoted much attention to the practical activities performed on an everyday basis by my interviewees. I would subtly instigate thick descriptions of daily interactions with their Russian or NATO counterparts, NRC diplomatic negotiations, military-to-military cooperation, and all sorts of innocuous activities that fill their daily lives as security practitioners. In this way, I was able to learn a great deal about what NRC practitioners do in and through practice, even though I could not attend their meetings.

My interview questionnaire was semi-directed; although I had a list of issues I wanted to touch on, I was prepared to follow interviewees in whatever direction they might want to take. Most of the time, interviews consisted of informal conversations articulated around a set of core questions. These questions evolved slightly through the interview process, which stretched over fifteen months. In total, I conducted sixty-nine interviews with security officials and experts in Moscow, Brussels, Washington, London, Berlin and Ottawa between February 2006 and May 2007.[107] In each of these locations, I made use of what ethnographers call the snowball method to meet with a variety of practitioners, a technique that worked quite well in Western organizations. In Russia, however, conducting interviews proved a lot more difficult, not because of linguistic barriers (I spoke a bit of Russian) but due to a very low proclivity, on the part of Russian officials, to meet with foreign specialists: "They will not talk to you," the Deputy Director of the Moscow Institute for the Study of Canada and the US told me, "because from the point of view of communications with the West, we are back almost in the Soviet times." In light of this obstacle, I found a number of "proxies" for Russian officials, in the form of think-tank directors, academic institute members and senior consultants who take part in Russian foreign policymaking at some distance.

In deciding on the number of interviews that I should do, I used two methods. First, on the Western side I selected a representative sample of countries and organizations. To begin with, I centered on the four core NATO countries whose voices are louder than any other at the North Atlantic Council (NAC) table: the US, the United Kingdom, France and Germany. I also wanted to include less powerful countries, which led me to choose Canada as a representative of smaller founding members, and Poland and Lithuania as newer members of both large and small size. I visited most of these countries' capitals or met with their representatives in Brussels. At NATO headquarters, I also met with several international civil servants and military officers from a variety of departments so as to better understand the organizational perspective. Finally, in order to grasp the specificities of the

---

[107] In the post-Cold War history of NATO–Russia relations, this period corresponds to a fairly difficult one, in the wake of the American intervention in Iraq. The year 2006 was certainly not as tense as during the Kosovo or Georgia crises, but it remained a rough patch at the political level.

NATO point of view, I also met with a few international civil servants from the EU (on EU–Russia relations) and the State Department (on US–Russia cooperation in disarmament). Admittedly, this sample does not add up to the exhaustive political sociology of the field of security that Didier Bigo recommends;[108] I will leave it to others to study in more depth the practices of "security professionals," to analyze their genealogy and to map the overall field of international security. In the more limited framework of this book, my use of Bourdieu is meant not to inventory the field but to find in it what explains the evolution of NATO–Russia diplomacy. And although my sample is not exhaustive, it is representative in terms of including a variety of countries and organizations.

In order to get as exhaustive a picture as possible, I employed a second method based on what ethnographers call the saturation point – basically, the moment when additional interviews do not yield significantly new insights compared to what was learned in previous meetings. After a number of interviews, I would usually conclude that I had grasped an important chunk of the shared background knowledge I was looking for. Of course, as will become clear in Chapter 4, in doing interviews I was not looking for big-T truth but for practical logics. My objective was to reconstruct NATO–Russia dealings as they exist from the practitioners' point of view – not from some god's-eye perspective. This raises different kinds of validity issues than in positivism. Generally speaking, I tried to probe discrepant views across my interviews but did not discount any as simply false. In what follows I do emphasize those story lines that I heard more often than others, but I also note more heterodox views. In fact, at times I would even hear different versions from inside the same building, just walking from one door to the next. Such, indeed, is the messiness and fluidity of intersubjectivity in social and political life.

Given that my focus in this study is on background knowledge, however, it is clear that my interviews served to record shared assumptions more than idiosyncratic opinions. What follows is not a study of partisan politics and I did not interview politicians from opposing factions in order to understand ideological debates. As interesting as this approach might have been, in this book I attempt to study the unsaid and the tacit – the groundswell

---

[108] Bigo (2000).

of Russian–Atlantic relations, so to speak; the deeper trends that inform its evolution underneath the sea foam of high politics and rhetorical skirmishes. Of course, even those rare senior diplomats who benefit from more autonomy are still quite heavily constrained by specific policy directions from their capital. But while a focus on decisionmakers is useful, as decades of IR scholarship have shown, in this book I make the wager that looking at those who *implement* these decisions is also worthwhile – if only because few studies have done so. This approach derives from my focus on the logic of practicality. In that context, interviewing international organization and foreign ministry officials as well as defense officers appeared the best way to capture the practical logics that cement practitioners across the board. After all, it is the gist of this research project to reconstruct a common stock of background knowledge *from* which differences become possible.

The task of recovering the *lambda* habitus of a collective raises a number of methodological issues. What does it mean, ontologically, to talk of a "Russian habitus"? Are states people too? It should be clear that there is nothing in this book that supports Wendt's claim that "states are real actors to which we can legitimately attribute anthropomorphic qualities like desires, beliefs, and intentionality."[109] To the contrary, and partly against Bourdieu, in what follows the only actors worthy of that name are made of flesh. In making this assumption, however, how can we make sense of the fact that the people who belong to the same group or organization, for instance the Russian state, tend to act as if they formed a corporate agent?

The methodological issue is "how to operationalize the habitus."[110] Ultimately, habitus is individual insofar as it describes inclinations inscribed in bodies. But as Wacquant recalls, "our categories of judgment and action, coming from society, are shared by all those who were subjected to similar social conditions and conditionings."[111] This means that collectives enter the picture in the form not of corporate agents, but of dispositional deposits that mark participant bodies with intersubjective traces. As subjectivized intersubjectivity, habitus makes the society present in each and every one of its members in the form of more or less conscious dispositions. In any groupings, there

---

[109] Wendt (1999, 197); see also Wendt (2004).
[110] Leander (2008, 21).   [111] Quoted in Vaughn (2008, 73).

typically exists a body of dispositions that similarly characterizes members due to their shared history.[112] *In fine*, it is through this dispositional mechanism that the illusion of corporate agency – that states are people too – becomes possible. That different agents belonging to the same collective tend to develop a similar habitus means that the orchestra of the state, to paraphrase Bourdieu, is able to play without a conductor, leaving the impression of a "superorganism" to the observer.

From a Bourdieusian point of view, the state is not an actor but a field: that is, a social configuration with a structure of positions inhabited by various actors that play by certain rules and compete over resources. Exposure to this game tends to reinforce certain dispositions among players; that is one reason why state elites, despite partisan politics, usually tend to think from a number of shared premises. But there is an even deeper reason why one can hypothesize that the citizens of a state will exhibit a limited number of shared dispositions. Because as a field the state is characterized by very high concentration of symbolic capital, it "possesses the means of imposition and inculcation of durable principles of vision and division that conform to its own structure."[113] The education system is the primary vehicle of this transmission, although the media and others also contribute to this symbolic domination. Given these processes, I speak of a "Russian habitus" not to suppress differences between Russian practitioners, but to map the dispositional similarities that a joint history inevitably brings about.

The illusion of state corporate agency is further reinforced by a peculiar process that Bourdieu calls the "mystery of the ministry."[114] In the state field, certain agents are endowed with enough symbolic capital to speak in the name of the masses. The mass becomes what the authorized speakers say, representing it as a corporate body. As Niilo Kauppi notes, for Bourdieu "the process of delegation becomes a case of social magic in which a person such as a minister, a priest or a deputy is identified with a group of people [which] no longer exists as

---

[112] In his study of the European Court of Human Rights, for example, Mikael Rask Madsen notes that due to their "collective habitus," Cold-War jurists "were generally inclined to deploy an approach consisting of both a diplomatic understanding of European human rights with a more or less self-sustainable and conceptual *Professorenrecht*" (Madsen 2007, 149).
[113] Bourdieu (1994, 9).   [114] Bourdieu (2001a).

a collection of individuals but rather, through this representative, as a social agent."[115] As a result, diplomats and state representatives come to embody the state in practice and give it a "narrative Self."[116] As a social scientist, my task is not to reify these narratives, however, but to contextualize and historicize them so as to explain their conditions of possibility.[117] By looking into the shared dispositions of given members of collectives, I acknowledge the importance of collectives as structures but also their fluidity at the level of agency. People act as if there were a corporate state and it is precisely this performativity that makes the state look like a reified thing.

I now want to turn to Chapters 5 and 6 (steps 2 and 3 of my subjective methodology) and the peculiar methodological challenges that they raise. In my attempt to historicize Russian–Atlantic relations, I had to narrow down my research and pick a specific issue area of interaction. Because it constitutes one of the key structuring axes of contemporary world politics, the post-Cold War relationship between Russia and the transatlantic security community is too vast and multidimensional to be entirely covered in one single study. Even after the end of the Cold War, this relationship remains unique in ranging from the Group of Eight's (G8) nuclear disarmament program to World Trade Organization (WTO) negotiations through global governance at the UN Security Council. Whether it is the Middle East peace process or the Kyoto Protocol, Russian-Atlantic political dynamics are part and parcel of almost any issue of interest on the global stage. Consequently, I had no choice but to narrow down the domain of inquiry, without of course losing sight of the bigger picture. The challenge was to select an issue area that is both theoretically and empirically pregnant.

Divided along a chronological logic, Chapters 5 and 6 trace the evolution of practices among Russian and NATO security elites around the question of the Alliance's "double enlargement."[118] Starting in 1994, faced with demands from democratizing central European governments and with the bloodshed in Yugoslavia, NATO undertook a series of unprecedented institutional transformations that were

---

[115] Kauppi (2005, 26). This process is akin to what Jackson calls "personation," "the social process by which someone is empowered to speak on behalf of (or 'in the name of') an entity, *thereby making that entity an actor*" (Jackson 2004, 286–7).
[116] Neumann (2004).   [117] Pouliot (2004).   [118] Asmus (2002).

to expand both its membership (geographical enlargement) and its missions (functional enlargement). Significantly, over the last fifteen years, NATO's double enlargement has consistently been the most difficult bone of contention between Russia and the Alliance. It has never left the agenda and has been the key driving force behind the many ups and downs of the relationship. At the time of writing, the double enlargement remains one of the thorniest problems between the former enemies. In other words, having occupied the center stage of the relationship for the entire post-Cold War era, the double enlargement is both a fruitful locus for understanding larger political dynamics and an area of particular policy relevance.

In terms of research design, Russian–Atlantic dealings over NATO's double enlargement constitute a hard case for the theory of practice of security communities that I outlined in Chapter 2. Similar to Harry Eckstein's notion of "least-likely case,"[119] a hard case is a series of interconnected practices that should, in principle, be difficult to account for within the rubric of a given theoretical narrative. While Eckstein and others[120] conceive of least-likely cases as means to validate theories, however, in my non-positivistic research design selecting a hard case is simply meant to demonstrate the incisiveness of the theory as convincingly as possible. Put differently, by selecting a case study on the basis of its counterintuitiveness, the researcher can illuminate new or at least under-researched aspects of world politics. In the Russian–Atlantic case, my attempt to recover practical logics in 2006 makes for a hard case because so many thorny disagreements plagued the relationship at the time. One can think of the fallout from the Anglo-American invasion of Iraq, the color revolutions in the Commonwealth of Independent States (CIS), the American ballistic missile defense project in central Europe, the row over the Conventional Forces in Europe (CFE) treaty, Kosovo's future and Iran's alleged nuclear ambitions. To probe the self-evidence of diplomacy in such a difficult political context is, I hope, more convincing than picking an easy case.

As far as contextualization is concerned, in Chapters 5 and 6 I combine discourse and practice analysis to study the evolution of Russian–Atlantic power relations over the post-Cold War era. In the Foucauldian tradition, I treat discourse as practice: that is, as a social

---

[119] Eckstein (1975).   [120] See George and Bennett (2005).

performance. Since I am primarily interested in intersubjectivity (sobjectivism's step 2), the beliefs or intentions *behind* discourse are less important, analytically, than the public utterance itself (although the intentions ascribed by others do matter as part of the social construction of reality[121]). In addition to discourse as practice, I also center my analytical focus on the various actions taken by NATO (and its member states) and Russia with regard to the double enlargement. I interpret these practices at the intersubjective level: that is, as part of a larger web of meaningful action that is spun over time by the agents involved. Since I am interested in official diplomatic interaction between the Russian state and NATO, I circumscribed my analysis to high-level officials (i.e. senior government or organization members).[122] Because my analysis primarily focuses on Russian reactions, I supplemented these data with a discourse analysis of the most important op-ed pieces by foreign policy experts and opinion-makers in Moscow. To access the data, I used official portals on the internet as well as the search engines of key newspapers' archives. For the Russian side, I primarily used the *Current Digest of the Post-Soviet Press* (which contains exhaustive digests of Russian-language newspapers translated into English by Eastview experts) and, subsidiarily, the *Moscow Times*. These sources cover all the most important Russian daily publications, including *Nezavisimaya Gazeta*, *Izvestia*, *Kommersant*, *Sevodnia*, *Rossiiskaya Gazeta*, *Moskovskiye Novostei* and *Trud*. Overall, I collected a few thousand Russian articles in order to get as incisive a grasp as possible of Russian practical and discursive reactions to NATO's double enlargement. The result is a sobjective account of the NATO–Russia power politics of diplomacy that sheds new light on its practical logics and relations of domination.

In terms of historicization, finally, in Chapters 5 and 6 I focus on the period ranging from the birth of post-Soviet Russia, in January 1992, to the Georgia War of summer 2008. Because my narrative seeks to explain the NRC practical logics as I recorded them through interviews in 2006, I mainly concentrate on the preceding decade and a half. The final section of Chapter 6 succinctly extends this analysis

---

[121] Goffman (1959).

[122] In Hansen's framework, my discourse analysis conforms to model 1 (analytical focus: official discourse; object of analysis: official texts and direct and secondary intertextual links) (Hansen 2006, 64).

beyond 2006 in order to show the continuity of recent NATO–Russia diplomacy. In both chapters, I trace one key constitutive mechanism over time: the aligning and misaligning of positions and dispositions in NATO–Russia diplomacy. This process-tracing entails, first, that I brush in broad strokes the evolution of capital and doxa in the field of international security. In this way, I am able to map the distribution of capital in the field from a structural point of view. I combine this positional analysis with a more dispositional one centered on changing dispositions on both the NATO and the Russian sides. Taken together, these two analytical focuses allow me to apprehend the degree of hysteresis in the Russian–Atlantic relationship, which is the key determinant, this book argues, of the limited development of a security community in the post-Cold War era.

PART II

The symbolic power politics of NATO–Russia diplomacy

4 | *The logic of practicality at the NATO–Russia Council*

Approaching Russian–Atlantic security relations from the practitioners' point of view, this chapter reconstructs insider knowledge at the NRC and its surroundings in 2006. By grasping the practical logics as they play themselves out during Russian–Atlantic security interactions on the ground, I seek to counter the representational bias (see Chapter 2). In terms of the sobjectivist methodology outlined in Chapter 3, I mainly perform the first step, which consists of the recovery of subjective meanings that comprise the logic of practicality. I proceed as atheoretically as possible and refrain from superimposing an analytical framework onto interview data. The theoretical narrative based on field analysis and the concept of hysteresis will become much more prominent in Chapters 5 and 6; for the moment I want to let practitioners speak for themselves with as little interference as possible.

In order to do this, I use two main methods. First, the chapter builds on sixty-nine qualitative interviews with security practitioners and experts in Ottawa, Brussels, Moscow, Washington, London and Berlin. These very rich data, comprised of hundreds of transcript pages and ethnographic notes, are complemented with a second method that can conveniently be called practice analysis. In the spirit of participant observation, I use a micro-focus on what Russian and NATO security officials do together at the NRC, in order to distil background knowledge from joint actions and respective practices. Where warranted, I also consider official declarations as discursive practices and add them to the data gathered in the field and through practice analysis. In order to evaluate the extent to which security practitioners at the NRC embodied diplomacy in 2006, I devise a set of three empirical indicators (see Table 4.1). These indicators are not mutually exclusive; their heuristic value is in organizing the vast amount of information collected across my several dozen interviews. Taken together, the indicators reveal the degree of self-evidence of the non-violent settlement of disputes.

Table 4.1 *Three indicators of the embodiment of diplomacy*

Indicator	Assessment questions
(1) Disappearance of the possibility of using force	How present is organized violence on the security practitioners' horizon of possibility? Do practitioners entertain scenarios of mutual confrontation? Are there mutual perceptions of threat? What means could practitioners conceivably use to alter the other party's course?
(2) Normalization of disputes	What is the nature of disputes? Do practitioners have dependable expectations that future disagreements can be solved peacefully? What lessons do practitioners draw from past and present disputes? How do practitioners handle disagreements and search for their resolution?
(3) Daily cooperation on the ground	What is the nature and focus of practitioners' daily interactions? What kind of background knowledge do routine practices embody? Do enacted practices foreclose certain courses of interaction? What institutional forms or routines do daily interactions take?

The chapter's main finding is that in 2006 diplomacy was a normal but not a self-evident way to solve disputes in Russian–Atlantic dealings. In other words, security practitioners on both sides had embodied the non-violent settlement of disputes as "the way to go" – although not the only possible way to go. In terms of a security community in and through practice, then, the evidence is mixed. On the one hand, most of the time security officials at (and around) the NRC thought *from* diplomacy instead of *about* its opportunity. My data confirm that there has been a sea change since the Cold War era, clearly in the direction of pacification. I provide ample evidence that diplomacy was something of a normal or ordinary practice in NATO–Russia relations, in the sense that it did not stand out as unusual in any way. But, on the other hand, a number of dispositions mitigated the embodiment of the non-violent settlement of disputes in 2006. Applying the three indicators in turn, I discover that the disappearance of the possibility of mutual force was countered by latent mistrust, the normalization of disputes was stymied by the elusiveness of the NRC diplomatic momentum and daily cooperation on the ground was thwarted by clashing organizational cultures. All in all, although Russia and NATO have undeniably moved away from the insecurity community of the Cold War, my analysis shows that the 2006 Russian–Atlantic relationship fell short of a security community in and through practice. Though normalized, the diplomatic practice was not self-evident at the NRC in 2006 – a finding later substantiated with the temporary suspension of the NRC's activities in the wake of the Georgia War in 2008.

I want to defuse three potential criticisms from the outset. First, it is clear that Russian–Atlantic security relations are much more complex than diplomatic interaction at the NRC will ever cover. This chapter makes no claim to present an exhaustive portrait of the relationship between Moscow and NATO member states. Diplomatic dealings at the NRC are not fully representative of overall Russian–Atlantic relations because central issues such as Iran, Iraq or North Korea, for example, are not typically addressed in this forum. Despite their obvious importance, these topics fall beyond this study's scope. That said, because this book deals with security community development in and through practice, a focus on the NRC is warranted insofar as it is a prime locus of diplomacy and dispute settlement. The NRC offers an exceptional vantage point on the logic of practicality in NATO–Russia politics.

Second, it is true that the very existence of the NRC already indicates that both Russia and NATO member states have at least a willingness to manage their relationship through diplomatic means. It does not, however, demonstrate in and of itself *how* diplomacy is becoming an ordinary practice in NATO–Russia dealings. After all, innumerable international forums have evolved into empty shells that fail to advance peace in any significant way. Alternatively, organizations such the UN host a diplomatic dialogue that does not always preclude the eruption of violent conflicts among its members. During the 1999 Kosovo conflict, for instance, the Permanent Joint Council (PJC) was sidelined and eventually suspended, as was the NRC in the wake of the Georgia War in 2008 (see Chapter 6). Clearly, the existence of a multilateral forum does not normalize diplomacy in and of itself. Formal diplomatic channels such as the NRC cannot be presumed to rest on the embodiment of diplomacy: this political process must be empirically demonstrated and documented.

Third, one could argue that diplomacy had already been normalized between the East and the West during the Cold War. But even though its roots can be traced back in history, the routinization of diplomacy and its enactment outside the shadow of a nuclear Armageddon is a new phenomenon in NATO–Russia relations. Of course, Alliance members and the Soviet Union repeatedly relied on diplomacy to resolve their disputes during the Cold War. There were even attempts at institutionalizing the practice, for instance through the Conference on Security and Cooperation in Europe (CSCE). The existence of a Soviet–American "condominium," based on a shared preference in Washington and Moscow for the bipolar status quo, also created fertile grounds for diplomatic negotiations. But, contrary to the current era, during the Cold War decades diplomacy took place in the ever-present shadow of nuclear and conventional deterrence. In the back of the minds of the negotiating diplomats loomed the very real possibility of a violent confrontation, a possibility that never receded for forty years. Threats of force were regularly issued on both sides even as diplomacy was practiced. In sum, the Cold War agreements that were reached may have been peaceful in nature but the political processes that made them possible, despite diplomatic appearances, remained grounded in a fundamentally violent landscape of interaction. Such was not the case in 2006, as the following pages demonstrate.

Indicator 1: the disappearance of the possibility of using force

Interview data and practice analysis demonstrate that in 2006 the possibility of violent confrontation was not part of Russian and Atlantic security practitioners' dispositions. This points in a particularly clear fashion to a partial embodiment of the diplomatic practice at the NRC. Generally speaking, security practitioners were not inclined toward the use of force, or threats thereof, in mutual dealings. They did not entertain scenarios of mutual violence either. That said, this peaceful habitus often coexisted with a fairly widespread mistrust on both the Russian and the NATO sides. One Turkish officer at NATO, for example, insisted that "the capabilities are still there," unwilling to take Russian cooperation for granted. Such suspicions suggest that fifteen years after the end of the Cold War, the possibility of force had not completely disappeared from Russian-Atlantic dealings.

"Gone are the days of nuclear threats and blackmail"[1]

Out of sixty-nine interviews with Atlantic and Russian security practitioners and experts, I heard only four officials affirm that they could not fully exclude the possibility of physical violence in Russian–Atlantic dealings. The overwhelming majority simply ruled out the possibility of a Russian–Atlantic military confrontation, whether asked explicitly or implicitly. "Not a possibility," "completely" or "categorically inconceivable," "never," "absolutely impossible": these are some of the ways to put it that I have heard most frequently from national delegations and international civil servants. "I can't see a rise of military violence at all at the moment," one top-level NATO official confidently asserted. "We have proceeded from the assumption that we don't have anything to fear from the Russian side," concurred a senior German diplomat. In several interviews, in fact, I gathered the impression that considering whether a Russian–Atlantic military clash could still be possible was perceived as out of place if not irrelevant. Many interviewees seemed to wonder just why I was asking about Russian–Atlantic military violence in the first place; it seemed as though the issue was not even worth considering. As Garfinkel showed, certain questions are simply out of place in terms of practical meanings (see Chapter 3). That the notion of Russian–Atlantic violence would appear displaced speaks volumes about the embodiment of diplomatic background knowledge at the NRC.

Most practitioners with insider knowledge maintained that scenarios of mutual violence were simply "not part of military and strategic planning and thinking anymore." On the Atlantic side, a senior NATO policymaker with direct connections to the Secretary-General assured me that "[t]here is no planning in NATO, of any kind, that engages Russia as a threat ... We don't get along with the Russians all that well, but it's not a problem." On the Russian side, he added,

---

[1] US State Department Chief for Russian affairs quoted in US Department of State (2006).

"I'm quite sure that none of their planning involves defending against a NATO attack." As one German official pointed out, since the early 1990s the Alliance's forces have been converted into deployable brigades (for peacekeeping purposes, mainly) that would be of limited use in case of a Russian conventional attack. This practice suggests that the Russian threat had receded from military planning. One State Department official observed a similar move on the Russian side: "Look at their military forces. If they thought the United States was a military threat, they wouldn't be focusing their military forces on how to win the Chechen war ... From our perspective, the relationship is demilitarized." Throughout my interviews in Brussels, I was struck by how widespread this assurance was, as well as by the fact that it reached the highest echelons of the NATO hierarchy. For instance, several national delegates ruled out any sort of military planning targeted against Russia, as did a top general from the NATO military committee. Most strikingly, a senior member of the Secretary-General's office went as far as to say that "Russia nowadays looks to the West rather the same way that the United States looks to Mexico or Canada. There are some issues, like soft lumber trade, but it's basically a very predictable environment."

Some Atlantic policymakers could still associate a number of potential threats with Russia, but none was of a military nature. In Washington, a senior policymaker could imagine Russia turning into a threat in any of three ways: by "using energy as a political weapon"; by giving rise to "instability and chaos should the government implode"; and through acts of mischief – "Russia's newly found assertiveness and post-imperial angst means it can cause a lot of problems as we try to solve things in the international community." He concluded: "Notice that military aggression or conflict is not one of the threats. I think Russians would be shocked if they could see inside our minds and NATO planning and realize how little we think about Russia." A member of the French delegation to NATO similarly affirmed that the only threat he could see coming from Moscow was the implosion of the state. According to a senior official at NATO's Moscow bureau, talk of military confrontation was nothing but "hogwash." On the Atlantic side, it seems as though the possibility of a military confrontation with Russia was simply not part of the possibilities entertained on a daily basis by 2006 security practitioners.

A similar picture emerged from Moscow. For instance, one former military officer asserted that "Russia's relations with its NATO neighbours are becoming demilitarized. A war between Russia and Germany is as unthinkable today as one between Germany and France." In the words of a well-known Russian academic, "negative feelings with respect to the Atlantic community are generated not by apprehensions of hostility or big conflict or nuclear war or whatever. There is nothing or almost nothing of this kind nowadays." Especially interesting was the recourse to Russian history to explain this certainty: "There could never be a return to confrontation. Historical experience shows it doesn't work. Russia has learned the lesson." In order to illustrate the impossibility of military confrontation, a senior Russian diplomat used the example of the very serious row over the American project to deploy ballistic missile defense components on Czech and Polish territory. During the Cold War, he argued, similar initiatives such as the American deployment of cruise missiles in the early 1980s would have caused further confrontation; but not anymore in 2006. "Now we will sit down, next week, and discuss the issue," the Russian official said. "We may disagree. We may get sore, both sides, but we are not afraid of war. Nobody's afraid. If somebody tells you he's afraid, he's either lying or he needs to see a head shrink. [Laughter.] I am dead serious. It was my business to know my guys on the left and my guys on the right."

But if this is indeed the case, why did certain segments of the military establishment still use confrontational language at times? One Russian expert proposed that military officers "don't perceive NATO as a threat, they just say it. They make scandals and declarations and noise." With her voice lowered, she continued that the Russian Chief of General Staff had recently confided to her: "Of course, I understand that no threat is coming from the West. But how could we explain this to our population?" Atlantic practitioners agreed that remnants of confrontational rhetoric among the Russian military could be explained by organizational logics instead of genuine apprehensions. A senior NATO official posted in Moscow opined that "remaining suspicions on the Russian side are rhetorical. It is a discourse that aims to value the army, just as it is the case in the United States with the military-industrial complex. Fundamentally a conflict with the West is inconceivable." For Atlantic practitioners, sticking to the traditional enemy sounded easier and more efficient in a dramatically underfunded military. Russia's continuing preoccupation with NATO was considered "a matter of political convenience. They focus on the familiar, old threat ... the bogeyman. It marshals political support among society and justifies expensive weapons procurement," in the mind of a State Department official. There was a dependable belief that the possibility of using force did not actively factor into both sides' military planning. For example, a German colonel who had spent years in Moscow confirmed that "the Russian military is not considering having a clash with NATO. They excluded it for the time being." This view was confirmed by a prominent Russian expert: "Even the most conservative, backward-oriented political forces in Russia could hardly consider 'Western aggression' a viable aggression, at least for the immediate and medium-term future." All in all, it is safe to conclude that in 2006 the possibility of a military clash with NATO member states had considerably receded from Russian practitioners' horizon of possibility.

Because background knowledge ought to be read between the lines, I also ascertained whether mutual confrontation was part of the Russian-Atlantic habitus through a variety of indirect means. For instance, I would introduce to the interviewees the scenario, very much topical in 2006, that a new color revolution had taken place in Belarus following the elections: could Russia possibly intervene militarily to defend the Lukashenko regime, and if so, would NATO take steps to defend demonstrators? Interestingly, a number of officials were convinced that Russia would not use force in such a case in order to avoid confronting the West. A Canadian official was a little more careful: "I think you can never dismiss the Russian potential for the use of force, but the parameters, the limits of Russian policy options are much narrower than they used to be; which is a good thing." According to another practitioner, even if Russia were to make a move, it would not elicit a response of force in return. But would NATO not intervene to stop Russia in the event of external mingling? "No. Frankly, no." Other solutions would be found outside the realm of military threats or violence, he thought. A senior NATO policymaker was more ambivalent: "What the reaction would have been I don't know, but it would have been negative and concrete. Nobody would have let this go." Noticeably, even this more forceful response stopped short of raising the possibility of a military clash.

On the Russian side, I probed the receding of military scenarios from practitioners' background knowledge by asking a number of observers what policies their state could implement in reaction to NATO's open-door policy toward Ukraine – clearly the most serious disagreement at the time of the interview (see Chapter 6). A Russian expert who was fiercely opposed to the Alliance's policy listed a variety of possible reactions, from anti-NATO demonstrations to energy pressures through meddling with Iran. He never mentioned threats of force; this seemed to be just beyond his otherwise suspicious mind. Even pondering such a fundamental dispute, which reaches extremely deep in the Russian psyche, Russian practitioners started their reflection from the assumption of non-violence. Similarly, when asked what tools Russia possessed to oppose the Alliance's decisions that went against his country's interest, a Russian official posted in Brussels responded "political dialogue" and "being a reliable partner." As he put it: "The only way for Russia to influence NATO is to be within [the NRC]." Overall, the diplomatic practice seemed to be in the process of becoming increasingly axiomatic.

This evolution finds its roots in the fifteen-year-long post-Cold War era, which was characterized by the absence of military confrontation between Russia and NATO. Even the one episode during which conditions were met for a potential clash – the Pristina airport incident in June 1999 (see Chapter 5) – was dismissed as insignificant by one senior Russian diplomat who was directly involved at the highest level: "That can happen, I don't know, between Great Britain and France. It wasn't anything dramatic ... You shouldn't disregard us if you want us to play along, like with Belgrade and others, like today with Kosovo. But we weren't close to war over Pristina. It wasn't the best point in our relationship, but it wasn't dangerous." When asked whether the specter of force ever appeared during that period, a Canadian official responded straightforwardly:

No, never; never threats of force. No, never even contemplated ... I think that the pattern has now been set with Russia – that you deal with each other through negotiation. You deal with each other through bringing the Russians into a system of rules and regulations and laws ... That's the way you deal with it and so, force, that's pretty well out of the question.

An American policymaker concurred: "There's no perception that there's been any threat to use force on either side." One senior British official in charge of defense policy put the matter in a very telling way:

If you want a really good idea of how in my view the world has changed for the better, it is that my predecessors would've spent one way or another somewhere in the seventy percent of their time thinking about Russia. I spend less than five percent of my time thinking about Russia. That's sixty-five percent different – it's representative of energy put to providing security goods in a more proactive way, in a more beneficial way and not in a senseless way ... I do not spend my time by and large worrying about a Russian threat.

On the Russian side, an in-depth study of Moscow's foreign policy similarly concludes that since the end of the Cold War, "[a]t no stage did it countenance armed conflict with the West."[2] By 2006 the possibility of using force against each other had considerably receded from the practitioners' point of view.

A *latent mistrust*

Despite this sea change, interview data and practice analysis also reveal that a non-negligible level of latent mistrust of mutual intentions remained in Russian–Atlantic relations in 2006. For instance, one German colonel believed that through its participation in Operation Active Endeavour (see below), Russia primarily "wants to gain intelligence" on NATO. Another Alliance official concurred: "Let's face it: it gives them a great insight into how we do business, a great intelligence gathering. They now have NATO secret communications on their ships, they see our standard operating procedures, they have our doctrine ... That's good stuff if you're Russia!"[3] This mistrust was undoubtedly reciprocal: for instance, one American officer confided

---

[2] Lo (2002, 154).
[3] Another NATO official would recognize the situation but without taking offence: "[The Russians] use NATO simply to know what's happening. So they're here, they're everywhere. They are represented with a lot of diplomats. They try to proliferate meetings. They meet with a lot of people. So what? This is basically information and intelligence gathering that they're doing here. Which is fine."

that "in private, many Russian officials ask about hidden motives behind NATO's willingness to cooperate." Trust, which stems from practical sense, formed a thin intersubjective basis for interaction at the 2006 NRC.

According to interview data, there seemed to be four main sources of mistrust at the NRC. First (and not limited to this case), it is an inherent part of the military habitus to plan for the worst contingencies.[4] Generally speaking, the military officers I interviewed were more careful than civilians in their assessment of the possibility of force in Russian–Atlantic relations. Entertaining worst-case scenarios, after all, is a habit that comes with their job. As a result, they were less prone to forget about the possibility of military confrontation. A British military officer, now a speechwriter at NATO headquarters, put the matter in perspective:

I think one has to differentiate between what is a threat and what is a risk. If you say a threat is more immediate, a threat is a combination of capability and intent. Now I would argue that at the moment, Russia still has the capability but not the intent. That is not to say that changes within the Russian Federation, in the future years, might not change this and that the intent would be there as well. But I reckon we would get enough indicators of that to be able to reorient ourselves as necessary ... If the threat is capability and intent, we are not there at the moment. I would say we are at a risk, which is where the capability exists, but the intent – there's always the potential for it to be re-instantiated, to reappear. But I do not think it will happen and I hope it won't happen, but as long as there's the possibility there, one has to protect.

This quote suggests a lower proclivity, from a military point of view, to take anything for granted beyond material capabilities. For the military officers with whom I met, there was no problem whatsoever in acknowledging that, in the short term, Russian–Atlantic relations seemed stable: but what about the long term? As a consequence of this professional disposition, the embodiment of diplomacy in military circles is bound to be slower. This is not to say that military officers do not actively cooperate on the ground, however. In fact, as will become clear below, in practice, military officers tended to establish working

---

[4] See, e.g., the debate on military planning during the Cold War in Heuser (1991); and Cox (1992).

relations more easily than civil servants. Military officers dislike the ups and downs of politics and they consequently adopt a much more down-to-earth attitude. For instance, one American NATO officer turned my question about the possibility of violence on its head in an attempt to temper his mistrust: "On the possibility of Cold War-like confrontation, one needs to be cautious. But what really is unthinkable is the fact that Russia is now at NATO headquarters!"

A second source of Russian–Atlantic latent mistrust is, quite obviously, the decades of Cold War confrontation. To be sure, lasting rivalry cannot but leave traces in habitus. These marks appeared especially pronounced among Eastern European security practitioners: "we still struggle with the question of whether Russia and the Soviet Union are two different terms or not." But remnants of confrontation were also widespread in other NATO countries: "Old habits die hard," as one State Department practitioner readily conceded. One of his colleagues was equally realistic: "I was brought up during the Cold War so I'm still skeptical of the Russians. Russia wants to influence NATO, and the NRC makes mischief making easier. Russia looks for opportunities to exploit differences among allies." Significantly, on the Alliance's side, this fear that Moscow could "exploit cracks" was in line with what was probably the most pervasive concern in Brussels during the Cold War. According to Ira Straus, in the post-Cold War era this fear for Alliance consensus has been the foremost stumbling block in creating a new NATO–Russia relationship.[5] My interview data suggest that this point is well taken.

Reciprocally, the Russians also inherited deeply ingrained dispositions of mistrust towards NATO. A middle-aged professor from one of Moscow's most prestigious schools told me, as if stating the obvious: "Of course NATO's main duty is to plan war against Russia. This is a well-known fact." Another security official depicted Cold War stereotypes in Russia "like the dead holding the living." To be sure, Russia's history of invasions from its western borders has left an important imprint on strategic thinking. On both sides, accusations of "outdated, Cold War-like thinking" abound – a practice that is clearly part of symbolic power struggles (see Chapters 5 and 6). During his tenure as American permanent representative to NATO, Nicholas Burns regretted that "[o]ne abiding legacy of the Cold

[5] Straus (2003, 234).

War has been a deeply entrenched suspicion of NATO's intentions, especially as the alliance has expanded eastward and struggled to redefine its mission in the post-Soviet world. This feeling of distrust might be best summed up by the idea that, if it is good for NATO, it must be bad for Russia."[6] Although mistrustful dispositions were found in just about a third of my interviews, they nonetheless add nuance to the finding that the recourse to force may be receding from practitioners' horizons of possibility.

Third, and contrary to what is often assumed, contemporary mistrust among NATO and Russian practitioners is not simply a remnant of the Cold War but also the result of post-Cold War interactions. In fact, today's mistrust in many ways runs deeper than during most of the 1990s. Throughout the post-Cold War era, both NATO and Russia have conducted a number of military interventions or deployments that have heavily affected the quality of the relationship (see Chapters 5 and 6). These practices sparked fears on both sides that the relationship might not be as demilitarized as had been thought. On the Russian side, two such NATO practices have especially curbed the embodiment of diplomacy. First, NATO's advances towards the east through successive waves of enlargement constituted at least an indirect threat for most Russians. "Without the enlargements the relations would be much better," argued one official posted in Brussels. Importantly, most Russians believed that enlarging NATO broke a promise made to Mikhail Gorbachev in 1990 over German reunification. An official from the Russian Mission to NATO in Brussels insisted that "Russia assesses capabilities, not intentions. If there is a deployment to the East, it arouses suspicions." According to a German delegate, the American announcement in 2005 of a deployment in Bulgaria and Romania was seen as another broken promise, as was the air policing of the Baltic countries' border on the very day after they became NATO members. The possibility that Georgia and Ukraine might follow in their footsteps sparked in Russia intense feelings of exclusion, humiliation and incomprehension (see Chapter 6).

Second, several experts in Moscow believed that NATO's intervention in Kosovo shattered Russians' confidence in the demilitarization of the NATO–Russia relationship. Operation Allied Force convinced most Russian practitioners that the Alliance was still ready to use

[6] Quoted in US Department of State (2004).

force to solve international conflicts and that Russia could eventually become the next target. In the words of a very moderate Russian expert:

Before Kosovo, ideas of confrontation were considered "vestige," remnants of Soviet propaganda ... In 1998, there opened an ideological struggle within the Russian society and those who predominated were anti-Western views and mentality. They were able to say: "Listen, you were telling us that the West is so nice and unable to do anything wrong. Now, look at Yugoslavia! ... They're delivering bombs on peaceful people!" This was a very serious fracture of Russian mentality. It reversed the burden of proof.

Among other things, NATO's intervention convinced the Russian military of the continuing relevance of a nuclear deterrent: "The difference between Russia and Serbia is that Serbia doesn't have nuclear weapons," according to a former officer. The fear that Russia could become NATO's target in the future deepened with the American-led intervention in Iraq. In the words of a Russian expert, "recently we discovered that [in the US] war is considered a rational tool in promoting home interests. It considerably undermined the authority of the West." In 2006, 40–45 percent of the Russian population harbored negative feelings toward NATO, primarily because of its perceived aggressiveness.[7]

On the Atlantic side, two sets of Russian military practices left officials under the impression that the new Russia may not be that much different from the Soviet Union regarding the use of force. First, from a Western perspective the Chechen wars confirmed as early as 1994 (and again in 1999) that the Russian military retained a lot of influence over the Kremlin's policies. According to a Russian observer, the speeding up of the enlargement process beginning in 1994 was a direct reaction to the first invasion of Chechnya: "For people suspicious of Russia's developments, this was a signal: Russia has not changed. It still prefers military solutions to political problems." Second, several Atlantic practitioners were discouraged by Russia's continuing use of arm-twisting tactics (often bordering on outright force) in its

---

[7] All-Russian Center for the Study of Public Opinion (VTsIOM) poll quoted in NATO (2006, 2). See also White (2006, 144–6); and White, Korosteleva and Allison (2006).

"near abroad": "Russia does have a more aggressive policy toward its neighbours, Ukraine, Belarus, Moldova," said a State Department senior policymaker. "And it's inclined to think in military terms to preserve its influence and status in that part of the world." For instance, NATO expressed concern over Russian troops stationed in both Moldova and Georgia despite repeated demands by these countries for their withdrawal (see Chapter 6). By 2006, officials were already expressing concern over Russia's forceful tactics in dealing with Georgia. While the odds of Russia using force against NATO members were generally non-existent, the opposite was true when it came to the ex-Soviet republics. As a senior American policymaker remarked, portending the Georgia War of 2008: "can we completely rule out that Russia can use force? Of course not: look at what they're doing in Georgia." Other officials also raised the possibility that force was still considered by Moscow in its "near abroad." All in all, a number of military practices on both sides significantly thwarted pacification in and through practice by raising doubts about the demilitarization of future joint dealings.

A fourth crucial factor in sparking mistrust and slowing down the embodiment of diplomacy at the NRC was the arrival of a dozen former Soviet satellites as new NATO members. In hindsight, it should be obvious that enlarging the Alliance to post-communist states would put a brake on the NATO–Russia pacification process: how could the possibility of using military force recede from practitioners' mindsets when the newcomers joined NATO precisely out of a fear of Russia? Eastern European and Baltic countries have a troubled history of relations with Moscow, including military occupation, which leads them to stay on guard, if not to be outrightly anti-Russian. In fact, as an Alliance diplomat recalled, these countries joined NATO precisely so as not to have to deal with the Russians – certainly not to be told almost on a daily basis, as they were to be by older Allies, that they ought to cooperate with Russia. The net result, in 2006, was that NATO's Russia policy was "frozen," in the words of a senior policymaker in Brussels: "There is no consensus inside NATO as to the future of the relationship with Russia. As a consensual organization it cannot move."

The habitus of practitioners from former Soviet satellites was characterized by a high level of mistrust toward Russia. A Polish representative bluntly recognized that her country's willingness to join

NATO came out of fear of another Russian invasion. As a result, one American official conceded, Eastern Europeans tend to focus on Article Five of the Washington treaty about collective defense. Once inside, the Polish representative continued, Poles have become "less allergic to Russia." Nonetheless, "[n]ot to take what Russians say at face value is a Polish habit." Officials from the Baltic countries shared a similar level of mistrust. Freshly confirmed as the new Commander in Chief of Estonia, Major General Ants Laaneots declared that "relations with Russia are indeed our biggest security problem."[8] Among NATO's international military personnel, I met a Lithuanian colonel who was a Red Army conscript in 1987; his dispositions were obviously heavily influenced by that experience. In a meeting with another Lithuanian delegate, I was told that "Lithuanians can read through the Russian mind." In general, the Balts felt that *they* were the ones inside NATO who could provide the most accurate picture of the Russians. It seemed clear to them that "Russia doesn't cooperate genuinely; they are just manoeuvering." Such dispositions inherited from history made the embodiment of diplomacy quite difficult at the NRC.

NATO staff and older members' delegations were acutely aware of this problem. One senior policymaker bluntly admitted that "the Balts and the Poles are less enthusiastic. They bring with them knowledge and a suspicion of Russian motives ... They don't get along: they bicker and fight all the time." A top military officer concurred that the Balts put "no trust at all" in the Russians, while a senior policymaker in Berlin observed that they "instinctively applaud everything, every signal, every move coming from the United States that takes a critical view on Russia." In fact, a number of delegations from founding members insisted that "new members have to evolve" because "their arrival in NATO has put a brake on NATO–Russia cooperation." Worse, argued a Canadian delegate, "upon their arrival new members such as Poland and the Baltic countries openly questioned the opportunity of a NATO–Russia dialogue." In view of this fundamental difference of approach, a German delegate conceived his country's role as that of "a bridge between these new members and the Russians." But it appeared very hard for new member states to get rid of their Soviet-era military establishment – "to weed out hardliners," as one

[8] Quoted in Shegedin and Zygar (2006).

top NATO military officer put it. Against that inertia, older European members "have to have [the new members] mature and go beyond that. This will play a very important part in the future" of Russian–Atlantic relations.

Because the new members' suspicions are often echoed by the US, in 2006 NATO's policy toward Russia boiled down to the lowest common denominator. As one senior NATO official summarized, "the span of policies toward Russia has enlarged. There was a time where the ease to reach a consensus was better. [But now] we don't really have an active Russian policy. We do things with Russia, we cooperate, but in terms of steering a course, it is very difficult because the span has widened so much. [It was] absolutely easier in the 1990s." On that basis, it seems appropriate to conclude that the entry into NATO of former Soviet satellites has put a strong brake on the post-Cold War Russian–Atlantic pacification process. So much so, said one senior NATO official, that "[i]t's hard to characterize NATO's approach to the Russians on a continuum because the change in membership has changed the character of the Alliance."

Several practitioners reported that there were "two factions inside NATO" as far as its Russia policy was concerned: on one side were countries such as Germany, France, Italy, Spain, Norway and Belgium, which exhibited a higher level of trust toward Russia; and on the other side clustered the US, the United Kingdom, Poland and the Baltic countries, which remained more mistrustful of Moscow. According to a Russian delegate who had been posted to Brussels for more than a decade, the new NATO members "simply do what 'Master' says," while countries from Old Europe are "more reasonable." I too could ascertain a division in my interviews, although I observed a particularly high level of variance among American and British practitioners. Generally speaking, however, London and Washington took a more cautious stance toward Moscow than other Western European capitals. All in all, in 2006 everything took place as if relations with Russia divided NATO member states a lot more than they cemented them.

Indicator 2: the normalization of disputes

The interview data gathered in the field reveal that in 2006 both parties to the NRC relationship appeared inclined to treat mutual disputes almost as business-as-usual. An American policymaker summarized this feeling well: "Yes, we still have disagreements, quite a few, but certainly nothing like the Cold War." A Russian counterpart reciprocated: "We do have disagreements today, all countries have. But we're not in the confrontational situation as prior to 1991." No doubt political leaders sometimes used abrasive language and heated rhetoric that suggested aggravated tensions. But in contrast to this political discourse, security practitioners adopted a more down-to-earth attitude and tended to play down antagonisms in the relationship. This normalization of conflicts reinforces the embodiment of diplomacy because it turns disputes into matters of routine. According to a seasoned American diplomat whose career spanned both the Cold War and post-Cold War eras: "Disagreements civil in nature and tone are far more possible. They don't put us on the brink of war."

Of cycles and sine waves

Russian–Atlantic relations have gone through a series of highs and lows over the last decade and a half, in which honeymoons (e.g., 1992–3, 2001–3) have been followed by rough patches (e.g., 1998–9, 2004–6) and vice versa. Interestingly, practitioners tended to understand this evolution in "cycles" (or "waves" or "stages") – an appraisal that led them to entertain dependable expectations that a low would inevitably give way to another high, and so forth. As one American policymaker put it: "The long term is not bleak; it's just we're in a rough patch now." From a wider perspective, one NATO official in charge of the Russia policy stated that:

the relationship has become much more stable and pragmatic. If I take a fifteen-year window, that was obviously a period of dramatic highs and lows. We got to know each other to an extent where we managed to rein that in a little bit and keep expectations real, maintain a level of transparency to ensure that nobody gets surprised by what the other side does.

In fact, from the practitioners' point of view, it seemed as though the inconsistent quality of Russian–Atlantic cooperation was quite normal in the everyday life of international security. As one NATO official put it:

You have these honeymoon periods where you ask, "how are you going to do this together?" I'd actually – let's be honest: after about six months you decide you've done as much as you can in that particular field and you sit back and twiddle your thumbs. And say "what else can we do?" You hit another sort of flat period where nothing is happening – then something else will happen and you'll say, "oh, we can do that together," and you go off again on another of your honeymoon periods where everything is hunky-dory and you're working closely together.

From the practitioners' point of view, then, a slowdown in cooperation was no tragedy but rather normal and even an inevitable consequence of a past surge.

In the same spirit, a handful of NATO officials described the relationship with Russia as a "sine wave." Despite highs and lows, they found that the relationship was becoming more stable over time. Engagement persisted in rough patches so that overall the lows were decreasingly low, so to speak. In fact, because the sine wave's amplitude decreased over the post-Cold War era, "a complete cut-off of relations is now less possible." Overall, NATO practitioners' understanding of the relationship as a cycle allowed them to normalize the "succession of upsurge and downsurge" in the relationship. Just like a "wave" on the seashore, argued one NATO official, "sometimes it's getting better, sometimes it's getting worse." The important point here is that solving disputes peacefully had entered the realm of practical sense: "We spent a lot of time in negotiations that set up the NRC, trying to imagine scenarios, and what we would do under this and that circumstance," argued an Alliance policymaker. "In practice it's been very pragmatic – we just know what it is when we see it, when a specific question comes up." Solving disputes at the NRC had become a routine matter in 2006.

In order to probe this view, I asked several officials whether they thought that another rupture of NATO–Russia relations (such as during and after Operation Allied Force in 1999; see Chapter 6) was currently possible. The general feeling was optimistic.[9] While the Georgia War and the ensuing suspension of NRC activities proved

[9] One interesting exception, however, was a State Department official who responded: "You always have to imagine such ruptures, because in diplomacy when there is a big crisis the response is often a rupture of relations. Look at Pyongyang, or Tehran: our embassies disappeared when

that expectation wrong, it is nonetheless striking that it was so widespread in 2006. For example, one NATO senior official replied that "that sort of spontaneous move is less likely today. You wouldn't hype a crisis into a rupture of NATO–Russia relations." One of his colleagues was equally convinced that today a rupture of relations "would be much more difficult to imagine." The capacity of the NRC forum to take the heat out of disputes – to provide a "safety valve," as one practitioner put it – had been proven in practice. Since 2002 NRC participants had discussed a number of contentious issues, including the Balkans, Afghanistan, Ukraine, Belarus, Central Asia, the Middle East, NATO's transformation, energy security and missile defense. By a Canadian delegate's account, these issues were reportedly put on the agenda in a tit-for-tat fashion – Russia accepted an NRC discussion on Georgia so long as the US assented to discuss Iraq, and so on. As a result, "[t]he dialogue at the NRC has become more entrenched. We've moved from all-out enthusiasm to more concrete progress ... There are no routines yet, but cooperation principles are emerging. Before we would not discuss controversial topics; now there is a willingness to do so," affirmed a NATO official. The same viewpoint could be heard on the Russian side: "The balance of the relationship is positive. We're now discussing things for which there was no will to discuss before. The political dialogue touches on any issues except internal matters." Significantly, a German delegate told me that, in the spring of 2006, the possibility of an NRC peacekeeping mission in the south Caucasus had even been raised – something the Russians had always refused to consider in the past. All in all, concluded the chairman of the NRC preparatory committee, "the NRC has evolved into a forum for serious dialogue on those issues where we do not see eye-to-eye."[10]

By far "the biggest gap the NRC managed to bridge," in a NATO senior official's words, had to do with the 2004 Orange Revolution in Ukraine. Significantly, in the post-Cold War era this event presented the highest risk of "evolv[ing] into a West vs. Russia, proxy type of conflict." Yet the NRC managed to solve the issue peacefully with a

things get too hostile. So yes it's possible, for instance if Russia takes military action against Georgia or something like that." The events of summer 2008 obviously proved him right.
[10] Fritch (2007, 2).

joint communiqué, on December 9, 2004, which "appeal[ed] to all parties to continue to avoid the use or instigation of violence, to refrain from intimidation of voters, and to work to ensure a free, fair electoral process that reflects the will of the Ukrainian people."[11] Given the stakes at play, this dispute constitutes a compelling counterfactual (but for X, then Y) that diplomacy had previously been normalized at the NRC. But for the prior embodiment of the peaceful resolution of disputes (X), the Orange Revolution could have led to a military standoff (or threats thereof) between Russia and NATO's member states (Y). At the NRC (and, notably, neither at the Organization for Security and Cooperation in Europe [OSCE] nor through the EU–Russia mechanism), Russia and NATO member states played down this deep-rooted conflict, agreeing to disagree. From the practitioners' point of view, what mattered was not so much the substance of the communiqué but "the fact that they actually managed to deal with" that issue. "We came to a common language, which proves that this framework works," concluded a German delegate.

The head of NATO's Russia policy explained this success by the fact that the NRC has turned Russia into a "stakeholder":

Look at the agenda of that meeting [December 9, 2004]: we agreed not only on that, but also on a very ambitious NATO–Russia Action Plan on Terrorism and the three big elements of prevention, combating, and consequence management; and we agreed on an exchange of letters for Russian participation in Operation Active Endeavour. These were deliverables that Russia was very interested in. We've managed to be successful, when we have, when we maintained enough substance to keep Russia engaged. It's not as easy as in Spring 99 to say: "the hell with all of you, we're walking away."

As another NATO diplomat continued, the Russians "have a very vested interest in making [the NRC] work ... they'd never go along and do something like that unless they felt it was in their best interest to engage on such a difficult topic. So I think [the communiqué on Ukraine is] a very revealing incident." In 2006, American and NATO practitioners considered that the NRC was Russia's "favorite forum" and that its officials "work[ed] seriously" there. As one British official

---

[11] NATO (2004a).

put it: "Russia actually likes its position of preference in relation to NATO. They like to have these discussions. They like to have this engagement and they like to be involved. [The relationship] has been wading through very, very deep mud and we're getting things out of the way [thanks to the NRC]."

In most (though not all) of my interviews, I had the feeling that practitioners strongly believed in the virtue of talking, whether that led to an agreement or not. Dialogue would not necessarily lead to a change of mind but it was worthy nonetheless, according to a NATO diplomat:

Does it mean that having that forum with them is going to sway their mind on certain issues? Any country is going to say, "No, we have our national interests and we're going to stick with them." But the chances are you're going to see it coming. You can work to get around it and talk to them about it but at the end of the day ... you're not going to sway them from that.

Talking eased the everyday life of security officials no matter what results it delivered. In the blunt words of a seasoned Canadian diplomat: "The idea that you always solve differences of views is dead wrong. Very often you paper over differences."

Contrary to the Cold War era, when both sides had to live permanently on the brink of nuclear confrontation, in 2006 disputes had become at least less alarming and at best normalized, by a senior Alliance practitioner's account. Russian and Atlantic officials felt much freer to discuss a variety of topics and express frank opinions: "There are disagreements, obviously, because we're talking about more things," confirmed a senior member of the Secretary-General's office. "Both sides are much freer to talk about what's on their mind. In the Cold War it was simply impossible to go there." Behind this evolution, Alliance practitioners perceived a new "degree of honesty" as well as an unprecedented "familiarity" in the relationship. Russian practitioners also believed that disputes were inevitable: "the common thing in international politics is not to be able to agree on everything. It's normal to disagree." Russian–Atlantic divergences, according to one Russian expert, were in that sense not so different from intra-Alliance disagreements. In this context, practitioners valued the possibility of sitting together around the same table and "talk, talk, talk," because "talking gets into habit."

In 2006, numerous tensions continued to surface and significant differences of international outlook remained. But a number of security officials emphasized that it often was just the same between France and the United Kingdom, for instance. The important thing, from the practitioners' point of view, was to be able to "air" differences and "talk [them] through." Thus it was the way in which these differences were bridged that made the relationship qualitatively different, not their number: "It doesn't always go very well, but at least we talk about it," summed up a senior NATO policymaker. To be sure, because the NRC was often used to "air the dirty laundry," there was a dramatic element to it, but it was judged useful as a sort of therapy. For instance, one British diplomat suggested that:

it's actually useful that we have a forum to have these arguments. If we weren't having these arguments in the NATO–Russia Council, where would we be having them? If we didn't have a means of Russia airing its concerns, what would we have instead? So it does feel difficult and destructive a lot of the time, but I think it's important for everyone that actually it's constructive to have these debates and it's constructive to air these problems.

In addition, several practitioners stressed the importance of the "boring" aspects of the NRC, such as a firm "timetable and a regular meeting schedule," which forced NATO and Russia to confront tough issues regularly. The NRC "provides a structure" to the diplomatic resolution of disputes, in an American practitioner's words.

At the institutional level, in 2006 the NRC comprised more than twenty-five working groups carrying forward concrete projects on security cooperation. Such a wide array of issue areas led the NATO bureaucracy to develop ties not only with the Kremlin and the Russian Ministry of Foreign Affairs, but also with the Russian Ministry of Emergency Situations, the Border Guards, the Interior Ministry, the Academy of Sciences, etc. "There are probably ten to fifteen thousand people within various parts of the Russian bureaucracy who are involved in one way or another in some NATO–Russia cooperative effort," reported one NATO official closely involved in relations with Russia. "That's a constituency." As they widened in scope and depth, relations between Moscow and the Alliance could not be disrupted as easily as in the past, he thought. Conflicts had to be solved through "normal" diplomatic channels. NATO prides itself on the fact that "[h]ardly a day goes by without an NRC meeting at one

level or another, which has led to an unprecedented intensity of contacts and informal consultations in many different fields."[12] As they
daily interact with foreign counterparts, practitioners bear in mind
that conflicts will not wither away overnight and that disputes cannot
be solved instantly. As one NATO military officer who spent years
working with the Russians insisted: "We need to continue and temper our expectations. We can only reach out through a step-by-step
approach. It will take a long time. It's better than doing nothing."
As they were going through cycles and advancing with small steps,
practitioners valued the NRC structure especially because it "[froze]
in time one of the high periods and institutionalize[d] enough of the
cooperative atmosphere that we can ride out the lows. We'll continue
in the behind-the-scene, low-profile way that doesn't always make the
headlines," insisted one NATO diplomat. Pacification in and through
practice has a different logic than an exclusive focus on high politics
would suggest: from the practitioners' point of view, what mattered
was that "[t]here is a de-dramatization of the whole NATO–Russia
relationship."

Although one should not overstate this evolution in light of the
Georgia War of 2008, in 2006 the NRC's working atmosphere
appeared less at the mercy of the overall quality of Russia–West relations than it used to be during the 1990s. In the words of an American
official: "The NRC is a hugely valuable tool to keep engaging the
Russians in dialogue, to keep working on practical projects where
our interests coincide, to keep a certain degree of momentum and
practical cooperation regardless of what is going on in the bilateral
political relation." These joint projects, according to a British diplomat, "progress quite well ... regardless of the difficulties we're having
in our strategic dialogue with Russia." A member of the Canadian
delegation to NATO similarly believed that "among the things that
were gained is that it has become impossible to lose the entire relationship all of a sudden. Sometimes the relationship is so banal and
normal that it looks just like relations with any other country." This
trivialization of Russian–Atlantic cooperation seemed quite significant in terms of pacification in and through practice – as were the
limits it faced in 2006.

[12] NATO (2007, 6).

An elusive momentum

As considerable as it may look from my interview data, the normalization of disputes at the NRC was considerably thwarted in 2006 by the fact that it remained partly hostage to the larger political relationship between Moscow and the West. The momentum described by a handful of practitioners appeared quite elusive to many others. As a NATO military officer posted in Moscow described the NRC diplomacy: "It's not a process that's self-propelling, with its own momentum. We really have to be creative ... you always need new impetus." Relatedly, certain practitioners expressed skepticism as to the capacity of the NRC to work in the absence of political will. While in 2006 the NRC still benefited from the "highest support" of key governments, it remained to be seen how much momentum the NRC practitioners' could keep going, and for how long, should political will falter. One imaginative interviewee in Washington elaborated: "I don't think one ever assumes that institutions and mechanisms can weather any and all storms ... You try to build the building to withstand the force of the vast majority of storms, but the exception may blow it down." With the benefit of hindsight, the Georgia War turned out to be such an exception, at least temporarily (see Chapter 6). A NATO diplomat in Moscow also perceived the two upcoming presidential elections in the US and Russia in 2008 as "clouding" the relationship. Change in political leadership, especially in the main countries represented at the NRC, mattered a lot from the practitioners' point of view. One NATO official recalled, for instance, that "you will see a particular country that is particularly pro-Russia one day after a set of elections and particularly anti the next – Germany being one." The reverse could now be said of the Obama administration as compared to the Bush years.

In addition, practitioners pointed out two other factors that exogenously determined the quality of the NRC relationship. The first was NATO's own process of transformation, which had been unfolding for a decade and a half and whose endpoint remained far from clear even to its own civil servants. When asked where they thought the NATO–Russia relationship would be in twenty years, several Alliance officials answered that the main difficulty was that "it's difficult to say what NATO will be in ten or twenty years." Because of its ever-changing mission, "NATO can't do that much [with Moscow] because it is so absorbed in its own crisis. NATO will not do anything because it lacks the capacity to institutionalize the relationship with Russia beyond what it already is. NATO considers that if Russia is interested, it is up to them to do something," affirmed a senior official posted in Moscow. The second external factor upon which the NRC diplomatic process depends is the future of Russia itself. In 2006, almost all practitioners would not venture to predict how democratic Moscow would be in the middle term. This created difficulties in day-to-day interaction, believed a NATO diplomat, because the Russians "haven't found an equilibrium in which they could say, 'OK, this is not Russia becoming something, this is Russia that *is*.'"

In terms of practical logics, a regular participant on the NRC preparatory committee evaluated that "we still don't have that inherent feel for political partnership." A number of NATO practitioners blamed the politicization of the NRC on the Russians, who, by a British official's account, "hold the practical agenda hostage to the strategic agenda." According to a senior official at the State Department: "The Russians make the NRC political. They want it to be a Foreign Ministry- and policy-driven thing. They're reluctant to let the military cooperation go. When they talk about [the NRC] and measure it, it's always in terms of the political relationship." The official illustrated his point with the discussions that were held in 2006 on the future status of Kosovo. In view of the difficulty of reaching an agreement, he lamented: "Half of what motivates the Russians on Kosovo is if the international community [meaning NATO] says Kosovo is going to be independent, then why not Abkhazia and Transdniestria? This is a self-interested concern we're not going to agree on. We won't solve that at the NRC. It hasn't gained any momentum of its own. It would be very nice if it did!" Another example of the politicized nature of Russia's cooperation with NATO, supplied by a British officer from the Ministry of Defense, was an NRC exercise that was supposed to be held on British soil but was later moved to France, allegedly because of soured relations between London and Moscow at the time.

In this context, practitioners expressed regret at the inflammatory rhetoric often uttered at the highest political levels. As one NATO official complained: "One of the problems that I find, from a policy professional who's been dealing with Russia for several years, is that Western policy toward Russia tends to swing widely between unrealistic euphoria and utter desperation. Those wide mood swings are not justified by facts." Similarly, on the Russian side, the political rhetoric about NATO was often not representative of the actual cooperation that was taking place on the ground at the NRC, according to a diplomat posted in Moscow: "The language that Russian authorities use at NATO and here is not coherent, which gives a completely schizophrenic impression. I live this daily. Whether this double language will continue depends on the overall relationship Russia has with the West." In her opinion, while NATO allies make the difference between Alliance issues and larger transatlantic or EU relations, Moscow does not: "For Russia the relationship with NATO is completely dependent – hence the schizophrenia – on the relationship with the United States and the West in general. It's not a different corridor: it's completely intertwined. It makes the relationship very vulnerable."

In order to lend momentum to NATO–Russia relations, one senior Russian diplomat emphasized the need to give concrete substance to NRC discussions by tackling "real challenges, not old myths about Russia attacking Washington with missiles." Alluding to the scenario of a terrorist attack on the London or Moscow subway, he continued: "This is something to deal with together. When we will resume this very serious and central dialogue, then I think we will have a certain security against rupture of relations." However, the same Russian practitioners argued that what ultimately prevents the NRC from gaining momentum was the fact that Russia remained excluded from NATO. Asked to explain why, three years after France's and Russia's staunch opposition to the American invasion of Iraq, trust was restored between Washington and Paris but not with Moscow, he lucidly answered: "They're inside the tent and we're outside. Yes, we have a mechanism with NATO, but it doesn't compensate for the feeling that you belong to the collective people." This profound feeling of exclusion, which was articulated throughout my interviews with Russian practitioners, is further discussed in Chapters 5 and 6.

The politicized nature of the NRC becomes especially obvious when it is compared to another example of institutionalized Russian–American cooperation: the Cooperative Threat Reduction program (also known as the Global Partnership since the 2002 G8 summit, and previously called the Nunn-Lugar program in the US). This multiyear program essentially aims to secure and dismantle weapons of mass destruction and their associated infrastructure in former Soviet Union states. Beyond its success, what was particularly striking about the Cooperative Threat Reduction program was its complete depoliticization: the quality of diplomatic interaction and military cooperation allegedly did not follow the overall mood of Russian–Western relations. As one State Department official stressed, his team worked on the program "non-stop through the 1990s. It survived all of that disruption. In fact, I would say that in general, the disruption and the instability, at least as a practitioner, drove us harder." In effect, he insisted that during crises such as Bosnia or Kosovo the level of cooperation counterintuitively "went up"; the program was "insulated" from other problems and consistently "dealt with in a very workmanlike way." The chief Canadian negotiator of the Global Partnership similarly assessed that negotiations with the Russians went "extraordinarily well" despite the fact that the issues were "extremely complex" and "most sensitive." This insulation of day-to-day interaction from overall politics was not as strong at the NRC in 2006, according to practitioners. This important finding leads me to explore the third indicator of the embodiment of diplomacy: daily cooperation on the ground.

Indicator 3: daily cooperation on the ground

Daily cooperation on the ground is an indicator of the embodiment of diplomacy because the logic of practicality is constituted in and through practice (see Chapter 2). Within a stable social configuration, the practical sense reads the way to go in the present and the future from past relations and practices. In the Russian–Atlantic case, there is one area in which cooperation has become more self-propelling: practical military-to-military cooperation. Although the NATO–Russia relationship was strained to a post-Cold War low at the time of the interviews, an American Lieutenant-General posted to NATO insisted that practical cooperation was "the best ever." A Canadian delegate agreed that the military-to-military dimension was clearly the NRC's "main added value." On the Russian side, military cooperation was similarly considered "the fundamental thing" – what supports political dialogue. According to a NATO representative in Moscow, practical cooperation such as counter-narcotics training in Central Asia – a Russian idea – worked very well because it is precisely what meets Russian expectations. It commits them to the NRC forum, which is good news for the Alliance. "The only way you're going to share a strategic perspective is if you do stuff together," observed a senior NATO policymaker. That said, in 2006 Russian and Atlantic security practices also embodied contrasting organizational cultures.

Doing stuff together

The very first practical cooperation between Russia and NATO began in October 1995, when a group of Russian General Staff officers arrived at Supreme Headquarters Allied Powers Europe (SHAPE) in order to prepare Russia's participation in the Implementation Force (IFOR) and later in the Stabilization Force (SFOR). In total, 1,500 Russian troops with 300 pieces of heavy weaponry went on duty in early February 1996, officially under the command of American General George Joulwan, who also happened to be NATO's Supreme Allied Commander Europe (SACEUR). As a number of practitioners recalled, although not formally integrated, Russian and NATO troops entered into joint patrolling, combat training, reconnaissance, etc. In the course of day-to-day work, several mechanisms were developed to ease communication and interaction on the ground. General Leonti Shevtsov, who commanded the Russian contingent, assessed the cooperation in the following way: "It has not been a smooth ride throughout, of course, but as a result of our joint work at SHAPE we are gradually learning to work together."[13] A detailed Russian–American assessment of IFOR gave "high marks" to cooperation on the ground, while also noting the need for improvement in operational coordination, decisionmaking procedures and planning process.[14] Interoperability – the ability of systems, units and forces to work effectively with others – was also flagged as an area for further improvement. Despite day-to-day interactions at the tactical level, a number of NATO officials emphasized that the peacekeeping operations were not run jointly, as the operational space had been divided between Russian and Allied forces.

The Kosovo Force (KFOR), which received a Russian contribution of 1,500 soldiers (the largest non-NATO contingent), was the object of a similar mix of plaudits and reservations concerning Russian–Atlantic cooperation on the ground. As Roy Allison reports: "At the operational level, issues of control in planning and coordination

[13] Shevtsov (1997, 4).   [14] Kipp *et al.* (2000, 56–9).

between Russia and other NATO participants arose periodically, although tactical-level cooperation appeared to be excellent, at least between Russian and US forces. NATO and Russian troops took part in joint training, joint patrolling, and joint de-mining tasks. Liaison functions developed on the tactical and strategic levels."[15] However, Moscow decided to pull out its contingents – both SFOR and KFOR – in the summer of 2003, thereby losing the opportunity for ground-level, day-to-day cooperation with NATO. But throughout the eight years of operational interaction, Russian and Atlantic practitioners succeeded, at least in part, in turning attention away from mutual disputes toward common fate and joint ventures. In this context, military officers were "able to find a common language when faced with a common mission."[16] To this end, many of the NATO officials I interviewed in 2006 were actively looking for new peacekeeping opportunities with the Russians.

Despite the lack of any active Russian–Atlantic peacekeeping operation in 2006, the NRC worked on a number of initiatives in preparation for an eventual mission. In September 2002, the NRC approved a document called "Political Aspects of a Generic Concept for Joint NATO–Russia Peacekeeping Operations." In September 2004, the NRC held a three-day procedural exercise on peacekeeping, in which the twenty-seven member states were confronted with a fictional international crisis situation that required the generation of a joint peacekeeping force to enforce an UN-sponsored peace agreement. In early 2005, Moscow announced the creation of a peacekeeping brigade comprised of 2,000 soldiers dispatched in three motorized rifle battalions, a reconnaissance battalion, and various support units. The brigade is now fully autonomous and has been involved in the NRC's operational compatibility program. Although not officially a peacekeeping operation, in 2006 NATO and Russia also cooperated on small-scale intelligence and defense functions with regard to Afghanistan (see also Chapter 6). A Canadian policymaker portrayed Moscow as "actively helpful in Afghanistan, not least in arranging American basing arrangements." Finally, the NRC's Counter-Narcotics Training of Afghan and Central Asian Personnel was initiated in December 2005 as a pilot project to train 350 officers to police Afghanistan's borders.

---

[15] Allison (2006, 111–12).   [16] Kujat (2002, 1).

In 2006, Russia and NATO were also participating in Operation Active Endeavour, a naval counterterrorist operation in the Mediterranean launched by NATO in the aftermath of September 11, 2001. In September 2006, under its own initiative Russia took part in this mission with a ship that was fully integrated under NATO command (another frigate, the *Ladnyi*, took its turn of duty in September 2007). Russia's participation in Active Endeavour is all the more remarkable in that it is an Article Five mission decided under the collective defense provision that was historically targeted against Moscow. In preparation for joining the operation, starting in 2005 the Russian navy participated in a number of training sessions with NATO members' fleets. By one NATO senior diplomat's account, the military integration required by the operation implied sharing secret communication codes, standard operating procedures, doctrines, and other information normally restricted to allies only. As an American delegate noted: "We've already done things we had never done before, such as exchanging officers between naval commands and sharing photographic equipment to put on board Russian vessels." Military cooperation and information-sharing on such sensitive issues suggest that the possibility of a mutual attack was not an overwhelming preoccupation on either side. In and through practice, the focus was on a common struggle.

In 2006 the NRC was in charge of a large menu of practical activities held both in Russia and on NATO countries' soil, including consequence-management exercises, joint responses to terrorist attacks, missile defense command post exercises and nuclear weapons accident response, among many other tasks. Russia also took part in an exercise called Sorbet Royal in 2005 that featured submarine rescue maneuvers.[17] Other examples of military-to-military cooperation included the Cooperative Airspace Initiative, which fosters NRC cooperation on airspace surveillance and airspace traffic management with the objective of countering terrorist threats to civil aviation. A live exercise with military transport aviation was held in Ramstein in July 2006, and a system of reciprocal exchange of air traffic data

---

[17] In the weeks following this exercise, Moscow requested help from the British navy in the rescue of one of its submarine crew near the Kamchatka peninsula. This success was often hailed by NATO officers as a concrete NRC deliverable from which Russia benefited.

was implemented in March. Other noteworthy initiatives include the Strategic Airlift Interim Solution, a joint Russian–Ukrainian venture to give NATO access to six Antonov aircraft, and the launch of a NATO–Russia Information, Consultation and Training Center for the Resettlement of Military Personnel Discharged from the Russian Armed Forces, which was expanded in 2003 to six regional branches across Russia in addition to its main office in Moscow. These joint ventures are tangible practices that demonstrate a considerable level of daily interaction on the ground.

In a similar fashion, Russia and NATO have been working for years on fostering interoperability among their militaries, which also points toward the gradual receding of confrontational thinking on both sides. As a retired American pilot, now part of NATO's international staff, optimistically described it: "the very willingness to develop interoperable forces suggests that mutual armed conflicts are no more possible." A German military officer agreed: "It would not be fair to deal together in these operations and at the same time think about confrontation in the future. The two cannot go along." In June 2005, for instance, the NRC Defense Ministers adopted a document entitled "Political–Military Guidance towards Enhanced Interoperability between Forces of Russia and NATO Nations," whose objective was to ensure that the forces of all services at the three levels of military command and operation (strategic, operational, and tactical) developed the ability to operate in synergy. The program led Russia and NATO to finally sign a Status of Forces Agreement in 2005 (ratified by the Duma in May 2007), which established a legal framework for reciprocal military transit over one another's territory free from visa regimes and related restrictions. Admittedly, these practical initiatives required fairly high levels of military transparency. In a similar vein, in June 2005 all NATO member states together with Russia published a "NATO–Russia Compendium of Financial and Economic Data Relating to Defense" listing defense expenditures of NRC countries since 1980.

In addition to military-to-military cooperation, in 2006 the NRC also hosted a few dozen workshops, roundtables and seminars on a variety of topics, ranging from fuels interoperability, terrorist tactics, defense reform and peacekeeping, to logistics, defense budgeting, area surveillance and maritime support. Academic exchanges were also organized at the NATO Defense College in Rome, where a group of Russian military officers taught for the very first time. The first academic year of a military-based defense reform course for active-duty military officers serving at the Russian Ministry of Defense also came to a successful conclusion in 2006. The course, approved by the NRC in 2004, had been developed jointly by NATO and a top-tier Moscow academic institute. During the same year, Mobile Education Training Teams took part in more than forty events, including another first: Russian military teaching at the NATO school in Oberammergau. The NRC's many working groups of experts also developed half a dozen detailed glossaries on matters of special operations forces (2006), peacekeeping (2006), combating terrorism (2006), defense reform (2005), or nuclear terminology (2004).

The NRC provided a physical locus of face-to-face, daily interaction among Russian and Atlantic security practitioners. In addition to its mission to the Alliance's headquarters, in 2004 Moscow also opened a liaison branch office in Mons as well as a small team within the Partnership Coordination Cell at SHAPE. As a senior NATO policymaker put it: "We now have a structural forum ... where they meet all the time on all issues and talk ... You start to cycle through officials who know you, you don't have such an ignorance of NATO and suspicion because they know how it works." The ongoing presence of Russian officials in Brussels, as well as their almost daily meetings with NATO counterparts, accounted for an important dimension of the NRC institutionalization. For instance, I was genuinely astonished to hear a Russian official express the view that "Russia sits around the table like any other country. It is a member of the family." He added that "there is this glue" at the NRC. Interpersonal bonds seem to work both ways. A British delegate admitted that in preparation for NRC meetings she would approach her Russian counterparts the same way she does her French or American ones. A French official told me a similar story, insisting that he calls his Russian colleagues in preparation for a meeting, asks for support or draws limits as he would for inter-Allied negotiations.

Institutionalization at NATO headquarters found its echo in Russia, though on a much smaller scale. The NRC was represented in Moscow through an Information Office and a Military Liaison hosted by the Belgian embassy. A "hotline" was also established in late 2003 between NATO headquarters and the Russian Defense Minister. On the civil side, NATO launched a website in Russian in order to speak directly to people within the country. In spring 2006, a NATO–Russia Rally was organized across Russia to promote cooperation with the Alliance as a key foreign policy interest of the country. With stops in nine cities from Vladivostok to Kaliningrad, the objective of the rally was to heighten public awareness of the NRC's goals and achievements. When I met with a senior NATO diplomat involved in the project upon her return to Moscow in May 2006, she said that although the project would not change Russians' perception of NATO overnight (very negative, according to her assessment), at least it was the first initiative of public diplomacy run jointly by NATO and the Russian bureaucracy on the Kremlin's soil. On the military side, the head of the Military Liaison revealed that in 2005 about 200 events had been organized in Moscow alone. NATO military representatives met at least twice a month with their counterparts at the Russian Ministry of Defense to discuss all sorts of military issues, including "contentious ones." Overall, these NRC mechanisms were perceived by practitioners as "a bridge to Russia" – "the proof that this Alliance is no longer directed against Russia," to borrow an American delegate's words.

Thanks to the NRC joint programs, hundreds of civilian and military personnel from Russia and Allied countries gathered to work together on a day-to-day basis. An American delegate judged these interactions on the ground as "very valuable, because they put us together and we go to the field together with real scenarios ... We're building trust, which is the fundamental thing ... It needs to be built both in my government and on the Russian side." From a British practitioner's point of view, the main gain earned from joint exercises was reassurance about intentions. As one German official confirmed, "we're coming together. The more we do it, in working groups etc., the more we work together on military-to-military level, have joint exercises on different levels, then the better it works. People stop thinking about the possible threat of the Russian army." On the Russian side, an analyst made a similar evaluation:

When I started in the middle of the 1990s, I couldn't have imagined that so soon, in seven to eight years – a very short historical period – NATO–Russia relations would be characterized by the Russian embassy as the most successful of all the directions of Russian foreign policy. With NATO we cooperate. Of course it's not sufficient, I would like to see more on the table. But this military-to-military cooperation, joint exercises, special status of forces, interoperability, all this is very important. These small steps create a new atmosphere in our relationship.

The net result was, to use the words of another observer in Moscow, the emergence of a *zdravyi smysl* (здравый смысл) or a "common sense" that the current NATO–Russia relationship had become safe from mutual violence. This was obviously a sea change from the Cold War.

For NATO practitioners, engaging the Russian army aimed to debunk certain enduring myths about the Alliance so as to foster a workmanlike atmosphere: "We made some progress in the Russian military," said one NATO official. "They are much more friendly to us and much more constructive than they were, I don't know, ten years ago ... You can't compare [Russia's Chief of General Staff Yuri] Baluyevsky with his predecessors, for instance – he's much better. Also the guys here at the Russian mission are different from the previous staff. They're ready to cooperate." According to one American policymaker, the NRC contributed to changing Russia's perception of the Alliance: "They've been too much around," he said. Judging from high-level declarations on Russia's side, there seemed to be some truth to these assessments: Defense Minister Sergei Ivanov declared, for instance, that "the NATO–Russia cooperation has outgrown the 'adolescence' age," hailing practical achievements on theatre missile defense and others.[18] Although these sanguine statements were often balanced by harsh criticisms of the Alliance, they represented a significant departure from those made by the otherwise more pro-Western Kremlin in the 1990s.

Also striking was the fact that discussions at the NRC created what a French delegate called a "variable geometry" of political coalitions, with Russia sometimes siding with certain allies and sometimes with others depending on the issue: "You come to a point at the NRC where we have lively discussions not only twenty-six plus one, but also among allies," confirmed an official from the German Delegation to the Alliance. This constituted a very important departure from the politics of the PJC, in which the NATO members' positions were "pre-cooked" in a prior NAC meeting. These Allied positions were

---

[18] Ivanov (2004).

then presented "en bloc" to the Russians, thereby creating a bit of confrontation. At the NRC, argued a British delegate, there was "very little coordination among allies." That said, the very nature of the Alliance created a very clear limit to the notion that the NRC comprises twenty-seven equal partners. In a German delegate's formulation, "solidarity inside the Alliance is a value we appreciate." The partnership with Russia remained subsidiary to collective defense; there were clear "red lines with Russia." As a French diplomat posted in Brussels confirmed: "Ultimately we are held to allied solidarity. I cannot embarrass my American colleague in order to support the Russians. Just the same, I can't say all I want to the Russians in front of my Allied colleagues. Some things need to be dealt with in private."[19]

Another important effect of day-to-day cooperation on the ground was the narrowing of NATO's and Russia's respective positions on a number of conflicts in the world. One NATO official insisted that cooperation on the ground breeds common interests. As an example, he listed all the ongoing operations that NATO was conducting at the time of the interview (in Afghanistan, the Balkans, Darfur, Iraq, and the Mediterranean) to conclude that "Russia in one way or another is not only smiling benevolently and kissing goodbye, they're explicitly supporting every single one of them to various degrees." After September 11, 2001, the convergence became especially significant (see Chapter 6).[20] That event led Russia and NATO to realize that they now faced a "common threat," affirmed a British diplomat: terrorism. Interestingly, this convergence was a rare instance of NATO moving in Russia's direction and not the other way around. Having advocated a more muscular fight against terrorism for years, the Russians were obviously happy about this turn of events, added a Canadian practitioner. That satisfaction seemed to be shared, at least to some extent, by NATO practitioners: "In general, they're a Western country in terms of thinking, in terms of approaching solutions. Especially after September 11, 2001, they're on the same side as we are." That said, a number of officials insisted on some remaining differences,

---

[19] According to one State Department official, "in theory the NRC works at twenty-seven and not twenty-six plus one. But in practice, Russia is not part of NATO. There exists allied solidarity. We can't let Russia too much in."
[20] Pouliot (2003).

noting for instance that "we will never get them to agree that you cannot solve terrorism in purely military terms." For a British official, deep differences in threat perceptions largely explained contemporary Russian–Atlantic distrust: "The Russians see the war on terrorism and the American definition as an excuse for American power to intervene where major oil reserves are." Equally, many Atlantic practitioners remained suspicious of "anti-terrorist operations" in Chechnya. Although in 2006 NATO and Russia were doing a lot of stuff together, more often than not their respective practices belonged to contrasting organizational cultures.

Contrasting organizational cultures

As much "stuff on the ground" as NATO and Russian practitioners may have been doing together in 2006, their prior common experience with working together remained extremely limited. As a result, the NRC institutionalization ran into two main obstacles at the practical level: a lack of substance and a clash of organizational procedures. To begin with the first problem, a number of officials were not convinced that the NRC was bringing about any tangible results in terms of Russian–Atlantic cooperation. One senior NATO policymaker put the matter this way:

My frank and honest feeling is that we've quadrupled the amount of bureaucracy, we've probably made the working level of meetings a bit more informal and relaxed, but in terms of actual effect on the ground – more cooperation and trust – my own feeling is that I haven't seen any improvement ... What I do see is a group of people who spend a lot of time with the Russians. People call them the Russian mafia – they're really into it ... But if you get past the meetings to see what the effect is, maybe they get along better and have beers, but I still don't see this great improvement in terms of more cooperation.

A similar skepticism could be felt on the Russian side: "Russians doubt the sincerity of NATO in engaging Russia. And they are skeptical about the results. Are we really doing something serious in this cooperative framework? Lots of words and discussions, working groups, symposia, and so forth; words, words, words. What about something serious and tangible? I'm not sure we have that." For another expert in Moscow, NATO's engagement with Russia was nothing but "the medicine for the Russians against NATO enlargement." The result, he insisted, is that few Russians believed in the sincerity of NATO friendship: "There are suspicions." Many Russians doubted that the Alliance was willing to do anything concrete with them beyond keeping the conversation going.

A familiar complaint among Atlantic practitioners was that the Russians are so focused on procedure that it often comes at the expense of substance. According to a Canadian delegate, the NRC did not deliver as much as expected because too many discussions remained embroiled in procedure to be productive. For instance, during the spring of 2006, the NRC conducted a stocktaking exercise in order to decide on its next priorities: "it has quickly turned into a fastidious exercise, without good news. It was reduced to a wording negotiation," complained a Canadian delegate. As one NATO senior military officer summed up, "rhetoric often trumps substance," adding that NRC activities belonged as much, if not more, to public diplomacy than to concrete achievements. "Events are showpiece, without real benefits," said a German colonel. "Take Active Endeavour: three years of talk for one frigate one week." Similarly, a senior American policymaker regretted that Russia asks the Allies to do many things in the NRC "but in the end you don't see Russia pursuing all of them. They're floating but never put together ... I think the Russians would be happy to say they're doing something without in fact doing anything." This concern with formalism also finds its expression in the multiplication of ad hoc committees under the NRC, whose added value was not always clear from NATO practitioners' point of view. "The Russians produce more papers than practices," complained a Lithuanian official, who told me of an Estonian joke that the NRC was becoming Soviet-like because too many people were happy to get paid without doing much work.

In 2006, the institutionalization of Russian–Atlantic relations at the NRC left certain officials with an impression of purposelessness. Some practitioners agreed that what was most direly lacking in the relationship was a genuine *finalité* or long-term goal. At the time, they felt that "staying engaged is the goal." NATO's attitude toward Russia seemed to boil down to "hold to engagement, for engagement's own sake," in an Alliance official's words. While institutionalizing engagement certainly has great value for pacification in and through practice, several practitioners wondered to what extent such a strategy was sustainable over the long run in the absence of any larger vision for the future. A Canadian delegate, for instance, proposed that "what's missing is still this notion of what's the long term plan." One of his colleagues opined that "the NRC doesn't produce that much because the Russians are happy with the status quo. They use the forum to better understand and eventually influence NATO."

In order to explain the persistence of Soviet-like practices and the alleged Russian difficulty in establishing transgovernmental relations with NATO, many Atlantic practitioners pointed to the fact that there had been no bureaucratic "purge" in Moscow at the end of the Cold War. After the implosion of the USSR, Russia's President Yeltsin quickly embraced the former Soviet Ministry of Defense and General Staff as the institutions of the new Russia. Still inhabited by the very same people who used to run the USSR, the Russian bureaucracy preserved an organizational ethos inherited from the Cold War. For instance, procedures of decisionmaking remained profoundly opaque. As one Russian interviewee revealed:

Many of these people are anti-Western by nature, by profession and career. They made their career out of it. These old stereotypes of the Cold War are still alive. I graduated from [Moscow State Institute of International Relations] and many of my former colleagues are now diplomats around the world. [At that point, the interviewee insisted that the conversation remained between the two of us as we both lowered our voices.] When we meet in private, they say: "In our mind, we know that you're right with your stance on cooperation, because Russia has no alternative. But in our heart, our soul, we cannot accept it."

Significantly, reciprocal ingrained dispositions were also evident on NATO's side in 2006, where a sizeable number of officials had been trained in Cold War thinking for decades – hence, for instance, the widespread fear of Moscow exploiting cracks in the Alliance.

One may be tempted to think that generational change will progressively ameliorate the situation, but this may turn out to be overly optimistic. For instance, a Russian researcher who had taken part in the NATO rally conferences expressed her confusion about Russian students' aggressiveness toward the Alliance. For the younger generations in Russia, the post-Cold War period has been one of chaos and humiliation. Unlike their parents, some of whom had wanted (and acted in favor of) perestroika, younger Russians only know democratic turmoil associated with (what they perceive as) Russia's international weakness and Western arrogance. A senior German officer who had been dealing with the Russians for many years explained: "I'm not sure this [generational change] will happen. There is no big difference in attitudes, because Russians have not broken with their past. Younger people speak English, but that doesn't change their minds. They still feel we don't understand, we don't like whatever they do. They do not feel respected. They have an outright problem facing reality and a very strong feeling of humiliation." Among Russian students, the objective of returning Russia to its past greatness on the international stage seemed consensually shared, another professor stressed.

The second and related obstacle to meaningful interactions on the ground originated from a mutual perception that Russian and Atlantic bureaucracies did not do things the same way when it came to security-related matters.[21] The contrast in organizational cultures expressed in 2006 was obviously the extension of age-old differences on both sides. Interestingly, however, it is mostly Atlantic officials who raised concerns about the Russian bureaucratic habitus, which they perceived as overly "top-down" and "rigid."[22] One American diplomat who had negotiated with the Russians for decades noted that they usually strive for a top-level agreement, whereas Westerners privilege low-level interactions and trust-building. For instance, a German officer who was actively involved in the opening of the NATO Information Office in Moscow in 2001 recounted that his team was given only one single contact point and telephone number inside the entire state apparatus. As the German practitioner recalled: "We told them from the beginning that this is not the way we are working, that we'd like to talk to the different project officers. But they have a different system: they still want to control everything."[23] The same story was heard from another NATO military representative in Moscow:

---

[21] On bureaucratic culture, see Barnett and Finnemore (2004).

[22] Of course, any Western characterization of Russian practitioners reveals as much, if not more, about the NATO *lambda* habitus. It is in this spirit that I record mutual perceptions of daily interactions.

[23] See also Williams (2005, 46).

In the military, we have [here in Moscow] a mentality different from what we normally experience in Western countries. There is a tendency to control events closely, to centralize everything. They still have a different attitude toward classification of information, taking decisions at the highest possible level ... There is a strong tendency to keep everything under control. I wouldn't talk of an obsession, but it's a very strong attitude inside the Russian military to execute central control over cooperation activities.

Even a top military officer in the NATO hierarchy complained that he was able to have very little contacts with the Russian General Staff.

In this context, NATO practitioners perceived that the main driver of NATO–Russia relations was located not in Brussels but in Moscow. Instructions were sent directly from the highest echelons and implemented on the ground, often against the will of diplomats. In the words of a Canadian diplomat:

NATO officials get the impression that the Russians don't give it their best energy. They're very rigid in meetings and negotiations. We get the feeling that we're dealing with an ancient mindset. It is probably instructions directly from Moscow, where certain people want certain messages through. But it does not belong to the dialogue we've been having over the last few years. They sometimes come out of the blue with some confrontational language.

As one Russian expert summed up: "if Putin orders, they will do it!" This obviously left little room for informal compromises and exchanges at the NRC. For instance, one senior military officer complained that during NRC meetings, the Russians strictly present national positions but refuse to exchange ideas in a casual way. Informal discussions are kept to a minimum. As one British officer illustrated: "Relations are always cordial. We smile and drink vodka ... But the relationship finishes right after the meeting."

Top-down control of NATO–Russia interaction was portrayed as a serious brake on practical cooperation on the ground. Even a Russian professor admitted that "[w]e have a very Byzantine organization. Routines are not possible! All decisions are taken in the Kremlin and then sent to the administrative level. [Bureaucrats] cannot push initiatives, only follow guidelines." As a result NATO was unable to reach a large number of Russian civil servants and militaries, especially at the lower echelons. As a senior officer posted in Moscow said,

"Russia's military still considers that the ability of senior officials to understand NATO policy and tactics could be sufficient to establish interoperability between our forces. We have a different view. We think it's necessary that to develop interoperability, we require an extended understanding within the officers' corps."[24] This was especially problematic because NATO officials "expect a snowball effect ... The more people get involved, the more it will become normality." More than this, it was considered a central trait of Russian culture that personal, friendly contacts are often necessary for anything to be solved, as one NATO diplomat recalled. Another veteran American envoy noted that, contrary to institutionalized Western repertoires, many things within the Russian bureaucracy happen *na levo* – on the side, through informal relations. Only a handful of Atlantic practitioners reported such interpersonal relations.

The second difference in organizational culture deplored by Atlantic practitioners regarded the formalism and secrecy of the Russian bureaucracy. A French delegate admitted that "on tough topics Russians get rigid and closed. It's not informal. They don't discuss freely because their system is still very controlled." He believed that a key to improving the relationship would be to make it more informal by organizing luncheons without note-takers, so that ambassadors could open up and show flexibility. "This is not the case with the Russians," he lamented. A Canadian diplomat concurred that NRC meetings "are not so open and free. It's very scripted." Rigidity also created problems of attitude, according to one NATO official: "Russia is still seen as a major headache. In my view it's a country that denies rather than creates, that tries to thwart what others are doing rather than coming with new good ideas ... Russia has the power to deny, but not the imagination and the power to create." This, he insisted, is "not the way to make friends." While the NATO organizational culture rests on informal exchange, transparency and non-confrontation, opined an Alliance practitioner, "Russia hasn't really used the NRC in a way that would generate understanding. It has been more a vehicle for complaining than a vehicle for engaging."

Russian and Atlantic practitioners perceived their respective negotiating cultures as quite different. One American official who had

---

[24] This interviewee added: "We get the impression that people who have taken courses at [a] NATO school or some Western institutes have not succeeded in their military as we expected."

been dealing with the Russians for decades believed that "the only language the Russians understand is that of strength. Respect comes with strength." For a NATO official posted in Moscow, another trait of the Russian culture was especially striking: "This is a country of opposites, which never gives in suppleness ... It doesn't support the middle – it's all or nothing. This is a socio-cultural trait but it affects external policies. Russian reactions are generated through this: always very strong reactions, in favor or not." Lionel Ponsard supplies a telling example, which also touches on the importance of language in diplomatic interaction:

Nyet is a simple Russian word that is often misunderstood. *Nyet* seems to be an almost automatic response by officials when asked if something can be done; what, in the West, is usually perceived as an obvious sign of unwillingness. One should know that an initial "no" in Russia is never definite. This is rather a simple – but effective – tactic aimed at gradually coercing the interlocutor to alter his position until the latter finally meets the Russians' satisfaction. This practice is very much stamped with the Russian culture.[25]

Yet in 2006 few NATO officials had an operational knowledge of the Russian language and culture, as surprising as this may seem. One officer regretted "a marked reluctance by individual Allies to provide suitably qualified Russophone liaison officers."[26] The problem was compounded by the fact that Moscow kept posting to Brussels ambassadors that had no knowledge of either French or English. Coming from a particularly polyglot Foreign Service such as Russia's, this situation sounded like bad faith to many NATO practitioners. At the time of the interviews, any conversation with the Russian ambassador, General Konstantin Totsky, had to be mediated by an interpreter, which obviously created serious barriers to communication and the free exchange of ideas, by a German delegate's report.

Several practitioners on the Alliance side were under the impression that the main stumbling block in developing informal ties with their Russian counterparts had to do with career prospects. As one German officer put it: "There's no informality with the Russians, because

---

[25] Ponsard (2007, 155).
[26] Williams (2005, 47 fn. 18). Major General Peter Williams was the first head of the NATO Military Liaison Mission in Moscow from 2002 to 2005.

getting informal with NATO officials means you're burnt within the Russian administration. We've tracked officers with whom we've been in touch: they're burnt. The Cold War is not over." A number of NATO officials were not comfortable in addressing this sensitive topic but they could not deny that they too had had that impression. Oksana Antonenko cites the example of General Shevtsov, who led the Russian contingent in the Balkans and was widely hailed for his success in cooperating with NATO's SACEUR. Upon his return to Russia, he was met with very little cooperation at the Ministry of Defense and was ultimately moved to the Interior Ministry.[27]

Finally, Atlantic practitioners also apprehended a culture of secrecy inside the Russian bureaucratic apparatus. A particularly telling example is Operation Active Endeavour, which gave Russians "a great insight into how we do business, a great intelligence gathering. They now have NATO secret communications on their ships, they see our standard operating procedures, they see our doctrines." Yet this openness was not reciprocated, according to a senior NATO officer: "They have a big access. Now the flip side is we get access to theirs too. It hasn't been the case yet." This view was echoed by a NATO military commander, who estimated that "we don't get back from Russia the openness we give. NATO is more forward." Another example was that Russian practitioners at the Brussels headquarters had access to the entire organization's directory, whereas NATO officials in Moscow do not benefit from similar conditions. In a similar vein, a British officer from the Ministry of Defence described the Russian reaction when given a tour of the building in London: "They're amazed. This doesn't happen in Moscow."

But Russian practitioners were not outdone when it came to criticizing the other party's organizational culture. The general feeling in Moscow was that NATO bureaucratic practices betrayed an insuperable hubris – a conviction that the Alliance is right and that Russia can only nod to it (see Chapters 5 and 6). A Russian official dispatched to NATO headquarters put it bluntly: "NATO puts a lot of pressure on Russia and puts her on the defensive. The United States keeps lecturing Russia. This is not welcome. It looks like *diktats* for losing the Cold War. But Russia didn't lose the Cold War: it was an internal choice.

---

[27] Antonenko (2007, 94).

Russia has no inferiority complex: it hasn't lost anything." Another expert described the American approach in equally harsh words: "If you only dictate and criticize, you don't have friends. You're lonely." Under the current NATO approach, she argued, Russia is "rejected" and subjected to "double standards." One professor described the Russian perception of NATO's practices thus:

> The West's main fault is that, for its own good, it has imposed a choice on Russia: either the West or the East … I don't think the West is being sincere in forcing this choice … The West likes to think of itself as the keeper of values and as a ruler. It wants everybody to act like it, like a steamroller … Yeltsin thought of himself as a pupil, but the government and the citizens felt insulted to be treated as such … The West wants to be a tutor: why? … What the West mainly lacks is the willingness to understand. It knows how to impose its own values but it doesn't want to understand that they are different in Western and Eastern Europe.

For the Russians, Atlantic diplomats were either unable or unwilling to take the legitimate interests of their interlocutors into account.

Exaggerated or not, these complaints about respective bureaucratic practices indicated not only differences in bureaucratic cultures, but also a kind of mutual resistance to adapt to (or recognize as legitimate) the other's organizational ways. As will become clear below, many of the diplomatic difficulties in Russian–Atlantic dealings find their roots in the intense and persistent symbolic power struggles between Moscow and Brussels. Take, for instance, this description by a French delegate of a typical negotiation at the NRC:

> On many issues it works the same. They begin by saying they want to do this and that with us. We respond that such programs already exist in the larger framework of the Euro-Atlantic partnership. They answer that they don't want to do it with the Georgians and everyone. They want an exclusive relationship with us, so we need to come up with a new document. We tell them we already have established this document and we offer it to Russia so that they can apply it. They reply that they're not NATO applicants and that they want a joint program of equals. They come from the Warsaw Pact where they were the kings. They don't want to work with NATO concepts, they want to add something Russian. But we say no. They are progressively getting to it and mindsets are evolving. They need time: one does not catch flies with vinegar.

This quotation reveals that, well founded or not, Atlantic and Russian complaints about one another's ways of "doing stuff" are not absolute but relational: they emerge from a deeper struggle over who gets to define the rules of the game at the NRC.

Conclusion: two masters in search of an apprentice

Alexandra Gheciu explains the success of NATO's socialization strategies toward Eastern European countries in part by the parties' mutual recognition of their respective roles as "teachers" and "students." Based on extensive fieldwork, Gheciu has discovered that "many pro-liberal elites in the former Communist bloc recognized NATO as a key institution of the Western community with which they identified, and, as such, as an authoritative, trustworthy source of expertise in the area of security."[28] As a result, the Alliance was successful in imposing its practices on the Czech Republic and Romania. In Gheciu's Bourdieusian "competence model of power," which is close to the one I outlined in Chapter 2, "the ability to exercise social influence is not inherently attributed to the resources possessed by a given entity. Rather, the power of actors depends on the recognition of their role of influence by other participants in social interactions."[29] Power is more than the possession of resources; it requires some sort of recognition by the dominated. For example, the power relation linking a master to his apprentice entails that the latter reproduces the former's practices because "this is the way the world goes round." The master's competence is felt by the apprentice, in and through practice, as a relation of immediate adherence to the nature of things.

Such was definitely *not* the case at the NRC in 2006: neither NATO nor Russia regarded the other as a master or a model to emulate. The next two chapters will explain the origins of these complex power politics by analyzing Russian–Atlantic relations over the post-Cold War era. In keeping with the logic of practicality, in this conclusion I want to document, with interview data, the awkward situation in which Russian and NATO practitioners found themselves in 2006: there were two masters but no apprentices around the NRC table. Across interviews, the notion of Russia as a Great Power had the most purchase in Moscow. Among NATO officials, there was an

---

[28] Gheciu (2005, 13).   [29] Gheciu (2005, 16).

equal tendency to associate the perspective of the Alliance with the "international community" and to naturalize Western values and policies as universally legitimate. As a result, both Moscow and Brussels took their teaching (and non-teachable) role for granted. Throughout my interviews, NATO practitioners were seen to be tired of Russia's insistence on Great Power status, while Russian officials took offense at the Alliance's condescending approach. The result was unremitting symbolic struggles over the very terms of the relationship, as well as an ineffectual power relation precluding the full embodiment of diplomacy as the self-evident way to go at the NRC.

According to Neumann, "[s]ince the early 1990s, Russia has struggled to find its role in the novel realities of international relations. In the various dimensions of Russian security policy, the concept of a Great Power stands out as a unifying formula for the conduct of affairs."[30] In effect, the narrative of Great Power has become the knowledge base from which security elites think in Moscow: for instance, one Russian expert argued that Russia "used to be a crucial player in international relations and so long as it exists, it will continue a grand strategy, not like small countries. It's traditional because Russia is unique. It's genetic in Russia. Most students – ninety percent, even more – are supportive of big politics and active involvement of Russia in world politics." In 2006, Yevgeny Primakov, who was instrumental during the 1990s in giving substance to the Russian Great Power disposition, expressed the notion clearly:

Considering Russia's history, intellectual resources, size, huge natural resources and, finally, the level of development of its Armed Forces, this country will not agree to the status of a state that is "led"; it will seek to establish itself as an independent center of a multipolar world ... Washington, relying on its present superiority, proceeds from the assumption that the United States will hold the central position in a future world system, while the rest of the world will have to follow the "rules of behavior" dictated by the Americans.[31]

Across my interviews with Russian practitioners and experts, it was a generally taken-for-granted "fact of life" that Russia belongs to this small club of nations that are bound to lead in international relations; such is the destiny of a Great Power.

[30] Neumann (2005b, 13).   [31] Primakov (2006, 2).

On the Atlantic side, the end of the Cold War sparked a widespread belief that the time had come for the West and its institutions to export their values to the rest of the world. NATO's success in socializing Eastern Europe bolstered this self-understanding as the role model of democracy, freedom and civilization. This evolution fostered a preexisting Western disposition towards universalism and bolstered organizations such as NATO in their role of teacher. In my interviews, I was struck by the extent to which many Atlantic practitioners would equate (unconsciously, for the most part) the peculiar policies advocated by NATO with the consensus forged in the "international community." As the embodiment of the international community, the Alliance should mold Russia to become a part of it, believed one senior official from State Department: "The long-term objective has to be Russia's integration into the Euro-Atlantic community, the international community, on all levels, based on shared values; joining the international club of democratic, market-oriented countries. There is no competing model for organizing political and economic life in the international community aside from liberal democracy, rule of law and market economics." The background assumption in these statements, which has consistently informed the Alliance's political discourse since the end of the Cold War, holds that NATO is bound to be the teacher. It is not Brussels that has to make compromises, but Moscow.

With Russia qua Great Power and NATO qua international community, there are two masters but no apprentices at the NRC. The Atlantic superiority complex is variously demonstrated in practitioners' understanding of Russian–Atlantic relations. For instance, one NATO official told me that "Russia still hasn't fully grasped the situation the world and Russia are in." Another policymaker in Washington regretted that "Russia has gone pre-Cold War in its mindset, in a kind of survival of the fittest." He continued with a particularly telling analogy picturing Russia as

this huge, seventeen year old male football player. He's big and strong and no adult would presume to force him to do anything ... The problem for everyone around him is that you want him to be a good neighbor and a productive member of society. You wanna talk him through all this anger and aggression and resentment. But everything you do and say, he just turns against you ... You have to wait for him to grow.

On many occasions during my interviews, Atlantic practitioners would depict Russian attitudes as "archaic" or "outdated," implying that Western thinking had "moved beyond" that. Some officials affirmed that Russians' "expectations are not in tune with facts and reality"; others claimed that political elites in Russia and Europe "live in different time zones," with Moscow striving "to join the Old World of fifty or a hundred years ago."

In 2006, NATO officials were having quite a hard time coming to grips with Russia's unrelenting quest for specificity in its dealings with Brussels. The equality status, for instance, was construed as "illogical" and "unmerited." Russia's self-understanding as a Great Power was deemed "irrational and emotional." Another officer in Berlin expressed puzzlement that at the NRC "the Russians took a lot of time to understand they had a voice, not a vote. Their feeling was that the NAC decided everything without them." Across my interviews in Brussels and other Western capitals, there seemed to be a widespread fear that granting Moscow a special status would only reinforce its quest for Great Power status. One NATO speechwriter insisted that Russia should "be treated in a *slightly* different manner from the way we treat Albania, Azerbaijan." This is unlikely to satisfy Russia's Great Power dispositions, but it looks as though it is the furthest NATO practitioners think they should go toward recognition. As one German official put it, NATO is "not willing to really change but to pay respect."[32] From the Atlantic practitioners' point of view, Moscow is not worthy of equal consideration: "What the Russians are doing is creating the image of trying to play in a game where they're not players anymore," concluded a Canadian diplomat.

Dozens of interviews with Atlantic practitioners left no doubt that in 2006 NATO member states did not consider Russia to be an equal, but were instead consistently trying, with limited success, to steer Russia's behavior in NATO's preferred direction. No

---

[32] At some point during the interview, this representative grabbed my recorder, shut it down, and lamented grudgingly: "Some say here at NATO that Germany is Russia's 'little friend': this simply isn't true." This preoccupation with not appearing too pliant with the Russians in front of NATO allies was shared by all the German officials and officers I met.

one expressed it better than a senior member of the Secretary-General's office:

We want a Russia bound to the international system, that plays by the rules, that has an interest in upholding the system, not calling it into question. We want it to be a conservative power in the best sense, that wants to conserve the order, rather than a power that feels in jeopardy as it felt before the First World War. It's not in our interest: we want to uproot this and have Russia bounded to a network and allow it to express its Great Power status instead of trying to subvert the Western – [here the interviewee catches the slip of the tongue] – not Western anymore – the international democratic order.

From this perspective, he added, the NRC "puts limits on how independent its actions can be because it has to go through these multilateral frameworks. We want to make those stronger to get Russia totally embedded." One Alliance official posted in Moscow was just as blunt: "It may be true we impose some stuff, but we do it with their consent. Otherwise, nothing gets done." As one German official who negotiated with the Russians on behalf of NATO throughout the 1990s recognized, "from their point of view, they have lots of reasons to complain and to say: 'Well, you do listen to us, but you don't take into account our argument.' That's what you continuously hear from them.'" Commenting on Russia's influence over NATO, he admitted that it has "[v]ery little, so objectively they have a point. There is very little that we've done in the past to accommodate Russian concerns."

In their relationship with NATO counterparts, however, the Russians did not suffer from any kind of reciprocal inferiority complex. In 2006, the dominant narrative of Great Power in Moscow meant that the partnership should be among "equals." As a result, NATO's self-attributed role as a teacher was not recognized by the Russians – in fact, it was rather despised. Since the end of the Cold War, NATO has tried hard to impose its views and steer Russia's course, with some success during the 1990s. But these attempts also fed a backlash, as resentment steadily built up in Moscow. As one expert observed: "The strong attitude in Moscow is that Russia was humiliated in the 1990s many times." For a Russian diplomat in Brussels, the main policy that the Alliance imposed despite Russia's opposition was NATO enlargement (see Chapters 5 and 6): "Russia's opinions were not taken into account. Here, actions mean more than

words: NATO puts forward a number of arguments but acts otherwise. This is not a question of putting soft words in people's ears. The
question is: why is NATO pushing?" In the words of one of the most
pro-Western experts I met in Moscow, "the West tried to press Russia,
to show that 'your game is over.'" The result was that ideological confrontation gave way to a new kind of competition, full of mistrust and
suspicion, based on a feeling that "Russia is considered as an element
of the international community which should be downplayed and
pushed, not allowed to become a strong international actor."

In 2006, Russia's reluctance to recognize NATO's authority produced
a very limited power relation in and through practice. So much so, in
fact, that in my interviews several Russian elites insisted on the need to
stay clear of a number of Alliance practices. The emphasis was rather
put on sovereignty and strategic independence. As Foreign Minister
Sergey Lavrov put it: "The foreign policy sovereignty of Russia is an
absolute imperative … Our country is not one [whose] foreign policy
could be directed from the outside. We are not out to be likable to everyone – we simply proceed from our own, understandable pragmatic
interest. Let us recall that our country particularly strove to be 'likable'
in the era of Nicholas I and in the last Soviet years: we know where that
led us."[33] Under such circumstances, most Russian experts advocated
a policy of Great Power independence, whether NATO liked it or not.
The post-Cold War terms of partnership, by which Moscow was sub-
servient to Brussels, had to be revised. The need for Western recognition had almost evaporated by 2006. As one expert put it, "now that
we are strong, the West has to accommodate us. Now we are ready to
compete with the Western states; we will not concede anymore."

In 2006, several Atlantic practitioners were taking note of their
increasing incapacity to exert authority over Russia's foreign policy.
One Alliance official expressed his feeling of impotence openly:

[Compared to other partners, Russia] is a tough case because, for instance,
in terms of defense reform, the Russians stated that "of course Russia is a
great country so we are doing our own defense reform. We will not simply copy what you're doing because of course we have our own ideas. Of
course we will learn what we want to learn from you but not everything."
In the case of for instance Ukraine and Georgia or those countries who

---

[33] Quoted in Ministry of Foreign Affairs of the Russian Federation (2007a).

become members it's much easier because we have our standards and we say, "if you want to become members of NATO you have to do this, this, and this" and they don't have a choice. They have a choice but the other choice is not really an option for them. But there is no leverage basically on Russia. [All that NATO can use is] well, logic, pure logic. We try to convince them that the way we are doing it is much more effective, much more efficient, actually affordable, etc. It's pure logic I think.

He continued: "When Russia was weak they were much more friendly, frankly, and it was much easier to deal with them. [During the Kosovo crisis] I don't think it was very difficult to deal with them anyway. We simply ignored their views. That wasn't really very difficult." Confronted with interminable arguments and symbolic struggles, however, in 2006 NATO practitioners expressed increasing disappointment and resignation. In the words of an American policymaker: "There is a certain feeling of impotence among allies when it comes to influencing Russian policy." One Canadian diplomat even compared Russia to "those big dump trucks [with] a sign at the back [that reads:] 'Do Not Push.'" In 2006, it looked as though Russia and NATO did not inhabit the same world: "Our objective is for Russia to be a normal country, like any other countries ... It's always frustrating that we're not mentally in the same place. Because the rest of the world is: China is in many ways more ready to act like that than Russia."

The fierce symbolic struggle between NATO and Russia over their respective status has had negative consequences in terms of the embodiment of diplomacy. The fact that there were two masters in search of an apprentice at the NRC rendered any power relation ineffectual. As far as the normalization of disputes is concerned, the rise of Russia's Great Power dispositions sparks perceptions of assertiveness, if not aggressiveness, among NATO's officials. Furthermore, the ever fastidious NATO–Russia negotiations over things as simple and banal as technical rules of military cooperation thwarted plans for joint exercises or missions between Moscow and Brussels. In the words of a French diplomat:

The Russians said they wanted to develop new joint procedures for peace-keeping. The United States and other allies said: "Enough! We draw different lessons and we can do this without these new procedures but by associating with you when there is a need." There was reluctance so the debate stopped. We don't talk about this anymore. The issue is not dead but it's on ice. That's the problem with Russia: everything that was easy to do, we've done. We've eaten all the meat on the bone, and now that we're at the bone we feel we've eaten enough.

In sum, in 2006 the Russian–Atlantic relationship was best captured, from the practitioners' point of view, by its very intense symbolic power politics. The key question then becomes: what are the historical origins of the 2006 symbolic struggles between Russia and NATO over the terms of the relationship? The next two chapters supply an answer by looking back at the evolution of this complex relationship over the post-Cold War era.

5 | The early steps: NATO, Russia and the double enlargement, 1992–1997

This chapter and Chapter 6 look back into history and seek to explain the main finding of Chapter 4 – that in 2006, NRC practitioners embodied diplomacy as a normal though not a self-evident practice in solving Russian–Atlantic disputes. Recovering the practical logics of NRC diplomacy raises the question: what made this practical sense possible in the first place? Since all socially constructed meanings emerge from past social struggles, one must add a diachronic dimension to the analysis and set meanings in motion (see Chapter 3). To do so, I analyze the historical evolution of NATO–Russia interactions with regards to the double enlargement – a vexing and persistent bone of contention in the post-Cold War era.

In order to shed light on practices, I combine field analysis with the interpretive study of habitus. In terms of the former, I locate Russia and NATO inside the field of international security and describe the evolving rules of the game in the post-Cold War era, in particular the changes in the conversion rates between forms of capital. For the sake of clarity, and in accordance with the recent evolution of the field's doxa, I reduce the range of capital in this field to only two types of resources. First, *material-institutional capital* refers to military forces, money and material riches (industrial capacity, demographics, etc.), as well as networks of allies, friends and other institutional ties. This form of capital was the main currency of Cold War realpolitik and balancing. Second, *cultural-symbolic capital* designates artifacts, narratives and symbols that define the meaning of the world (what is real, true, etc.) and legitimize it (what is right, good, etc.). These resources are the staple of the post-Cold War, democratic peace era. Below I explain this doxic shift in more detail; the important point, at this stage, is that mapping the distribution of material-institutional and cultural-symbolic forms of capital paves the way to positional field analysis. In a historical perspective, I analyze the relative positions of Russia and NATO and combine this objectified view with a reconstruction of dispositions over time.

My historical narrative hinges on the evolving alignment and misalignment of positions and dispositions (see Chapter 2) experienced by NATO and Russia in the post-Cold War international security field. In the first section, I explain what the new NATO-imposed rules of the post-Cold War international security game consist of and how the Russians zealously implemented them until late 1994. The early post-Cold War years were characterized by an exceptionally strong homology between the field's structure and the players' habitus, thanks to which Russia accepted its weak position while NATO was disposed toward assuming the leadership. The second section then shows how the Alliance's decision to enlarge functionally and geographically put an end to this pattern of domination: in Russian eyes, these practices contravened the new rules of the international security game. As a result, although mutual disputes continued to be solved non-violently, Moscow became decreasingly disposed to accept NATO's domination in the field of international security. Russian dispositions were progressively misaligned with Moscow's position in the Alliance-dominated field. In the third section, I explain how the resurgence of the Great Power habitus in Moscow sparked intense hysteresis effects, which severely strained negotiations over the 1997 Founding Act between NATO and Russia.

Overall, while Williams and Neumann are right that, for a time, NATO was "able drastically to narrow the field of politically viable options available to Russian policy-makers,"[1] by the mid-1990s the diplomatic order of things was already starting to weaken. Despite the prevalence of the non-violent settlement of disputes in the post-Cold War era, security community development stalled early on due to the increasing mismatch between the positions occupied in the field by NATO and Russia and their respective dispositions in playing the international security game.

[1] Williams and Neumann (2000, 372).

The new rules of the international security game

In this first section I make two related arguments. First, I characterize the new rules of the international security game, in the aftermath
of the Cold War, as a shift from the external to the internal mode
of pursuing security. NATO and its member states were the main
proponents *and* beneficiaries of this evolution in that it consolidated
their already dominant position in the field. Second, I demonstrate
that from 1992 until mid-1994 Russia very zealously adhered to the
new rules of the game, in its foreign policy discourse as well as in its
actions. During that short-lived period, the strong homology between
positions in the field and dispositions in habitus created fertile conditions for doxa and the self-evident practice of diplomacy in NATO–
Russia dealings.

NATO order: security from the inside out

The end of the Cold War was a watershed in the history of international
security. After decades of bipolar confrontation, the whole structure
of political interaction underwent radical changes prompted in large
part by the demise of the USSR. At the intersubjective level, the rules
of the game of international security were considerably redrawn. As
Gheciu insightfully argues, the principle of sovereignty, which forms
the normative basis of contemporary international society, enables
two distinct modes of pursuing security.[2] The *outside* mode, which
was prevalent during the Cold War and constitutes the traditional
focus in security studies, is based on geostrategic arrangements such
as alliance-making and power-balancing. In this scheme, the military instrument is the main tool to enhance security. Throughout the
Cold War, NATO's doctrine relied heavily on this approach, emphasizing conventional and nuclear deterrence of the Soviet threat. By
contrast, the *inside* mode of pursuing security proposes that stability
in world politics relies on states' domestic institutions and order. In
the Kantian tradition, for instance, democratic regimes are valued as
efficient means to achieve international security. To be sure, given its
liberal origins NATO has always espoused this view in its discourse.
However, in the post-Cold War world, security-from-the-inside-out

---

[2] Gheciu (2005, 4–9).

gained an "unprecedented importance" in the field of international security.[3] Traditional realpolitik became secondary to democratic peace as a means to achieve security. As a result, the capital conversion rate was basically reversed: in the new rules of the game, cultural-symbolic not material-institutional resources formed the sinews of power.[4]

This intersubjective change became evident in the early 1990s when the principles that had given birth to the CSCE in the mid-1970s were consolidated and extended. Mostly under the initiative of Western countries, the CSCE had been an early proponent of the inside mode of pursuing security. Its agreed political principles enshrined several of the basic ideas that still underpin the security-from-the-inside-out paradigm. Most importantly, the CSCE process is based on a comprehensive approach to security in which politico-military issues are only one dimension along with human rights and freedoms and economic and environmental well-being. These various dimensions of security are construed as interconnected and interdependent. Furthermore, in the CSCE spirit, security is indivisible, mutual and must be pursued by cooperative means. The tools of cooperative security, including mutual transparency, accountability and confidence-building, have to do not only with foreign policy but also, and in fact primarily, with domestic politics. For instance, traditionally domestic concerns such as human rights and freedoms have now become part of the international security game. In this sense, the CSCE approach constitutes the opposite of deterrence and balancing – that is, the external mode of pursuing security.

With the end of the Cold War, the inside mode of pursuing security gained even more political prominence within the CSCE process. The Paris Charter, signed in 1990, proclaimed democracy to be the only legitimate form of government in Europe, and promulgated the protection of human rights as the only way to organize the relationship between member states and their citizens. In turning domestic politics into a central concern for international security, the Charter was a turning point in the history of international security.[5] As part of the newly constituted OSCE, an Office for Democratic Institutions and Human Rights was set up and a High Commissioner for National

---

[3] Gheciu (2005, 9).   [4] Williams (2007).
[5] Adler (1998); Flynn and Farrell (1999); Ghebali (1996).

Minorities was nominated with mandates to monitor the internal political situation of member states. Other similar initiatives were taken in the following years, including the establishment of a Code of Conduct on the Role of the Armed Forces in Democratic Societies or the designation of a Representative on Freedom of the Media. Adopted in 1999, the Istanbul Charter for European Security went as far as to recognize human rights not as an end in itself, but as a means to strengthen member states' territorial integrity and sovereignty. The OSCE's *droit de regard* in domestic affairs, accompanied with proper follow-up means, attests to the rise of the inside mode of pursuing security in post-Cold War international politics.

The OSCE's practices and its approach to security from the inside out quickly diffused to other international institutions in the post-Cold War era.[6] They inform, for instance, the agenda of "human security" promoted by a number of countries as well as by some UN agencies. The internal mode of pursuing security is also a central component of the EU's Neighbourhood Policy, which puts democracy and human rights at the forefront of its external relations. As the 2003 European Security Strategy states: "The quality of international society depends on the quality of the governments that are its foundation. The best protection for our security is a world of well-governed democratic states."[7] Finally, and perhaps most importantly, the internal mode of pursuing security came to constitute the basic rationale for the political processes that are the focus of this chapter – NATO's functional and geographical enlargements. As Gheciu notes, "at the end of the Cold War, the international promotion of Western-based liberal democratic norms in Central/Eastern Europe was regarded within NATO as both an important recipe for enhancing Euro-Atlantic security and as a viable project."[8] NATO's double enlargement was – and still is – designed to be part and parcel of the new rules of the game in the post-Cold War international security field.

From the outset, NATO positioned itself at the forefront of the "doxic battle" that led to the intersubjective transformation into security-from-the-inside-out.[9] In fact, the Alliance promoted the shift,

---

[6] Adler (2008).   [7] Council of the EU (2003, 10).   [8] Gheciu (2005, 5).
[9] Villumsen defines doxic battles as "basic struggles determining what is valued in the field and what is considered worthless" and based on the mobilization of capital (Villumsen 2008, 81).

which significantly contributed to consolidating its dominant position in the field. For one thing, the demise of communism (both in the USSR and elsewhere in the world) directly benefited NATO by creating an opportunity to change the rules of the game toward the internal mode of pursuing security. In contrast to free-falling post-Soviet countries, the Alliance stood as an island of stability amidst the structural shifts of the end of the Cold War. Given its successful history, NATO imposed itself as a "locus of accumulated [capital]": "The alliance provided a uniquely powerful venue in which the new situation could be defined, policies pronounced, forces mobilized."[10] First, despite important military cuts at the end of the Cold War, NATO benefited from a growing military superiority, in relative terms, while retaining a unique institutional strength as a tightly knit alliance that had triumphed, in many Western eyes, over a decades-long rivalry. Second, the Alliance boasted a new civilizational identity as the spearhead of democracy and human rights on the international stage. As Williams explains, "the West appropriated the claim to represent democratic values, and asserted its own inherent peacefulness. In short, the idea of the democratic peace allowed the military conflict of the Cold War to be transformed into a cultural struggle, thus contributing to the exercise of specific strategies and forms of cultural power."[11] Third, and relatedly, in reifying democracy and human rights as natural and universal, the Alliance concealed its domination under the guise of a disinterested advocate of universal values. As a result, with unparalleled stocks of both material-institutional and cultural-symbolic capital, NATO enjoyed a strong position of preeminence in the internal mode of pursuing security.

Positional agency (see Chapter 2) helps us understand why NATO was bound, in a sense, to push in the direction of the internal mode of pursuing security. In the aftermath of the Cold War, the organization boasted a huge superiority over the rest of the world in terms of cultural-symbolic capital, representing itself as the standard-bearer of democracy and human rights. Its relative advantage, in fact, was probably greater in these resources than it was even in terms of material-institutional capital. Given its superior position in a field of international security defined in cultural terms, it was only "natural," in terms of practical sense, for the Alliance to use its cultural-symbolic

---

[10] Williams (2007, 41).   [11] Williams (2007, 40–1).

resources to foster its domination. Field analysis helps understand why, and how, NATO was able to wield so much symbolic power as to redefine the doxic rules of the game toward the internal mode of pursuing security. It also sheds light on the practice of enlargement per se, which allowed the organization to become a sort of club of democracies, thus wielding even more power over its neighbors and, in general, the many players in the field whose dispositions were in tune with the security-from-the-inside-out paradigm. The double enlargement ultimately derives from the liberal habitus embodied by NATO member states as well as from the Alliance's cultural-symbolic domination of the post-Cold War field – a combination that provided a rare opportunity to exert power and magnetic attraction over other players by defining the very conditions of admission into the "club."[12]

Under the new rules of the international security game, promoted in large part by NATO itself, talk about power-balancing became *passé* and illegitimate. It was replaced by the promotion of democracy and human rights as the best means of ensuring security. As Williams continues: "Through an appeal to the centrality of culture in the new security context – by invoking the triumph of Western culture, the universality of liberal ideals, values and institutions, and even the end of history – a new set of power relations became dominant."[13] In this context, the Alliance legitimated its transformation with the principles of cooperative security and human rights embodied by the CSCE process. With the USSR still alive, NATO's Secretary-General Manfred Wörner promoted "a more diffuse concept of security in which economic integration and assistance and the internal democratization of states become as important as traditional military defense in maintaining security."[14] The first push toward transforming NATO came at the 1990 London summit where Allies explicitly embraced the idea of indivisible security. The Alliance also enunciated for the first time what would become one of its fundamental tasks in the post-Cold War era – partnership: "The Atlantic Community must reach out to the countries of the East which were our adversaries in the Cold War, and extend to them the hand of friendship."[15] At the Rome summit, one year later, NATO established the North Atlantic Cooperation Council

---

[12] I am indebted to Michael Williams for helping me formulate this argument.
[13] Williams (2007, 40).   [14] Wörner (1991, 8).   [15] NATO (1990).

(NACC), a forum designed to make partners of former enemies and foster transparency, confidence and inclusiveness.

After the demise of the USSR, several American pundits and politicians began to chant a new slogan: "NATO must go out of area or it will go out of business."[16] In 1993, the geographical dimension of enlargement was only just beginning to receive public scrutiny. The attention was focused on the Alliance's mandate, which some proposed should expand in two main directions: partnership and peacekeeping. With regard to partnerships, noticeable initiatives include the NACC, the Partnership for Peace (PfP, launched in 1994), and the Euro-Atlantic Partnership Council (EAPC, founded in 1997 to replace the NACC). Several of the PfP's objectives are directly in line with the internal mode of pursuing security (e.g. increasing transparency in defense planning and budgeting or fostering democratic control of the military). As for peacekeeping, at the 1991 Rome summit, Allied member states mentioned for the first time the possibility of deploying forces for "crisis management" in addition to collective defense missions. Six months later, in Oslo, the NAC formalized this functional turn by stating its readiness to support peacekeeping activities under the responsibility of the CSCE. Within a year of the demise of the Soviet threat, NATO had already taken on a new lease on life while progressively imposing itself as the dominant organization in the field of international security.

The junior partner: Russia's early embrace of the new rules of the game

In its first few years as an independent country, Russia enthusiastically embraced the internal mode of pursuing security, even to the point of supporting NATO's transformation in that direction. When in 1992 the Alliance proposed establishing military contacts with former Warsaw Pact countries, reactions in Moscow were initially positive. In a similar way, at first the Russians were quite supportive of NATO's functional transformation toward peacekeeping. The Charter of Russian–American Partnership and Friendship, signed in October 1992, called for the creation of a Euro-Atlantic peacekeeping force under the political authority of the CSCE and the NACC.

---

[16] Asmus, Kugler and Larrabee (1993, 31).

While some Russian officials expressed concern that the Oslo summit could reinforce NATO's position of strength in European security, these fears concerned the Alliance per se, not the internal mode of pursuing security that the organization had come to profess. Clearly, the new Russian elites who came to power in 1992 arrived at the Kremlin strongly disposed to support the new rules of the international security game.

These proto-liberal dispositions were largely inherited from Gorbachev's "New Thinking." Heavily inspired by the CSCE process, the New Thinking was premised on the notion that security ought to be mutual or common.[17] According to the doctrine of cooperative security, the existence of the security dilemma means that security cannot be pursued unilaterally. In addition, resorting to force was deemed neither legitimate nor effective as a means of solving international disputes. These principles were in line with the internal mode of pursuing security by repudiating force and encouraging domestic reforms. Several actions taken by Moscow in the late 1980s, including asymmetric and unilateral reductions in nuclear and conventional forces, as well as the surrender of the Soviet glacis in Eastern Europe, were obvious manifestations of these ideas. This is not to say that Gorbachev was an idealist politician who weakly surrendered to the West: there is no doubt that the New Thinking was an attempt to renew communism at a time of severe domestic and international crisis and give Moscow a higher moral ground vis-à-vis the West.[18] Breaking with the Cold War logic, Gorbachev and his team began pursuing security by other means – eventually losing control over the new dynamic they had unleashed.

After the implosion of the USSR in December 1991, the new ruling elites in Moscow essentially followed the precepts of New Thinking and the internal mode of pursuing security. In an article published during the summer of 1992, Foreign Minister Andrei Kozyrev explained how the notion of human rights had become the backbone of Russia's foreign policy:

The realization of human rights in our country is inseparable from our policy to integrate Russia into the global family of democratic states. We

---

[17] Checkel (1997); Evangelista (2002); Lévesque (1995); Thomas (2001).
[18] Welch Larson and Shevchenko (2003).

will combine our efforts with those taken by all states which recognize that respect for human rights and fundamental freedoms is an essential component of peace, justice and well being. This principle has become one of the mainstays of the foreign policy of the Russian Federation ... The supremacy of human rights is indeed the basis on which states should seek to discover a common language, a sort of "humanitarian Esperanto."[19]

Kozyrev took special pride in the fact that at a recent meeting in Moscow, the CSCE's Commission on the Human Dimension had approved a provision to the effect that concern for human rights did not amount to interference in the internal affairs of states. He also recalled that in January 1992 the CSCE had taken as its main objectives the protection of human rights and democracy and the promulgation of the rule of law. In order to show that this policy was being implemented, the Russian Foreign Minister explained how the Russian delegation advocated more effective mechanisms for introducing standards of democratic human rights into the internal political life of individual states during the forty-eighth session of the UN Commission on Human Rights. "Progress in human rights is a precondition for creating an atmosphere of stability, justice, security, cooperation and lasting peace," Kozyrev concluded passionately.[20]

In the immediate aftermath of the Cold War, Russian statespeople spoke and behaved like very strong advocates of the internal mode of pursuing security. The team in power at the Kremlin, personified by Yeltsin and Kozyrev, was disposed to recognize the new order of things imposed by NATO. In the post-Cold War era, democratization was to replace power-balancing as the primary means of achieving security. According to Robert English's in-depth study of the origins of the end of the Cold War, these dispositions had historically formed in Russia during the Nikita Khrushchev "thaw" in the 1960s, when a group of young apparatchiks were socialized into a different way of looking at the world.[21] Clearly, these democratic inclinations remained the preserve of a small elite in Moscow under Gorbachev and later Yeltsin,

---

[19] Kozyrev (1992, 289). Note that my discourse analysis does not presume that speakers necessarily believe what they say; there is no way to probe what is between people's ears. However, the very performance of this discourse in public speaks volumes about the Russian elites' "sense of their place" in the early 1990s.

[20] Kozyrev (1992, 290).   [21] English (2000).

although an increasing proportion of the Russian population seemed
disposed toward them in the early 1990s. Institutionally empowered
in the new Russia, it is this liberal habitus that led to a striking homology between Russian dispositions and the country's weakened position in the new field of international security.

In the absence of hysteresis effects, NATO's domination over
Moscow went unchecked. Because of the homology between their
habitus and the field's new doxa, the Russian elites were disposed to
play the Alliance's game of security-from-the-inside-out. For almost
two years, from 1992 to mid-1994, NATO was able to steer Russian
foreign policy in a way reminiscent of the archetypical master–
apprentice relationship. Two sets of issues show especially clearly how
much the Russians emulated NATO practices in a consistent way.
The first is the Alliance's functional transformation from collective
defense *stricto sensu* to collective security, of which the Russians were
so supportive that at first they even showed interest in joining the
organization. At the very first meeting of the NACC, in late December
1991, Yeltsin wrote a letter declaring his country's readiness to examine the issue of Russia's membership of NATO in the long term.
Because NATO officials never responded to this gesture, Moscow
had to retract and claim that Yeltsin's letter had been mistranslated.
But throughout 1992 and into the first half of 1993, several Russian
officials informally tested the grounds for membership. The NATO
answer, however, was negative, reportedly because of American reservations. That did not prevent several pundits from arguing that in
the post-Cold War era, Russia firmly belonged to NATO, its "natural
ally."[22] Writing in the *NATO Review* in early 1993, Kozyrev argued
that his main foreign policy guideline was to "join the club of recognized democratic states."[23]

Equally striking is the fact that Russia's sanguine attitude toward
NATO's functional transformation did not harden when it became
obvious that, by taking up new functions of partnership and peacekeeping, the Alliance was giving itself a new lease of life. Of course,
most Russian specialists and politicians had first expected NATO to
disband just as the Warsaw Pact had done, and be replaced with the
OSCE as a pan-European security institution. The Alliance dissipated
all doubts, however, when in 1991 it stated its objective of remaining

---

[22] Sergei Blagovolin quoted in Guk (1992).   [23] Kozyrev (1993, 3).

the essential forum for consultation among the Allies. While this should have logically tempered Moscow's enthusiasm, for a time the enlargement of NATO's functions to peacekeeping and partnership was still considered by the new Russian elite as fitting the security-from-the-inside-out approach. For instance, the inclusive and cooperative spirit of the NACC was in line with the CSCE's cooperative security approach and seemed to suit Russian interests quite well. In October 1993, when the Americans first floated the idea of the PfP with the Russians, the initial reaction was still quite favorable. Yeltsin was reported to approve the outreach initiative toward the post-communist world insofar as it included Russia. Everything took place as though the Russian apprentice would nod in response to whatever the Atlantic master said or did.

NATO's domination over Russia was also obvious in Moscow's early actions with respect to the civil war in Yugoslavia, as the Alliance did not lose much time in putting its new peacekeeping function into practice. The Bosnian civil war provided Brussels with its first test case of the collective security doctrine. NATO became involved in the conflict very gradually. During the summer of 1992, presidential candidate Bill Clinton was the first to mention the possibility of Allied air strikes against Bosnian Serbs in combination with the lifting of UN sanctions against the Bosnian government (the "lift and strike" strategy). European allies, however, were not convinced and favored the UN-sponsored Vance–Owen plan, which finally faltered in mid-1993. NATO then undertook two operations intended to support UN Security Council resolutions on the deployment of the UN Protection Force (UNPROFOR) in Bosnia. After the bombing of Sarajevo's market in February 1994, the UN Secretary-General asked the Security Council to mandate NATO air strikes on Bosnian Serb positions. Starting in April, Alliance forces led by the Americans intensified their bombing of Bosnian Serb forces until the Srebrenica massacre, during the summer of 1995, which led to Operation Deliberate Force and a total of about 3,500 sorties. The Dayton Accord was finally concluded later that fall under strong American leadership.

The most striking aspect in NATO–Russia dealings over the Alliance's involvement in the Bosnian civil war is the explicit support that the Russian government offered in the beginning. Until February 1994, Russia shared "the predominant Western interpretation of events in Bosnia: that Serb expansionism and aggressive

ethnic nationalism was directed against the legitimate government
of a sovereign and independent state."[24] Significantly, this supportive approach was translated into deeds, as demonstrated by Russia's
alignment with the Western members of the UN Security Council.
Recall that in September 1991 Gorbachev's Soviet Union had voted
in favor of Resolution 713 imposing an arms embargo on all warring parties. That was already a tangible demonstration of the new
strength of cooperative security. In the first months of 1992 the new
Russian government pursued this alignment by voting in favor of
Resolutions 727, 740 and 743, among others. The Russians also supported the Vance–Owen plan, whose key effect would have been the
partition of Yugoslavia against the will of the Serbs. In May 1992,
Moscow went further in agreeing to Resolution 757, which imposed
sanctions on Belgrade. But the most significant gesture demonstrating
Moscow's support for the Atlantic approach came in early June, when
Russia agreed to UN Security Council Resolution 836 authorizing the
deployment of peacekeepers to protect Bosnian safe areas and threatening Serbia with "tougher measures, none of which is prejudged or
excluded from consideration."[25] This crucial vote indirectly backed
NATO's repeated threats to strike if violations continued. In total,
throughout 1992 and 1993, Russia and the NATO countries at the
UN Security Council jointly adopted more than fifty resolutions on
Yugoslavia. That said, Russia's support was not unequivocal and some
differences remained: for instance, Moscow systematically opposed
the use of force and was critical, at times, of what it perceived as the
West's anti-Serb bias. But overall the alignment remains striking.

    In the immediate aftermath of the Cold War, there was a very strong
homology between Russia's position in the new field of international
security and the empowered dispositions at the Kremlin. The new
elites' disposition toward the internal mode of pursuing security and
their readiness to play the junior partner were in tune with Russia's
diminished status in the NATO-imposed order of things. In terms of
capital, Russia's position in the newly defined field of international
security had severely weakened in the early post-Cold War era. At the
material-institutional level, with its economy in total disarray and its
industrial basis seriously undermined, the country went through one
of the most dramatic material declines in recent human history. The

---

[24] Headley (2003, 211).   [25] UN Security Council (1993).

entire institutional network built by the USSR also crumbled within a few years, which placed Moscow in a friendless situation. Its army was also left to decay for at least ten years; the Russian nuclear deterrent was actually the only significant "hard" resource remaining. As for cultural-symbolic capital, in the new game of international security premised on democracy and human rights, Russia could not but be a pupil, given its authoritarian past. The new Russian government had everything to prove and it did not benefit from any significant symbolic resources to legitimize its practices. Instead it had to look for external legitimacy. Kozyrev's disposition to play the junior partner was thus in tune with the country's position in the field, which favored the doxic enactment of diplomacy. Until early 1994, the Alliance symbolically dominated Russia to the point of obtaining its support on a number of practices that would otherwise have aroused frustration. This pattern was to change rather abruptly at the turning point of 1994.

Critical juncture: the Russian pupil goes awry

The year 1994 was a turning point in post-Cold War Russian–Atlantic security relations: thereafter, NATO and Russia progressively embarked on the uneasy path of symbolic power struggles that continues to this day. The window of opportunity opened by NATO's unprecedented domination and Russia's acquiescence, between 1992 and 1994, was abruptly shut when the Alliance launched its geographical enlargement and implemented its new collective security functions in Bosnia. Taking the Russian perspective, I will demonstrate that NATO's unilateral decisions to bomb Yugoslavia and to take on new members were construed as contradicting the professed new rules of the international security game. In the next section, I will show how these practices helped revive Russian Great Power dispositions and sparked hysteresis effects in the relationship.

The double enlargement takes off

The first major crisis in post-Cold War Russian–Atlantic relations occurred in February 1994, after a Sarajevo market was shelled, presumably by Bosnian Serb forces. In reaction, the UN Secretary-General called for NATO air strikes, a move that was rejected by the Russians. When NATO officially accepted the request, the Russians expressed outrage at being sidelined and refused to accept the Alliance's interpretation of UN Security Council Resolution 836, which had threatened "tougher measures." They also warned that they would veto any further resolution at the UN Security Council. In a phone call to President Clinton, Boris Yeltsin reportedly said that the crisis could worsen to the point of involving nuclear weapons – a clear signal that Moscow would not stand being ignored. Indeed, when the UNPROFOR command ordered a Russian battalion to move into Bosnia on February 14, the Ministry of Defense in Moscow refused the order on the grounds that Russia had not been consulted in the management of the crisis. In order for Russia to recover its position in Balkans diplomacy, Yeltsin finally proposed to Belgrade that the Bosnian Serbs should withdraw as requested by NATO in order to let the Russian battalion in. When the crisis finally defused, the Russians celebrated a diplomatic victory, while NATO gloated that the threat of force had been decisive in obtaining the Serbian pullout.

In pursuit of diplomatic relevance, in April 1994 Yeltsin pushed for the creation of the Contact Group with France, Germany, the United Kingdom, the US and later Italy. Although coldly received at first, the initiative eventually guaranteed Moscow's inclusion in key diplomatic negotiations, temporarily softening tensions over Bosnia and leading to a few diplomatic successes. For instance, Russia did not formally protest when NATO bombed a Serbian airfield in Croatia in November 1994. In fact, on that occasion Yeltsin categorically condemned the Krajina Serbs' bombing of Bihać while instructing his representative at the UN Security Council to vote with NATO countries. But evidence suggests that NATO countries had accepted the idea of the Contact Group because it conveniently provided a *facade* of inclusion. As US Assistant Secretary of State Strobe Talbott remembers: "its real purpose, in the mind of the Allied foreign ministers, was to keep Russia, as they variously put it, inside the tent, on the reservation or, in [Warren Christopher's] phrase, sullen but not obstructionist."[26] Ultimately, then, including Russia worked only

---

[26] Talbott (2002, 123). Equally telling is the conclusion drawn by James Goldgeier and Michael McFaul on the basis of dozens of interviews with American officials: "On Bosnia, most officials in the U.S. government just did not want to have to worry about the Russian angle" (Goldgeier and McFaul 2003, 199).

to the point that effective decisionmaking remained firmly in the Alliance's hands. For instance, when Serbian forces surrounded the town of Gorazde in early April 1994, NATO carried out its threats and used force for the very first time in its history. Alliance members justified the bombing on the grounds of Resolution 836, to which Russia had previously acquiesced. Informed after the fact, Russia protested loudly, but in vain.

After a year-long lull, in July 1995 the Bosnian civil war came back to haunt NATO–Russia relations when Bosnian Serb forces took Dutch peacekeepers hostage and encircled Srebrenica. At a London meeting of the Contact Group, Russian Defense Minister Pavel Grachev signed up to an American proposal to give NATO the authority to bomb Serbs if they attacked Gorazde again, while Kozyrev declared that Russia would not veto a resolution reinforcing UNPROFOR. As Talbott remembers: "Key to [William] Perry's argument was a promise that Russia would have a 'dignified and meaningful' role in the peacekeeping operation that would take over once NATO had forced the Serbians into negotiations."[27] But during the negotiations with the warring parties, the Americans insisted that the Alliance, not the UN, would lead the peacekeeping mission in Bosnia. Russia's opposition could only deliver a minor concession: by a complex command chain arrangement, the Russian troops in Bosnia would be put under the orders of American General Joulwan, acting not as NATO's SACEUR, but as the American Commander in Chief in Europe (Joulwan formally wore both hats). "On matters of peacekeeping and virtually everything else," concluded Talbott, "Russia wanted inclusion but not subordination."[28] At the time, though, the Russians felt they were given the latter, not the former; and these feelings continued to grow in the wake of Operation Deliberate Force during the summer of 1995.

As to geographical enlargement, the impetus originally came from a number of former members of the Warsaw Pact shortly after the implosion of the USSR. In mid-October 1992, Czechoslovakia, Hungary and Poland formed the Visegrad Group with the aim of speeding up their integration into Western institutions, including NATO. At the time, however, the George H. W. Bush administration made clear that it had no intention of moving NATO eastward.

[27] Talbott (2002, 170).   [28] Talbott (2002, 186).

In December 1992, the NAC closed the door to Eastern enlargement by praising the NACC as the proper forum for consultations on security matters. Consequently, NATO officials initially remained careful in reaching out to Eastern European countries, an approach that was praised in Moscow. But the mere possibility of enlarging NATO was enough to spark doubts. When officials from the Baltic countries joined the fray in the ensuing weeks, the Kremlin expressed concern. Sergei Stankevich, a political adviser to Yeltsin, wrote that "maintaining the status of a Western outpost called upon to restrain Russia's 'aggressive aspirations' would enable the architects of a Baltic 'cordon sanitaire' to count on substantial long-term aid from the Atlantic community."[29] For the Russians, enlarging NATO would revive Cold War logics of confrontation and represent a step backward from the internal mode of pursuing security heralded in the early 1990s.

As early as the spring of 1993, a number of high-profile politicians in the West, including US Secretary of Defense Les Aspin and German Defense Minister Volker Rühe, began to publicly advocate NATO's enlargement to the Visegrad states. Within the newly elected Clinton team, National Security Adviser Anthony Lake quickly emerged as the main advocate of enlargement as part of his philosophy of democracy promotion. The proponents of enlargement presented the issue as one of survival for NATO. The Alliance was portrayed as a community of states bound by a liberal identity, values and norms, which "naturally" had to expand to like-minded countries. As Schimmelfennig observes: "By presenting the policy of enlargement as a policy that was based on the fundamental values of NATO member states and on the membership rules of the Alliance, the proponents of enlargement made it *difficult for the 'brakemen' to openly oppose this policy* without harming their credibility as community members."[30] For some months, the debate was fierce as a number of officials in the US and abroad harbored reservations about the policy. In late 1993, Clinton decided to put enlargement on temporary hold and instead to launch the PfP in order to reach out to potential future candidates.

On their side, the Russians consistently opposed the Alliance's expansion save for one occasion, when Yeltsin declared during an official visit to Poland in late August 1993 that Warsaw joining the

[29] Stankevich (1992, 5).   [30] Schimmelfennig (2003, 244).

Alliance "would not be in conflict with the process of European integration, including the interests of Russia."[31] In the next few days, the Russian Foreign Ministry tempered the president's declaration, adding that expanding NATO would be counterproductive while acknowledging the sovereign right of every state to choose means of ensuring its security. In an obvious act of retraction, in September Yeltsin wrote a letter to the main Western capitals warning against a mechanical expansion of the North Atlantic bloc and instead proposing that NATO and Moscow jointly guarantee the security of Eastern European countries. The Russian president also argued that enlargement would be illegal in view of the terms of German unification and that relations between Russia and NATO should always be "a few degrees warmer" than those between Brussels and ex-Soviet satellites.[32] Yet the damage was apparently done: Yeltsin's declaration in Warsaw had opened a window of opportunity for the proponents of enlargement. For instance, Secretary-General Wörner, who had been a timid supporter until then, began to endorse the policy more openly.

Russian diplomats tried hard to back-pedal and state Moscow's strong opposition to the Alliance's expansion as clearly as possible. In November 1993, the Federal Security Service released an important report on NATO enlargement. Written under Primakov's leadership, it epitomized the dominant thinking in ruling circles at the time. First, the report noted that "many of Russia's apprehensions associated with NATO's entry into the countries of Central and Eastern Europe would be removed or eased if there were guarantees of priority development for the process of changing the alliance's functions." In the report's analysis, not only were such guarantees never given, the Alliance's threats of force with regards to the Bosnian civil war only compounded Russian concerns about NATO's functional evolution. Second, the report regretted the "fixed nature of stereotypes of bloc thinking, which is especially characteristic of a number of representatives of the military leadership in the Western countries." Third, while acknowledging that it would be "incorrect to proceed from [the premise] that NATO's geographic expansion would serve to create a staging ground for inflicting a strike on Russia," the report emphasized the "objective

---

[31] Quoted in Parkhomenko (1993).   [32] Quoted in Asmus (2002, 47).

necessity" for Russia to review its defense posture as a result of it "regardless of the fact that in a political sense NATO is no longer regarded as an adversary." Fourth, the report alluded to the possibility that enlargement could play into the hands of anti-Western forces inside Russia and curb democratic reforms. Fifth and finally, Primakov's report acknowledged that "Russia has no right to dictate to the sovereign states of Central and Eastern Europe whether or not they should join NATO."[33] All in all, while many NATO officials construed Russia's opposition as "outdated Cold War thinking," for the Russians it was rather premised on a rejection of such a confrontational mentality.

In late 1993 and early 1994, NATO's stance regarding enlargement was left ambiguous. When enlargement was officially taken off the agenda in favor of the PfP in December 1993, Kozyrev and his team celebrated the launch of this vast program of partnership and cooperation. Yet only days later, Germany's Defense Minister Rühe declared at the opening of a meeting of the NATO Defense Planning Committee: "There is no question as to the advisability of expanding NATO. We have only to determine when this will happen and whom it will involve."[34] A similar ambiguity surrounded the Brussels summit of January 1994, where heads of state and government agreed "to reaffirm that the Alliance remains open to the membership of other European countries." The bulk of the summit, however, was devoted to the PfP, an initiative enticing partners to "work *alongside* the Alliance."[35] For the Russians, expansion and the PfP were opposite initiatives because one was exclusive and the other inclusive. NATO could take one or the other direction, but not both at once. In a press conference with Clinton, Yeltsin emphasized that "all those countries must be integrated together, in just one package. This will make everyone more secure. If, however, you try to dismember us, accepting us and admitting us one by one – that will be no good. I'm against that; I'm absolutely opposed to it. That's why I support the president's initiative for Partnership for Peace."[36] In the same spirit, Kozyrev signed the PfP framework document in June 1994 and agreed with NATO member states to engage in a discussion about a special partnership with Russia "corresponding to its size, importance, capabilities and

---

[33] Quoted in Poleshchuk (1993).   [34] Quoted in Yusin (1993).
[35] NATO (1994a) (emphasis added).   [36] Quoted in Talbott (2002, 115).

willingness to contribute to the pursuit of shared objectives."[37] When the American and Russian armies held their first ever joint peace-keeping exercises on Russian soil in September, everything was taking place as though a cooperative Russian–Atlantic *modus vivendi* was developing.

And yet, a series of events in December 1994 showed this to be a cruel illusion. On the first day of that month, the NAC issued a communiqué initiating "a process of examination inside the Alliance to determine how NATO will enlarge, the principles to guide this process and the implications of membership."[38] This decision, which took many senior officials by surprise including the American Secretary of Defense, came as a huge blow to the Russians. For one thing, Clinton had promised Yeltsin that American policy with respect to enlargement would be guided by three noes: no surprises, no rush, and no exclusion. For another, the internal deliberations inside the Alliance had led most observers to conclude that enlargement was still off the agenda: the "Russians had good reasons to be confused about America's real intentions," conclude Goldgeier and McFaul.[39] Coincidentally or not, on the day of NATO's announcement, Kozyrev was in Brussels to sign an Individual Partnership Program as well as a document fostering NATO–Russia dialogue. Claiming that no one in Brussels had forewarned Moscow of this upcoming decision, Kozyrev finally declined to sign any document and, under Yeltsin's direct instructions, froze all further progress in institutionalizing cooperation with the Alliance. For the Russians, the unilateral decision to expand reflected a NATO pattern of offering "Russia a fait accompli, a final position of the 'take it or leave it' type."[40]

Within a few days, this about-face led to one of the most emblematic moments of post-Cold War Russian–Atlantic relations: the Budapest CSCE/OSCE summit. The Russians had hoped that this summit would consecrate an inclusive European security architecture based on a strong pan-European organization – the strengthened OSCE. Their hopes had just been shattered by NATO's December 1, 1994 communiqué. The new security order premised on the Alliance's functional and geographical enlargement seemed bound to relegate Russia to the margins of Europe. Despite all the NATO talk of partnership,

---

[37] NATO (1994b).   [38] NATO (1994c).
[39] Goldgeier and McFaul (2003, 184).   [40] Kozyrev (1995, 9).

Alliance practices in late 1994 appeared, for Moscow, to go against the professed cooperative security order of the post-Cold War era. In Budapest, lamenting the rise of a "cold peace," Yeltsin denounced the exclusionary consequences of the Alliance's double enlargement:

Europe, even before it has managed to shrug off the legacy of the Cold War, is risking encumbering itself with a cold peace ... NATO was created in Cold War times. Today, it is trying to find its place in Europe, not without difficulty. It is important that this search not create new divisions, but promote European unity. We believe that the plans of expanding NATO are contrary to this logic. Why sow the seeds of distrust? After all, we are no longer adversaries, we are partners. Some explanations that we hear imply that this is "expansion of stability," just in case developments in Russia go the undesirable way. If this is the reason why some want to move the NATO area of responsibility closer to the Russian borders, let me say this: it is too early to give up on democracy in Russia![41]

For the first time, the Russian frustration with the Alliance's activities was stated at the highest level. On the plane to Washington from Budapest, the Clinton team tried "to figure out if [Yeltsin's speech] was a long-term change or a brief interruption in what had been very close and friendly relations between Washington and Moscow."[42] With the benefit of hindsight, December 1994 constitutes the crucial point when Russian–Atlantic relations became a lot more uneasy. Only days after the OSCE summit, Russian troops began invading Chechnya.

Breaking the rules: Russian interpretations of the double enlargement

Why did Russia, despite its acceptance of the new rules of the international security game, react so negatively to NATO's double enlargement policy? Clearly, NATO's practices were not received in Russia with the same spirit in which Brussels enacted them. For the Alliance, geographical and functional enlargement was in line with the new rules of the game it was imposing after the end of the Cold War – the security-from-the-inside-out paradigm. For the Russians, however,

---

[41] Quoted in Goldgeier and McFaul (2003, 191).
[42] Interview with Burns quoted in Goldgeier and McFaul (2003, 192).

NATO's dual expansion meant exclusion and humiliation; such practices were reminiscent of Cold War realpolitik far more than of a new world order allegedly premised on cooperative security.

From a Russian point of view, NATO's February 1994 ultimatum to Bosnian Serbs contradicted the very essence of the new rules of the international security game premised on inclusiveness and mutuality. As Gorbachev, certainly no hawk, complained: "Russia was confronted with a *fait accompli*. It was treated as a junior partner that is expected only to nod its head and support the choice made by others, contenting itself with a pat on the shoulder."[43] While NATO thought it had a free hand in the Balkans, the Russians could not countenance being sidelined from solving a problem of European security when they felt they had been promised just the opposite with the NACC, the PfP and other allegedly inclusive Atlantic initiatives. It thus came as a shock to the Russians that NATO's functional enlargement to embrace peacekeeping, which they had been supporting in 1992 and 1993, in fact turned out to be conducive to Moscow's exclusion from the management of European security. The new rules of the international security game, heralded by the Alliance and the Russians alike, were supposedly premised on inclusion and cooperation. Starting in February 1994, however, NATO's own practices in the Balkans did not seem to match the internal mode of pursuing security to which the new Russia had subscribed. No one has better expressed the change of attitude in Moscow than Kozyrev in a spring 1994 article in *Foreign Affairs*. It is worth quoting at length in order to compare it with the views he had defended in 1992:

If a partnership is built on mutual trust, then it is natural to recognize other rules as well: the need not only to inform one another of decisions made, but also to agree on approaches beforehand. It would be hard to accept an interpretation of partnership in which one side demands that the other coordinate its every step with it while the former retains complete freedom for itself. Partners must have mutual respect for each other's interests and concerns.

This is a key lesson from the decision-making process that led to the lifting of the siege of Sarajevo in February. NATO's threat to bomb Bosnian Serb positions if the siege was not lifted by a certain date was made without Russian participation. It immediately became apparent that Russia could

---

[43] Gorbachev (1994).

not and should not be excluded from the common efforts to regulate the conflict in the Balkans, a region where Russia has longtime interests and influence. Ultimately the advantages of partnership were illustrated when Russia and the West coordinated their efforts to persuade the warring parties to make peace. But the initial lack of consultation and coordination meant that first both sides had to run the risk of returning to the old benefactor–client relationship that had played such a pernicious role in the regional conflicts of the Cold War era.[44]

For the Russians, the fact that NATO took it upon itself to decide on the use of force in Bosnia went against the grain of the new rules of the international security game based on inclusive partnership.

In late August 1995, when NATO's Operation Deliberate Force began, Russian officials similarly decried their exclusion from prior consultations. Yeltsin denounced the Alliance for breaking with the cooperative security discourse it was simultaneously preaching: "In proclaiming its 'peacekeeping mission,' the North Atlantic alliance has essentially taken upon itself the role of both judge and jury."[45] For the Russians, NATO was guilty of duplicity: while claiming to include Russia in diplomatic talks through the Contact Group, it was simultaneously making unilateral decisions to use force without Russia's participation. As a result, many in Moscow came to construe NATO's functional enlargement not in terms of the internal mode of pursuing security, but as a shrewd strategy intended to strengthen the Alliance's profile in the post-Cold War era. Even the father of New Thinking protested "a desire to expand de facto NATO's sphere of operation far beyond its historical borders. All this has very little in common with humanitarian ideals of restoring peace in Bosnia."[46] Doubts about NATO's promise of an inclusive security order began to emerge – to be compounded by NATO's decision to enlarge.

Despite all the Alliance talk to the contrary, the December 1994 decision to enlarge seemed to Moscow to breach the three basic CSCE principles that had been so fundamental after the end of the Cold War – that security is indivisible, mutual, and cooperative. It looked as though the NATO-professed rules of the post-Cold War international security game were scorned by the Alliance itself, whose actions, as Moscow understood them, smacked more of realpolitik

[44] Kozyrev (1994a, 66).   [45] Quoted in *Rossiiskiye Vesti* (1995).
[46] Gorbachev (1994).

than cooperative security. For one thing, from a Russian perspective expanding NATO created new dividing lines in the European security system. NATO's claim that an enlarged alliance would not lead to new demarcations in Europe made little sense for Moscow: one is either inside the tent, or outside. Russia remaining on the margins of a tightly knit alliance that arrogated to itself the central role in European security could not but lead to its exclusion. The Russians felt they were unfairly excluded from a place they thought they belonged to.

In a similar vein, expansion seriously undermined the chances of developing a pan-European security institution with teeth, in which Russia could exert influence. To counter this view, many Atlantic officials insisted that the door would always remain open for Russia to eventually join NATO. Clinton repeatedly told Yeltsin that enlargement could, in theory, also embrace Russia. Yet there are grounds to doubt that such a policy could have been implemented – not least because Brussels turned down all Moscow's declarations of interest in 1992, 1996 and 2002. The German Defense Minister offered a more accurate expression of the dominant view in the Atlantic world in September 1994: "Russia cannot be integrated, neither into the European Union nor in NATO ... if Russia were to become a member of NATO it would blow NATO apart ... It would be like the United Nations of Europe – it wouldn't work."[47] Inside the Alliance, most member states feared that involving Russia could only mean the end of the transatlantic consensus. In any event, Russian officials concluded that their country was excluded from NATO's geographical enlargement in contravention of the principle of indivisible security.

Moreover, the Alliance's expansion defeated the principle of mutual security. For the Russians, the move sparked new security dilemmas regardless of the overall quality of their relationship with member states. If Moscow was not part of the Alliance, then it was inevitably relegated to its external periphery. The main fear was that, in gaining even more strength, NATO would be able to force any and all policies on Russia. In Defense Minister Igor Rodionov's words: "I do not think that NATO is expanding to start a war, but it is becoming a military alliance whose power cannot be matched by anybody. We fear that as it gains strength and moves closer to Russian borders, NATO will try to impose on us its conditions – political, economic

---

[47] Volker Rühe quoted in Yost (1998, 139).

and others."[48] Instead, mutual security implies that one country's security cannot be enhanced at the expense of others'. For the Russians, NATO's unilateral decision to enlarge plainly contravened this principle. As Primakov explained: "we don't need to be convinced that NATO is not preparing to attack us. We do not intend to attack the United States, either. But let us suppose, purely hypothetically, that we were to conclude a military alliance with Mexico, Venezuela and Cuba. Surely that would elicit a negative reaction from the United States."[49] At issue were not intentions but the fact that increasing one side's forces necessarily has consequences for the other. If security is mutual, according to Russian officials, then the Alliance cannot be strengthened without affecting the security of its neighbors.

Despite all NATO claims to the contrary, for Moscow expansion retained an insuperable anti-Russian flavor. In fact, many officials in Washington did not hide their suspicions about the new Russia under Yeltsin. In a 1995 op-ed, Strobe Talbott wrote that "among the contingencies for which NATO must be prepared is that Russia will abandon democracy and return to the threatening patterns of international behavior that have sometimes characterized its history."[50] Turning NATO into the central security pillar of the new architecture appeared to be an efficient means of blocking any return to Russia's past imperialism. This rationale also informed the strong Republican support for enlargement in the US: Senator Richard Lugar, for instance, "was convinced that the West had to lock in the gains of the end of the Cold War before they were frittered away."[51] In a similar vein, the main reason why post-communist countries were so eagerly begging for admission was indubitably their fear of Russia. Fully aware of this, the Russians tried to convince Atlantic officials that in this context expansion amounted to setting in motion a self-fulfilling prophecy.

Finally, in Russian eyes NATO expansion contradicted the very principle of cooperative security by which international order could be achieved only through negotiated settlement. Russian officials felt that the decision to enlarge was imposed on them and that the policy failed to take their country's legitimate security interests into account. Most strikingly, the 1995 "Study on Enlargement" appeared "deliberately provocative in offering almost no concessions

[48] Quoted in Black (1997).   [49] Quoted in Kondrashov (1996).
[50] Talbott (1995, 6).   [51] Asmus (2002, 32).

to Russian interests. Enlargement was confirmed as an open-ended process; nothing but full membership was countenanced for applicant countries; and these applicants were also expected not to 'foreclose the option' of foreign troops and nuclear weapons being stationed on their territory."[52] Seen from Moscow, the Alliance's refusal to alter its policy based on Russian concerns meant that "a new world order was emerging while their country stood by as helpless observer."[53] In his memoirs, Yevgeny Primakov recounts a one-on-one conversation with Warren Christopher in early 1996: "My discussion with Christopher left no doubt that our opinion would be ignored during the expansion of NATO. It was not the process of expansion that would have to take Russia's position into account but Russia that would have to adapt to the process."[54] The symbolic inequality of NATO–Russia diplomacy became increasingly hard to accept for Moscow.

NATO's proactive approach was driven in large part by the conviction that any concession to the Russians on the issue of enlargement would amount to showing weakness. As Talbott recalls: "if the Russians knew that the prospect of a collision would cause us to hit the brakes on enlargement, they'd have no incentive to acquiesce in our going forward."[55] Contrary to the spirit of cooperative security, any substantive compromise with Russia to accommodate its concerns was excluded from the outset. The net result was that, throughout the enlargement row, Russia basically faced the facts as NATO laid them out. Resentment started to increase among Russian elites: Andranik Migranyan, a Yeltsin adviser, regretted that "Russia's reward for destroying the totalitarian Soviet empire is not a return to civilization as a respected and equal partner, but the isolation and serious weakening of the country."[56] Instead of cooperating, NATO appeared to be exploiting its partner's difficulties to secure cheap gains.

Moscow elites have always rejected the notion, particularly popular in Western conservative circles, that NATO had won the Cold War. From the Russian point of view, the Alliance did not defeat them; it was their own rulers who brought the USSR down. As Kozyrev wrote in March 1994: "Victory in the cold war was won not by NATO's military machine but by the CSCE's democratic principles."[57] In a

---

[52] Dannreuther (1999–2000, 152).   [53] Ponsard (2007, 91).
[54] Primakov (2004, 135).   [55] Talbott (2002, 99).
[56] Migranyan (1994).   [57] Kozyrev (1994b).

similar fashion, Primakov affirmed in 1996: "Peoples on both sides of the Iron Curtain rid themselves of the policy of confrontation through joint effort."[58] Consequently, post-communist elites expected to be welcomed as equals by the Alliance. The expansion of NATO sent them the exact opposite message, reminiscent of the Cold War's "containment" policy.[59] The promises of cooperative security were left unfulfilled, the diplomatic order of things was shaken, and the trend toward a security community started to weaken.

All in all, seen from Moscow, NATO's double enlargement seemed to contradict the very premises by which the Alliance sought to justify the practice. Several Western pundits echoed Russian criticisms of the exclusionary dynamics engendered by NATO's enlargement. In an open letter to Clinton in June 1997, fifty former American senators, cabinet secretaries, ambassadors and foreign policy specialists denounced "a policy error of historic importance." The process is plagued with a "central contradiction," argued one pundit, because it "emphasize[s] cooperative security in Europe as a whole, but insist[s] on the right to enlarge an organization designed for the collective defense of one part of Europe against the other."[60] In reality, expansion would "resurrect Europe's dividing lines" and bypass the "chance to build a European security community that included Russia."[61] A *New York Times* editorial went so far as to call for Russian membership in NATO in order to avoid such a stalemate in European security.[62]

But NATO did not alter its course – quite the contrary. In September 1995, the "Study on NATO Enlargement" confirmed the "open door" policy, adding: "No country outside the Alliance should be given a veto or *droit de regard* over the process" of enlargement.[63] Coincidentally, the study was published at about the same time as NATO was conducting its air strikes on Bosnia. Starting from 1994, NATO's double enlargement practices were to leave an indelible mark on the Russian habitus – one that persists to this day.

Hysteresis: NATO and the Russian "Great Power"

Starting in the mid-1990s, age-old Russian Great Power dispositions resurfaced among policymakers in Moscow, prompting a misalignment

[58] Quoted in *Rossiiskaya Gazeta* (1996).   [59] Kozyrev (1995, 13).
[60] MccGwire (1998, 34–5).   [61] Kupchan (1994).
[62] *New York Times* (1994).   [63] NATO (1995).

with the lower position occupied by the country inside the Alliance-dominated field of international security. While in 1992–4, Yeltsin, Kozyrev and other members of the Russian government had incorporated the new rules of the international security game, acting and thinking *from* Russia's weakened status, later the situation began to change in part as a result of NATO's practices of double enlargement. Despite its verbal promotion of the internal mode of pursuing security, in reality NATO appeared to follow a different logic, especially because of the exclusionary consequences of the double enlargement for Russia. As a result, the Russian proto-liberal habitus that had rendered possible the Alliance's domination in the immediate aftermath of the Cold War gradually gave way to deeply embodied Great Power dispositions.

The Russian Great Power habitus was never too far from the surface, even during the 1992–4 honeymoon. For more than forty years, Moscow had been the center of a huge empire and enjoyed a privileged dialogue with its superpower counterpart in Washington. Such an enduring position of domination in the international security field left deeply ingrained dispositions among Russian policymakers. Despite New Thinking policies and post-communist Russia's early embrace of the NATO order, the Great Power habitus has deeper historical roots than any other in the Russian political soil. Nonetheless, for about a decade, from Gorbachev to Kozyrev, Great Power dispositions were remarkably muted inside the Kremlin. This raises the important question: what explains the fact that in the mid-1990s the dispositional balance in Moscow was tipped in favor of the Great Power habitus? I argue that NATO's practices with regard to the double enlargement played an important role in this change.

This is not to say that the Alliance bears sole responsibility for the resurgence of Great Power attitudes in Russia; several other factors contributed to this evolution. First, as I just explained, for historical reasons Russian soil is uniquely fertile for this habitus of *grandeur*.[64] Second, NATO is only one among many international interlocutors

---

[64] An eminent group of scholars identifies a number of other "historical patterns marking the long haul of Russian foreign policy," including "the powerful but often perverse impact of absolutism, the impulse and burden of shapeless borders, the effect of perennial economic backwardness, the consequences of empire in lieu of more modern national forms, and the allied and ultimately most poignant influence, Russia's permanent and sometimes agonizing quest for identity" (Legvold 2007, 20).

for Russia (although it is a particularly important one in Self and Other dynamics). Furthermore, NATO–Russia relations are heavily influenced by the larger dynamics between the West and "the rest" at the systemic level. Finally, domestic politics – both in Russia and in NATO countries – have certainly played an important role. Throughout the 1990s, Russian society went through unprecedented economic and political turmoil and its political institutions were often taken over by corrupt elites. In sum, several factors combined to prompt the reemergence of the Russian Great Power habitus. I contend that NATO–Russia dealings with regard to the double enlargement significantly contributed to tipping the balance in favor of Great Power disposition in Moscow.

How can we ascertain that the brunt of the change was not of domestic origin, especially given the consecutive victories of nationalistic forces in the 1993 and 1995 Duma elections? New elites did come to power in Moscow in the mid-1990s: in foreign policy, for instance, Primakov came to typify the Russian Great Power habitus. But a closer look at timing and the precise sequence of events in the mid-1990s suggests that much of Russian domestic change *followed* (instead of preceded) the events described in the previous section. Two examples should drive this point home. First, Moscow did not become more assertive immediately after the 1993 elections and the arrival in force of nationalistic deputies in the Duma. During the first half of 1994, Russian officials were still taking a conciliatory tone toward NATO, supporting much of its diplomacy in the Balkans as well as its partnership initiatives. The real change in Russian foreign policy came only after December 1994, once NATO had announced its enlargement and as it prepared for its large-scale military intervention in Bosnia. The second example that demonstrates that elite change in Moscow was in part a reaction to Russian–Atlantic dealings is the Russian invasion of Chechnya – the first genuinely praetorian practice of the post-communist Kremlin. Again, Moscow's decision was taken *after* the Alliance had officially kicked off the enlargement process. While there is no doubt that Moscow's behavior in the Caucasus sparked fears in the West, it cannot be said to have been the catalyst of the enlargement process because military orders were given after NATO's decision had been publicly announced.

Looking at the double enlargement from Russia's perspective does not mean that NATO's point of view is of less value. For instance, a number of Russian practices, from Yeltsin's shelling of the White House in October 1993 to the invasion of Chechnya in December 1994, revived Western fears that Russia's democratic transition might be very fragile after all. In this context, enlarging NATO appeared to be a sound policy. This may very well have been the case. I focus on the Russian perspective for analytical, not normative reasons – because this is the best way to trace the origins of hysteresis in post-Cold War Russian–Atlantic security relations. Looking at the double enlargement through Moscow's eyes helps better understand how and why NATO's own practices have been particularly deleterious to its dominant position in relation to Russia. I leave it to others to account more extensively for the Alliance's point of view.[65]

Russia's Great Power habitus

In concluding Chapter 4, I argued that in 2006 Russian practitioners took for granted the Great Power status of their country. At the intersubjective level foreign policy discourse similarly assumed that Moscow belonged to a small club of the most powerful nations. Across the political spectrum, Russian elites generally thought *from* their country's Great Power status: it formed a Russian commonplace. To be sure, this disposition is primarily a historical substrate. For the last three centuries at least, Russia has constituted a pole of power in international politics. From Peter the Great's arrival in European society to the Soviet superpower, the Russian habitus is imprinted with a sense of belonging to the restricted circle of Great Powers.[66] Historians also note that this narrative has often played the role of a fallback position in Moscow: "The breadth of popular and elite consensus on Russia's 'greatness' as a sine qua non of its identity as a state appears clearly in the crises that have arisen from international failures."[67] Until the end of 1991, Moscow remained the premier center of the communist world. Remarkably, this disposition did not completely wither away with the fall of the USSR, despite the fact that, thereafter, Moscow occupied a much lower position in the new field premised on the internal mode of pursuing security. With

---

[65] For Bourdieu-inspired explanations of NATO's transformation in the post-Cold War era, see Gheciu (2005); Villumsen (2008); and Williams (2007).
[66] Neumann (2008b).   [67] McDonald (2007, 163).

New Thinking falling into disrepute, this disconnect between Russian dispositions and the country's weakened position was bound to spark hysteresis effects. Starting in the mid-1990s and increasingly so to this day, the Russian habitus appeared better attuned to the dominant position that the country enjoyed in the past than to the post-Cold War configuration defined along lines of democracy and human rights. The Russian Great Power habitus is attuned to the external mode of pursuing security – that is, the traditional rules of the game in the field of international security centered on power-balancing and alliance-making. In the early 1990s as Russian dispositions lost touch with the country's low position in the hierarchy, this misalignment led Russian officials to decreasingly recognize the order of things in international society imposed by NATO. This hysteresis lies at the root of today's intense symbolic struggles and seriously undermined security community development.

Despite its long history, the Russian Great Power habitus had mostly disappeared from foreign policy discourse and practice in the immediate aftermath of the Cold War. It was only in the ensuing years that it made a progressive comeback. In March 1994, for example, Kozyrev adopted a new tone with NATO member states: "Some people in the West have actually succumbed to the fantasy that a partnership can be built with Russia on the principle of 'if the Russians are good guys now, they should follow us in every way' ... [But] the Russian Federation is doomed to being a Great Power ... it can only be an equal partner, not a junior one."[68] Starting in the mid-1990s, the assertion and reassertion of the country's Great Power status became a mantra among Moscow's elites – a discursive practice that arguably revealed a lack of self-confidence in the status being deserved and recognized. In this connection, Bobo Lo describes "the Potemkinization of Russian foreign policy," arguing that the Great Power discourse was part of Moscow's "mythmaking" after the end of the Cold War.[69]

Nothing better illustrates the resurgence of Russia's age-old Great Power disposition than the nomination, in January 1996, of Primakov as Foreign Minister in replacement of Kozyrev. At his very first press conference in his new capacity, Primakov expressed the attitude quite

---

[68] Kozyrev (1994b).   [69] Lo (2002, 5 and 7).

clearly: "Despite the current difficulties, Russia has been and remains a Great Power, and its policy toward the outside world should correspond to that status."[70] He also insisted on the need for equitable partnership with the West and reasserted that there was no victor in the Cold War, as overcoming it had been a joint victory. Starting with Primakov, Russian foreign policymakers appealed to the historical notion of *derzhava*, which Andrei Tsygankov translates as "the holder of international equilibrium of power."[71] Accordingly, the main constitutive elements of the Russian narrative of Great Power are calls for equality, multipolarity, spheres of interest and balance of power. Geopolitical thinking also plays a prominent role in this habitus.[72]

The gist of my argument consists of linking the revival of Great Power dispositions in Russia to NATO's practices with regard to the double enlargement. I want to substantiate this correlation with four interrelated arguments. First, NATO's double enlargement led to an unprecedented foreign policy consensus in post-communist Russia around 1995. In the immediate aftermath of the Cold War, there was a lot of debate on Russia's new identity. Starting in 1994, however, these different foreign policy opinions gave way to a broad-based agreement based on the notion of *derzhava*. Thereafter, the Russian elite struck a position that repudiated much of the New Thinking of the early 1990s and instead integrated several items from the age-old Russian habitus of Great Power. An insider to these debates, Dmitri Trenin confirms that "the turning point came in 1994 with the decision in principle by NATO to admit new members. Most groups within the Russian elite, otherwise deeply divided on the issues of policy, were suddenly united in portraying this decision as essentially anti-Russian."[73] Crucially, the consensus around the notion of Great Power emerged *after* NATO's official launch of the process of geographical enlargement.

Second, NATO's practices regarding its double enlargement played a significant role in disempowering those elites that had been disposed to follow Western leadership and recognize its cultural-symbolic superiority. Epitomized by Primakov's nomination as Foreign Minister, the institutional empowerment of the Great Power habitus that took place in the mid-1990s was accompanied neither by any significant

---

[70] Quoted in *Moskovskiye Novosti* (1996).   [71] Tsygankov (2004, 93).
[72] Tsygankov (2003).   [73] Trenin (2000, 13–14).

changes in the material conditions of the Russian population, nor by any obvious upheaval of the international structure. What, then, could have led to this foreign policy shift? In a detailed study of elite and mass opinions about foreign policy in Russia, William Zimmerman observes: "Russia's orientation to the world had changed considerably in the two years between 1993 and 1995. The era dominated by those sometimes termed the Atlanticists in Russian foreign policy had passed."[74] The author makes a link between this finding and the decision to enlarge: "NATO expansion both in numbers and in role has very likely deterred those Russian elites who from a Western perspective warranted being deterred *and* has disabused Russian elites who would have been likely to respond favorably to policies designed to reassure."[75]

Western practitioners' recollections of events also provide evidence that NATO's double enlargement contributed to reviving Great Power dispositions. For instance, one insider of the Clinton White House believes that the policy has been "the real culprit" in the deterioration of Russian–Atlantic relations.[76] Building on dozens of interviews with American diplomats and politicians, Goldgeier and McFaul similarly conclude that "[while] it is hard to measure the negative impact of NATO enlargement for US–Russian relations on other security concerns ... it is true that the cooperative pattern of problem solving on issues like Baltic troop withdrawal and the India rocket deal established in 1993–94 were [sic] not repeated after the NATO enlargement process began to move forward."[77] With the benefit of hindsight, then, several practitioners on the NATO side realized that something had changed in Russian dispositions after 1994; and they identified enlargement as the probable trigger of that change.

Third, because of its belittling consequences, the Alliance's double enlargement contributed to a return to Russia's Great Power narrative. As Talbott was selling the case for a NATO intervention in Yugoslavia, Kozyrev responded: "it's bad enough having you people tell us what you're going to do whether we like it or not. Don't add insult to injury by also telling us that it's *in our interests* to obey your orders."[78] Playing the junior partner turned out to be unbearable for

---

[74] Zimmerman (2002, 93).   [75] Zimmerman (2002, 206).
[76] Blacker (1998, 179).   [77] Goldgeier and McFaul (2003, 355–6).
[78] Quoted in Talbott (2002, 76).

Moscow given NATO's inclination to further reinforce its dominant position. To make matters worse, the Russians felt that as soon as they did not agree with Allied member states' policies, they were accused of reverting to Russia's imperial past. In 1995, Kozyrev expressed his irritation:

> the firm, sometimes tough protection of [national] interests by Russian diplomacy should not be seen as an exercise in superpower rhetoric. When the United States and its allies in Western Europe or Japan have political differences or even trade wars, no one thinks of accusing this or that country of having imperial ambitions or of giving up on democracy. Why is it, then, that when Russia disagrees on something with its Western partners, the alarm is immediately sounded and partnership with the West is declared to be either falling apart or totally impossible?[79]

All in all, the double enlargement left the Russians under the impression that playing by the new rules of the international security game was bound to make Russia's position weaker while NATO's grew stronger.

Fourth, from the Russian point of view NATO's practices of functional and geographical enlargement were reminiscent of the Cold War game. Progressively, many Russian elites came to feel that NATO's discourse of democracy and cooperative security was in fact a cover-up for collecting its geopolitical trophies. In other words, the Alliance seemed to use a double language, advocating idealpolitik in words but implementing realpolitik in deeds. In reaction, ingrained realpolitik dispositions took precedence over the thinner habitus that had flourished from Gorbachev to Kozyrev. The double enlargement policy, in other words, triggered Great Power dispositions at the expense of those that had informed Russia's foreign policy in 1992–4. As Vladimir Baranovsky remarks: "The predominant feeling is that even if Russia could not retain its position in Europe, it certainly did not deserve to be forced out ruthlessly and treated as a defeated country."[80] Under such circumstances, Great Power dispositions appeared better adapted to playing the game of international security with NATO member states. When one adds to these processes the practical imperatives of positional agency, by which Russian

---

[79] Kozyrev (1995, 8).   [80] Baranovsky (2000, 449).

elites were structurally oriented toward making use of the resources at hand (military capital but very few cultural-symbolic resources), then clearly practices associated with the external mode of pursuing security had a better chance of prevailing over the medium term.

The resurgence of the Russian Great Power habitus was gradual throughout the 1990s. It was only with the Kosovo crisis and the ensuing resignation of Yeltsin that it became wholly dominant among decisionmakers (see Chapter 6). In the meantime, the coexistence of Great Power dispositions and of cooperative security inclinations created intriguing tensions in Russian foreign policy, between the desire to integrate Atlantic structures and a drive to retain as much independence as possible. On the one hand, as a Great Power Russia should be an autonomous pole of the international system; on the other hand, as a weak player in the post-Cold War international security game, Moscow continued to value democratic norms and cooperation as means of pursuing security. Positional and dispositional effects pushed diplomatic practices in different directions. To an extent, this puzzling ambivalence characterizes Russia's external relations with the West to this day.

Mind the gap? Institutionalizing NATO–Russia ties

The diplomatic interactions that led to the NATO-Russia Founding Act, signed in May 1997, illustrate particularly well the intense hysteresis effects that started to grip Russian–Atlantic relations in the mid-1990s. Throughout the negotiations, NATO practitioners considered Russia's assumption of Great Power status nonsensical, while Russian officials could hardly bear the Alliance's condescending approach. The mismatch between positions in the field and each party's dispositions was striking – almost as much as at the NRC in 2006 (see Chapter 4). The following pages identify two concrete hysteresis effects on Russian-Atlantic interactions. First, the negotiations turned out to be much more tense and difficult than they had been earlier in the post-Cold War era. By both sides' accounts, the dialogue was characterized by fierce symbolic power struggles. In particular, the Russians turned out to be far more difficult partners than NATO had imagined because they consistently insisted on the need for equality. Second, given its disconnect from the structure of the international security field, the Russian Great Power habitus sparked "Don Quixote effects" in the form of a series of diplomatic initiatives that seemed out of touch with the reality of the international security field.

Starting in the mid-1990s, hysteresis effects showed up in Russia's determined quest for NATO's recognition of its equality and in the Alliance's blunt dismissal of that claim. Viewed from Brussels, Moscow's weakness was plain; as a result, Atlantic diplomats expected the Russians to be happy to defer to NATO's lead in the field of international security. But such was not the Russian perspective after the Great Power habitus began to resurface in the mid-1990s. As Trenin notes, Moscow's objective in institutionalizing relations with the Alliance was crystal clear: it never aspired to be a normal partner and not even a normal ally, but rather the "first among equals, with the only possible exception of the United States."[81] This was plainly out of the question for NATO officials. The Russians had simply lost the sense of their place, it appeared, rendering them impossible inter-locutors. Officials in Moscow harbored reciprocal feelings about their NATO counterparts.

Already in 1994, when NATO invited Russia to join the PfP, the Duma Committee on Defense recommended joining "only if consid-eration is given to [Russia's] special status."[82] President Yeltsin quickly added his voice to the chorus, declaring that "by virtue of its scope and substance," Russia deserved a partnership with NATO "differ-ent from relationships with other countries. The idea is to conclude a special agreement with NATO in keeping with Russia's place and role in world and European affairs and with our country's military power and nuclear status."[83] During the very first ministerial meet-ing of 16 + 1, in May 1994, Defense Minister Grachev handed to his NATO counterparts a list of proposals for institutionalizing their ties, including a consultation mechanism. In his private meeting with the American Secretary of Defense, however, he was told that no special conditions would be given to Russia. Put back in his place, Grachev reportedly answered: "It wouldn't be correct for Russia to set forth special conditions [or ask for] a warmer place in the sun. A civilized nation would never set such conditions."[84] In early 1994, Russia was still willing to play the junior partner, although Great Power disposi-tions were clearly on the rise.

[81] Trenin (2005, 282).   [82] Rodin (1994).
[83] Quoted in *Nezavisimaya Gazeta* (1994).   [84] Quoted in Schmidt (1994).

The Russian–Atlantic negotiations over the Founding Act took place against the background of NATO's geographical enlargement. For the Russians, this was a damage-limitation exercise, whereas for the Alliance it was a way to have the Kremlin swallow the pill without balking. The main strategy adopted by the Alliance was to grant Russia some of the symbolic pomp of equality but without the substance. After much hesitation, and only once it became clear that Moscow would not sign the PfP otherwise, the Alliance finally accepted the beginning of formal negotiations on an individual partnership program with Russia in June 1994. In May 1995, NATO and Russia agreed on a document called "Areas for Pursuance of a Broad, Enhanced NATO/Russia Dialogue and Cooperation," which envisioned "dialogue through ad hoc 16 + 1 meetings" on matters of peacekeeping, nuclear weapons and crisis management. At the first 16 + 1 meeting between Foreign Minister Primakov and his NATO counterparts, held in Berlin in early June 1996, the Alliance made its first significant concession by granting Russia a further three years in meeting the CFE flank limits.

Throughout the negotiations, NATO officials appeared willing to concede some ground to the Russians, but never at the expense of the Alliance's freedom. More often than not, accommodations were symbolic and non-binding. As Talbott recalls, during spring 1996 "Primakov began dropping hints about three conditions that, if accepted by NATO, might make enlargement palatable to Russia: a prohibition against stationing nuclear weaponry on the territory of new member-states; a requirement for 'co-decision-making' between Russia and NATO on any issue of European security; and codification of these and other restrictions on NATO and rights for Russia in a legally binding treaty."[85] But the Founding Act fulfilled none of these conditions (except perhaps the first one, which the Alliance conceded in a unilateral declaration). Given hysteresis effects, NATO officials considered these demands "out of place"; for the Russians they were simply the logical consequence of their country's status. In the mid-1990s the Alliance still enjoyed enough authority over Russia to discipline its expectations and grant it seeming concessions that in fact only reinforced domination. This is especially clear when one examines the fate of Primakov's three demands in the negotiating process of the Founding Act.

---

[85] Talbott (2002, 218).

First, as regards nuclear weaponry, one of the key accommodations granted to Russia was a NATO declaration made at the opening of a 16 + 1 Defense Ministers meeting in December 1996. On that occasion, US Secretary of Defense Christopher declared that "in today's Europe, NATO has no intention, no plan, and no need to station nuclear weapons on the territory of any new members, and we are affirming that no NATO nuclear forces are presently on alert."[86] This political commitment obviously had no legal force. In addition to its non-binding character, the Alliance's declaration was seriously restricted by its contextual clause ("in today's Europe"). The implicit restriction here is that any change in current circumstances would license NATO to renege on its pledge if needed. The move was all the more dubious for the Russians since they had had their fingers burnt after Gorbachev had similarly been promised in 1990 that NATO would not enlarge to the east. This time, the Russians wanted more than verbal promises and good intentions; yet that was all the Alliance was ready to offer.

The Alliance dealt with Primakov's second request (co-decisionmaking) in a similar way. During a tour of Europe's main capitals, including Moscow, in February 1997, Secretary of State Madeleine Albright finally agreed to the creation of a consultative council with Russia. She made clear from the outset, however, that this mechanism would provide Moscow with a voice, not a veto. Recall that throughout the post-Cold War era, NATO's worst fear in dealing with the Russians had always been a weakening of the transatlantic consensus. Created by the Founding Act, the PJC was to provide for consultation and, "where appropriate," for joint decisions. In practice, however, the PJC allowed any member at the table to withdraw any topic from discussion. Consequently, even NATO's pledge to consult with Russia was seriously blunted by restrictive clauses. This limit was highlighted less than two years later, when the PJC proved incapable of hosting effective negotiations between NATO and Russia in the run-up to the Kosovo crisis.

Primakov's third demand – that the content of the NATO–Russia agreement be codified in a legally binding treaty – proved to be the toughest one. For reasons already mentioned, the Russians were not willing to rely only upon the Alliance's political guarantees. In Yeltsin's opinion: "A document on the parameters of NATO–Russia

---

[86] Quoted in Goldgeier and McFaul (2003, 203).

relations must be binding. We intend to submit it for ratification, since we cannot, in view of past experience, be content with nonbinding assurances."[87] NATO diplomats proved unmoved, however: time was on their side after Russia had been put on notice, in December 1996, that the enlargement would proceed, with or without a prior agreement with Moscow. By mid-March, Russia had dropped several of its key demands in light of NATO's inflexibility, including political membership for new members and the legally binding nature of the agreement. In exchange, NATO offered a fourth "no," to the effect that "NATO had no intention, plan or need to introduce substantial forces onto the territory of the new members."[88] As with earlier commitments, the Alliance limited its application to "the current and foreseeable security environment." Again, the pledge would be valid only so long as member states wanted it to be. In the colorful words of Migranyan: "The West made a firm commitment to just one thing: not to make, on any question, any commitments that in the future might tie its hands in relations with Russia."[89]

During NATO Secretary-General Javier Solana's next visit to Moscow, in mid-April, Primakov insisted on his demand that NATO should not expand infrastructure, including lines of communication, airfields, military bases and stockpiles of weapons, onto new members' territories. With US Secretary of State Madeleine Albright in the Russian capital, Primakov proposed placing limits on the number of tanks, armored personnel carriers, and artillery that an expanded NATO would be allowed to possess. The proposal was once again turned down by Alliance officials, who also rejected Russia's demand for a ban on force deployment on new member states' territories and of limitations on military infrastructure. Two more rounds of negotiations in Luxembourg and Moscow did not bear fruit and Russia withdrew its demands when told by NATO that there would be no more concessions.[90]

The negotiation of the Founding Act illustrates hysteresis effects in international relations particularly well. From the Alliance point

---

[87] Quoted in *Rossiiskaya Gazeta* (1997).
[88] Quoted in Goldgeier and McFaul (2003, 205).   [89] Migranyan (1997).
[90] It is worth noting that this unresolved issue of armament ceilings for new members still haunts Russian–Atlantic relations, and it helps explain Moscow's moratorium on the implementation of the treaty on Conventional Forces in Europe (CFE); see Chapter 6.

of view, Russia was attempting to punch well above its weight with its extensive and legally binding demands. Moscow was in no position to dictate any provision and should have been happy that NATO opened a diplomatic negotiation with it in the first place. The Atlantic compromises granted to the Russians were mostly symbolic in nature and they did not restrict the Alliance's freedom whatsoever. From the Russian perspective, as a Great Power what mattered most was to be treated as NATO's equal. This imperative at times appeared even more important than obtaining genuine concessions from Brussels. Particularly striking is the emphasis that Russian elites consistently put on the need to save face. For instance, Primakov regularly had to defend himself against accusations of watering down Russia's position in the hope of achieving an agreement with NATO. More than anything else, for Moscow the Founding Act was meant to get Russia's Great Power status publicly recognized.

In addition, Russia's practices illustrate quite well positional agency in international diplomacy. Where you sit is what you do: given that post-communist Russia had very little cultural-symbolic capital – the resources that had become the prime currency in the internal mode of pursuing security – it was structurally inclined to resort to the means at hand, which were mostly military. In the new rules imposed by NATO, however, military capital had been considerably devalued and even deemed *passé*. As a junior player in terms of democracy and human rights, Moscow could only have a losing hand in this security-from-the-inside-out game. However, despite all its problems in the 1990s, given its thousands of nuclear weapons the Russian army retained a strength superior to almost any non-Western country in the world. It was thus the country's position in the field (low cultural-symbolic capital, fairly high military resources), in addition to resurging Great Power dispositions, that drove Russia's response to the double enlargement, which often appeared ill-adapted from the standpoint of the dominant players. By the new doxa, reliance on outmoded and even illegitimate military resources in the international security field was deemed awkward if not altogether disingenuous by the Alliance. As a result, Russia's positional agency appeared all the more hysteretic to those players whose habitus and resources were better aligned with the field's structure.

The Founding Act negotiations gave birth to a number of quixotic practices on Russia's part. Because of hysteresis, the Russians had to publicly prove their status and avoid as much as possible backing down in front of NATO. The Russian stance was all the more difficult because diplomatic interactions were taking place against the background of the Alliance's enlargement. Even before the negotiations formally opened in December 1996, the Russian government had listed five countermeasures that it was prepared to implement should enlargement proceed: (1) the revision of military doctrine; (2) the creation of a defensive alliance, within and beyond the CIS framework; (3) a significant build-up of the southern, western and northwestern groups of force, the CFE treaty notwithstanding; (4) a build-up of new tactical nuclear weapons to be retargeted against new NATO members; (5) the withdrawal from START I and II.[91] There was an obvious tension – very much characteristic of hysteresis – between this tough approach (and its heavy reliance on military resources) and the negotiations that were taking place on the ground, where Russia was playing with a losing hand. Overall, Russia undertook four main sets of quixotic practices that were doomed to fail given the field's structure: counterproposals, hindrance, soft balancing and veiled threats.

Throughout the negotiation process, the Russians made a number of counterproposals so as to keep the initiative and obtain concessions from NATO. For example, in March 1996 Primakov proposed to Poland that NATO give it security guarantees that would stop short of full-fledged membership. In April, the Kremlin suggested the establishment of a Baltic–Black Sea Nuclear-Free Zone, to be codified legally and comprised of the Baltic states, the Visegrad Four, Belarus, Ukraine, Moldova, Romania and Bulgaria. Shortly thereafter, Yeltsin put forward a "French scenario" providing for the admission of new members to the bloc's political structures only without their joining military structures. Primakov even visited Norway and Denmark to demonstrate how some established NATO member states had never allowed bases or troop deployments on their territories. In July 1996, Yeltsin wrote a letter to Clinton consenting to NATO enlargement to Poland on the condition that Baltic states would be excluded from any future enlargement. Several months later, in his summit with Clinton in Helsinki, the Russian president tried that line again as part of a gentleman's agreement. Ultimately, NATO and its member states did not seriously consider any of these Russian counterproposals.

[91] Rodionov (1996).

The second strategy that Russia followed was one of hindrance, at times bordering on obstruction. Under Kozyrev, Moscow had often sought NATO's cooperation by underlining how Russia's political and economic weakness could become a potential threat. In the mid-1990s, the Russians went further and took measures intended to hinder certain Allied member states' initiatives. In January 1996, for instance, the Duma delayed ratification of the Strategic Arms Reduction Treaty (START) II, invoking the problem of NATO expansion. In September 1996, at the very last minute, Russia refused to participate in PfP Black Sea exercises with Bulgaria, Romania and Turkey. In October 1996, the Duma adopted one of several resolutions against NATO expansion, warning that an enlarged NATO would undermine the validity of the CFE treaty. Again in February 1997, the Duma refused to ratify START II because of enlargement. Even after Yeltsin had confirmed that he would sign the Founding Act at the Paris summit in May, the Duma passed two resolutions strongly condemning NATO's planned expansion.

In this connection, the new National Security Concept adopted in early May 1997 registered a fundamental change of tone in Russian foreign policy doctrine toward NATO. In the 1993 Foreign Policy Concept, Russia had been faced with only internal threats, from separatism to drug trafficking. The document downplayed military factors and assumed "the end of the East–West confrontation."[92] Where NATO was mentioned, it was only in the positive context of setting objectives for cooperation. By 1997, Russia's official security doctrines incorporated two new long-term threats absent from previous documents: interference in internal Russian affairs (a reference to Western criticism of the Chechnya intervention, certainly, but also to NATO's functional enlargement); and expansion of military blocs and alliances. In fact, the 1997 document stated that "the NATO expansion to the east and its becoming a dominant military and political force in Europe [is] extremely dangerous."[93] Significantly, the first four threats to Russian security listed in the Concept were all directly related to NATO's practices with regard to the double enlargement: the marginalization of the UN and the OSCE, the weakening of Russia's influence in the world, the strengthening of military blocs, and the appearance of military bases on Russia's borders.

---

[92] Quoted in Kassianova (2001, 830).   [93] Quoted in Kassianova (2001, 832).

Third, Russia also took a number of foreign policy initiatives akin to what realists call "soft balancing" – limited and indirect balancing strategies of coalition-building and diplomatic bargaining within international institutions, short of formal alliances.[94] In April 1996, during a Sino-Russian summit in Beijing, the parties adopted a declaration premised on the notion of strategic partnership. A year later, Moscow and Beijing adopted a Joint Russian–Chinese Declaration about a Multipolar World and the Formation of a New World Order. Interestingly, the text emphasized sovereignty and non-intervention as the key principles of international relations, while dismissing universal standards of human rights. That was the first time Moscow openly contested the NATO rules of the international security game – a trend that accentuated sharply in the wake of the Kosovo crisis. In addition to China, Russia also joined with Belarus to contest the Alliance's practices. In March 1997, the two countries declared themselves united in their unwillingness to accept NATO's plans to advance eastward, and even took steps to plan joint military exercises. In yet another display of hysteresis, NATO officials immediately dismissed these maneuvers as not credible – once again Russia was tilting at windmills.

Fourth and finally, Russian officials also issued a handful of veiled threats that were, in hindsight, nothing but trial balloons – typical behavior from agents trying to punch above their weight. For example, in February 1996 an unidentified official from the Ministry of Atomic Energy was quoted as saying that Russia could target nuclear weapons against NATO military bases set up on the territory of East European countries. In a similar bullying tactic, Primakov threatened to cut off all relations with NATO if any country from the former Soviet Union was invited to join. Again, at the time none of this could have deterred NATO from proceeding with enlargement as planned because Moscow's moves appeared simply out of place. What must be emphasized, however, is that Russia's newly found assertiveness – at the time in words if not in deeds – was strong testimony to the resurgence of the Great Power habitus and the resulting decline in the Alliance's domination of the international security field. This new dynamic, however, was fully displayed only a few years later in the wake of the Kosovo crisis.

---

[94] Paul (2005).

In the meantime, in Paris in late May 1997, NATO member states and Russia gathered with much pomp to sign the Founding Act on Mutual Relations, Cooperation and Security between NATO and the Russian Federation. By the agreement, the parties solemnly pledged to "build together a lasting and inclusive peace in the Euro-Atlantic area on the principles of democracy and cooperative security. NATO and Russia do not consider each other as adversaries. They share the goal of overcoming the vestiges of earlier confrontation and competition and of strengthening mutual trust and cooperation."[95] Despite the symbolic talk and ceremony, however, hints of hysteresis could be gleaned during the summit. In his declaration, Yeltsin emphatically insisted on the need to act as equals at the PJC just created. On their part, NATO leaders took great pains to show how much of a gain the agreement was for Russia, with Clinton stressing his determination "to create a future in which European security is not a zero-sum game – where NATO's gain is Russia's loss, and Russia's strength is our alliance's weakness. That is old thinking."[96] The performative social magic that allowed this celebration to happen quickly ceased to operate, however, when Kosovo took center stage in Russian-Atlantic relations, a topic to which I turn in the next chapter.

Conclusion: a stillborn security community?

The limited development of a Russian–Atlantic security community owes much to the critical juncture of late 1994, when NATO launched its double enlargement policy. Given the dire effects that this turn of events had on the development of diplomatic doxa, the probability that a genuine pacification process could ensue, in and through practice, was seriously undermined. Starting in the mid-1990s, Russian elites stopped being well disposed toward the NATO order of international security. With the resurgence of the Great Power habitus in Moscow, the domination pattern that is necessary to turn diplomacy into a doxic practice started to crumble. To be sure, disputes continued to be solved peacefully; but in the longer run, even "successful" diplomacy contributed to weakening the homology between Russian dispositions and the country's position in the new field of international security. Field analysis, which looks not only at what players say and do, but

---

[95] NATO (1997).   [96] Quoted in *New York Times* (1997).

also at the structural location from which they do so, suggests that with its very limited resources, Russia was in no position to play the Great Power game in NATO's eyes. Likewise, NATO's practices of double enlargement, largely the result of the organization's unchecked domination of the field of international security, were bound to arouse the Russian habitus. Self-evident diplomacy gave way to strong hysteresis effects, with two masters but no apprentice in the relationship.

In using the language of critical juncture, I want to emphasize the path-dependent nature of social and political relations, whose future depends on their past because history develops like a branching tree. Because of positive, reinforcing feedback loops, early steps tend to lock into a certain trajectory and eliminate alternatives that were originally open. Arguably, the end of the Cold War was one of those rare historical instances when the world found itself at an intersection where several paths were available. As Kissinger writes: "When an international order first comes into being, many choices may be open to it. But each choice constricts the universe of remaining options. Because complexity inhibits flexibility, early choices are especially crucial."[97]

The evidence presented in this chapter suggests that, for a short time between 1992 and 1994, everything took place as if Russia was going to integrate into the new NATO world order. At that point, "[t]he ideas of Russian messianism and the pursuit of an independent role in line with its Great Power heritage were either understated or even denied."[98] Many paths were therefore possible, including the one toward a security community. Things abruptly changed in 1994 when NATO took two initiatives that set its relations with Russia on the bumpy track that continues to this day. For the Russians, the double enlargement amounted to NATO reneging, in practice, on its own discourse of inclusive, mutual and cooperative security. Because the move was reminiscent more of realpolitik than of the professed internal mode of pursuing security, Russian Great Power dispositions gradually resurfaced. With rising hysteresis and symbolic power struggles, the policy amounted to signing the nascent security community's death warrant.

Using a Bourdieu-inspired theoretical framework gives an important edge in matters of critical junctures and early steps because it supplies

---

[97] Kissinger (1994, 26–7).   [98] Ponsard (2007, 62).

not only a structural mechanism for path dependence (the field) but also an agent-level process: as a historical distillate of embodied dispositions, habitus explains self-reinforcing practices. The historical constitution of habitus, in effect, is characterized by a "relative irreversibility": "all the external stimuli and conditioning experiences are, at every moment, perceived through categories already constructed by prior experiences. From that follows an inevitable priority of originary experiences and consequently a *relative* closure of the system of dispositions that constitute habitus."[99] The practical sense, as a result, builds on past experiences to feel what is to be done. The dispositions comprised in the habitus, constituted by subjective and intersubjective past experiences, in part constitute future practices. As a result, the path taken at certain historical junctures may make other paths more or less likely in the future. Such has been the case in post-Cold War Russian–Atlantic relations: partly because of the resiliency of Russia's Great Power habitus, which was reactivated by NATO's double enlargement, today's symbolic power politics are in great measure the fallout from the early steps of 1992–7.

[99] Bourdieu and Wacquant (1992, 133).

6 | *The fallout: NATO and Russia from Kosovo to Georgia, 1998–2008*

Hysteresis and symbolic power struggles continued to plague NATO–Russia diplomacy well into the twenty-first century. Pursuing the historical analysis of practices, in this chapter I focus on the period stretching from NATO's intervention in Kosovo to the war between Russia and Georgia. During this decade, the Alliance continued its double enlargement policy by conducting a range of new military operations outside the Euro-Atlantic zone and admitting ten new member states. Because my objective is to trace the roots of the practical sense of diplomats at the NRC as I recorded it in 2006 (see Chapter 4), I mainly concentrate on the period up until that year. In the final section of the chapter, I briefly extend my narrative to more recent NATO–Russia diplomacy and show that it basically followed the same pattern of increasing symbolic power struggles that began back in late 1994.

Despite the fact that Russia and NATO member states successfully dealt with their fierce disagreements over the double enlargement in a non-violent manner, hysteresis was compounded between 1998 and 2008 as the disconnect between positions and dispositions increased consistently. After the Kosovo crisis, Great Power dispositions grew stronger among the Moscow foreign policy elites, even though the country's position remained weak by NATO standards. Then, in the wake of September 11, 2001, the rules of the international security game partly shifted back to "hard security," an evolution that temporarily played to Russia's advantage. For a short while, its dispositions were better aligned with its enhanced position, prompting a short-lived improvement in the relationship with NATO. But when a new wave of double enlargement shattered this fragile alignment in the ensuing year, the road was once again open for the intense symbolic power politics that still prevails today. It is in this light, I conclude, that we should understand the Georgia War of summer 2008: as they powerlessly witnessed Russia's ruthless actions in South Ossetia, Alliance members reaped what they had sown. Moscow's defiant assertiveness and its new deafness to Western criticism are testimony to the fact that one generation after the end of the Cold War, the NATO–Russia relationship is plagued with so much hysteresis that security community development now seems remote.

Hitting rock bottom: the Kosovo crisis

During the Kosovo crisis, hysteresis effects reached unprecedented levels in Russian–Atlantic post-Cold War relations. For Alliance officials, there was simply no question of letting Russia distract the Alliance from its new collective security tasks. If Moscow did not like NATO's actions, it simply had to learn to live with them. On the Russian side, resurging Great Power dispositions came to drive foreign policy practices more than at any time since the end of the Cold War. It is worth recalling that NATO's double enlargement culminated with the Kosovo crisis. In geographical terms, the Alliance formally admitted three new members – Poland, Hungary and the Czech Republic – in the middle of its bombing campaign on Serbia. At the functional level, Operation Allied Force constituted the first attempt by NATO to exert its new collective security mandate despite external and internal opposition. Furthermore, during the Washington summit of March 1999, the Alliance adopted a new Strategic Concept formally enshrining its out-of-area missions. The Kosovo crisis thus lies at the confluence of the key tensions in post-Cold War Russian–Atlantic dealings.

Russian–Atlantic diplomacy during the Kosovo crisis was one of brinkmanship. On top of particularly acrimonious language and an official cutoff of NATO–Russia relations, the events also led up to the only moment when there was the possibility of a violent confrontation: the seizure of Pristina airport by Russian paratroopers in a dash to beat NATO peacekeepers to the Kosovo border. In terms of domination patterns, this suggests that hysteresis effects gained strength in 1999 compared to the mid-1990s. In effect, NATO's practices in and around the Kosovo crisis led the Russians not only to question the doxic rules of the post-Cold War international security game, but also to increasingly reject them outright as Great Power dispositions consolidated in Moscow. In sum, the Kosovo crisis was both constituted by, and constitutive of, fast-growing hysteresis effects in post-Cold War Russian–Atlantic relations.

Worlds apart: NATO–Russia diplomatic brinkmanship over Kosovo

Although Kosovo had been considered a potential hot spot for years, armed clashes between the Kosovo Liberation Army and Serbian forces erupted only in March 1998. On March 31, the UN Security Council voted, with Moscow's support, for Resolution 1160 condemning Serbia's excessive force and imposing an arms embargo on Belgrade. By the end of May, NATO had taken up the question and discussions were held on the possibility of sending peacekeepers to Kosovo. At a PJC session in late May 1998, Russia was confronted with the fait accompli of a NAC position issued on the previous day. Even at that early point, the Russian–Atlantic clash to come was already discernible in Primakov's ensuing press conference statement: "We must not set a precedent in which NATO acts outside the territory of the NATO countries without a decision by the UN Security Council."[1] When, in late June, NATO sent aircraft to Macedonia and organized (despite Moscow's objection) a one-day military exercise on the Kosovo border, Russia recalled its representative to the Alliance. In Moscow, the main Defense Ministry official in charge of cooperation with NATO, General Leonid Ivashov, warned that military intervention without a UN Security Council resolution would amount to "unleashing a new cold war in Europe": "NATO not only is not listening to the views of its partners, it is unwilling to put the resolution of crisis situations in Europe into anyone else's hands."[2] Russia's uneasiness with the Alliance's position of strength was already palpable.

In August 1998, when Moscow agreed to join a NATO exercise in Albania, it insisted that simulated air strikes be removed from the scenario. But the Alliance's plan was made clear when Germany's Defence Minister Volker Rühe called for "early NATO military intervention in Kosovo, even if this means acting against Russia's will."[3] In September, Russian Foreign Minister Igor Ivanov delivered a personal message from President Yeltsin to the White House, threatening that Russia would "not countenance" air strikes – "a phrase that in diplomacy goes beyond disapproval and carries with it at least the option of reprisal."[4] In October, Russia nonetheless joined with

---

[1] Quoted in Gornostayev and Katin (1998).
[2] Quoted in Mukhin (1998).   [3] Quoted in Sysoyev (1998).
[4] Talbott (2002, 300).

NATO members of the UNSC (while China abstained) to call for the international monitoring of an immediate ceasefire and to threaten "to consider further action and additional measures to maintain or restore peace and stability in the region."[5] In an official comment on that vote, the Russian representative to the UN Security Council declared: "there are no provisions in [Resolution 1199] that would directly or indirectly sanction the automatic use of force."[6] A few days later, however, NATO representatives argued during a PJC meeting that the resolution had described the situation in Kosovo as a threat to regional peace and stability, thus opening the way to military action based on Chapter VII of the UN Charter. In a strong rebuff, Foreign Minister Igor Ivanov declared that Moscow would exercise its veto, while Defense Minister Igor Sergeyev warned that a NATO operation in Kosovo would signal the start of a new cold war. Sergeyev also threatened to break relations with NATO and freeze the process of START II ratification. Unshaken, NATO issued a new ultimatum to Belgrade in mid-October, prompting Moscow to recall its ambassador once again. Vladimir Lukin, then chairman of the state Duma's International Affairs Committee, went as far as to float the idea that Russia might offer military support to Yugoslavia in case of an Alliance military operation. With the Alliance systematically dismissing Russia's objections, political discourse in Moscow reached new levels of nervousness.

Looking for ways to regain the initiative, Russian diplomats supported an agreement between Serbia's President Slobodan Milošević and the Contact Group on establishing the OSCE Kosovo Verification Mission. This mission proved a double-edged sword, however, when, in mid-January 1999, the discovery of the Račak massacre confirmed Atlantic suspicions of Belgrade. Nonetheless, Moscow pushed the Contact Group to organize a conference in Rambouillet in mid-February. Given hysteresis, however, diplomatic accommodation appeared out of reach. According to one Russian insider: "all Western attempts to establish within the Contact Group a common understanding of the concrete parameters of the agreement met with a kind of slack resistance on the part of Russia."[7] Given its weak position, obstruction seemed the only way for Moscow to exert some kind of

---

[5] UN Security Council (1998a).   [6] UN Security Council (1998b, 11).
[7] Levitin (2000, 136).

influence on the diplomatic process. Despite Igor Ivanov's last-minute push in Belgrade in mid-March, the Milošević regime finally rejected the Rambouillet agreement. The road was open to NATO bombings, which formally began on March 24.

Upon learning the news while flying over the Atlantic en route to Washington, Prime Minister Primakov ordered his plane to turn back to Moscow. The Russian government immediately recalled its ambassador to NATO, froze all NATO–Russia cooperation under the PfP, discontinued PJC activities, expelled two NATO information officers posted in Moscow, and allegedly retargeted its nuclear weapons toward the NATO members that were taking part in the air strikes. In a televised statement, Yeltsin fumed with anger:

> Russia is deeply outraged by NATO's military action against sovereign Yugoslavia, an action that is nothing short of undisguised aggression ... Not only the UN Charter, but also the Founding Act on Mutual Relations, Cooperation and Security Between Russia and NATO, has been violated. A dangerous precedent for reviving the policy of diktat based on the use of force has been set, and the entire modern-day system of international law and order has been threatened. This essentially amounts to an attempt by NATO to enter the 21st century wearing the uniform of world policeman. Russia will never consent to this.[8]

In a dramatic fashion, Yeltsin added that Russia "has extreme measures it could take but we have decided not to take them." That language was unequivocally the harshest ever used in post-communist Russia with regard to the Alliance.

On March 26, Russia introduced to the UN Security Council, with the support of India and Belarus, a draft resolution calling for an immediate cessation of the use of force against Belgrade. The result of the vote was a complete disaster for Moscow's diplomacy: only three states (Russia, China and Namibia) supported the text, while twelve voted against it. A few days later, Moscow sent a high-profile delegation to Belgrade while also dispatching an intelligence-gathering ship to the Adriatic. In the end, NATO quickly rejected the peace plan that the Russian delegation negotiated with Milošević during the trip. On April 7, the Duma adopted a resolution urging Yeltsin

---

[8] Quoted in *Rossiiskaya Gazeta* (1999).

to supply Belgrade with weapons, followed by another on April 16 approving the political union of Russia, Belarus and Yugoslavia. Other brinkmanship initiatives on Russia's part included a special (Russian) Security Council session to discuss the country's nuclear-technical complex, a review of military doctrine, the planning of the largest military exercises since Soviet times and the reinforcement of the defensive alliance with Minsk, including the establishment of a single defense space.

Unprecedented in the post-Cold War era, these Russian gestures signaled an increasing restlessness as well as the decline of NATO's symbolic domination of Moscow. That said, it is equally significant that Russia did "only" that: despite the escalation of rhetoric and much domestic criticism, the Yeltsin team stopped short of taking any significant military measure during the bombings. Instead, it maintained open its diplomatic channels with Washington and other Western countries. It also made much use of the Contact Group. For instance, on April 7, a senior Foreign Ministry officials' meeting was held in Brussels, and then in Dresden, at the political directors' level, on the next two days. On April 14, Yeltsin named former Prime Minister Viktor Chernomyrdin as his presidential envoy – a clear rebuff to the nationalistic opposition in Moscow as well as to Prime Minister Primakov. Everything was taking place as if conflicting dispositions and positions were simultaneously informing Russian foreign policy, making for an awkward mixture of quixotic rhetoric but restrained actions.

Chernomyrdin immediately began a diplomatic shuttle that significantly contributed to ending the conflict and moving Russia and NATO closer together. In Oslo, Albright had communicated to Igor Ivanov NATO's three non-negotiable conditions to terminate bombings: the end of violence in Kosovo, the withdrawal of Serbian forces and the return of refugees. In preparation for the G8 meeting of Foreign Ministers, Talbott and Chernomyrdin travelled between Moscow and Washington to find common ground. In Bonn, the G8 agreed on seven principles for a political settlement that were to serve as the basis for a future UN Security Council resolution. One stumbling block, however, concerned the composition of the peacekeeping force and whether it would be under NATO or UN leadership. A few days later, the diplomatic process made headway thanks to the Russian suggestion to involve a neutral third party in the negotiations with Belgrade.

The Americans proposed President Martti Ahtisaari from Finland, whom Moscow quickly endorsed. The first trilateral Chernomyrdin–Ahtisaari–Talbott talks were held in Helsinki in mid-May (i.e. a few days after Yeltsin had fired Primakov as Prime Minister). As with the Bonn G8 meeting, the main difficulty was settling NATO's role in the future peacekeeping force. The US would not accept anything but primary command for the Alliance. Flying from Belgrade to Moscow to meet again with Talbott and Ahtisaari, Chernomyrdin finally had no choice but to concede to NATO's demand to be "at the core" of the peacekeeping force. That deal, extracted against the will of many members of the Russian delegation, effectively put off the most problematic aspects of the negotiations. In the meantime, Milošević had come to accept the G8 broad principles and on June 3 the Serbian parliament voted in favor of the Chernomyrdin–Ahtisaari–Talbott agreement.

For all that diplomacy, hysteresis did not wane or disappear. When the G8 Foreign Ministers gathered in early June, Igor Ivanov complained that the draft UN Security Council resolution gave center-stage to NATO. His reaction was to submit some twenty objections to a text that was only thirty-three paragraphs long. After two days of intense negotiations, Moscow finally caved in to most of the NATO demands, including a Chapter VII mandate authorizing the use of force by peacekeepers. These negotiations paved the way for Resolution 1244, which the UN Security Council voted for on June 10, with China abstaining but Moscow approving. At the operational level, however, a wide rift still separated NATO's military command from Russia's. As one Talbott aide recalls: "The Russians repeatedly objected to the notion that their forces would have to serve under NATO command and pushed for their own peacekeeping sector, 'just as is proposed for the big NATO powers.'"[9] The Americans, for their part, favored the Bosnian model by which Russian contingents operated under indirect Allied command – basically a technical arrangement that in reality kept the Russians under a tight leash. This disagreement quickly took on a symbolic dimension, with the Alliance unwilling to budge and the Russians deciding to have their own way this time. As Talbott recounts: "Ivashov reacted to that attempt to save Russian face the same way he had

[9] Norris (2005, 144).

in the Petersberg talks: It was insulting and unacceptable. Russia would not 'take orders' from NATO; it would not settle for anything less than its own sector and certainly would not 'beg for scraps from NATO's table.'"[10] For Atlantic officials, such demands were simply out of place.

The following day would see the ultimate demonstration of hysteresis in Russian–Atlantic relations – as well as the most dangerous episode in the post-Cold War era. In a stunning move, a Russian contingent of 175 SFOR peacekeepers secretly rushed through Serbia during the night of June 11 en route to Pristina airport in Kosovo. At the same time, about 800 Russian paratroopers were scheduled to land there. In so doing, the Russians were able to beat NATO forces into Kosovo. At the time, conflicting accounts emerged from Moscow, with Foreign Minister Igor Ivanov assuring NATO that the deployment was a mistake and would be reversed. But reports from the theatre said otherwise. During the night, NATO SACEUR General Wesley Clark asked and received permission from the Pentagon to explore possible military responses to the Russian move. When he ordered British General Michael Jackson, who was commanding the KFOR's planned deployment, to prepare to seize the airport, a serious row erupted between the two generals. With the support of the British Defence Ministry, Jackson refused to execute the order of the Alliance's supreme commander. Meanwhile, the Americans applied enough political pressure on Hungary, Romania, Bulgaria and Ukraine to ensure that they would not clear overflight requests to Moscow (six IL-76 transport planes with 100 troops and equipment each were scheduled to land in Kosovo by way of Eastern Europe). As a result, within a few days the Russian contingent was left without a supply line of food and water and had to be resupplied by NATO forces.

It later became known that Operation Trojan Horse, as the Russians codenamed the dash to Pristina, had been planned in the utmost secrecy by the Russian military with Yeltsin's approval. Ruffled by NATO's intransigence throughout the crisis, the Russian Great Power habitus made any further capitulation unthinkable. Amidst flurries of celebration throughout Russia, Duma member Lukin commented on the Pristina stunt: "The action is also valuable from the standpoint

---

[10] Talbott (2002, 333).

that the West has finally started to realize that it can't treat Russia like some lackey. We're partners, not lackeys."[11] Recall that the Pristina move happened simultaneously with the extremely tense negotiations on KFOR between Talbott and his team of American generals and Sergeyev, Ivashov and Chief of General Staff Anatoly Kvashnin. Under these circumstances, the operation was meant to create a fait accompli on the ground and offer better leverage to Moscow in its negotiation with the Alliance. The Russians were pleading for "equal rights" in the operation like those enjoyed by NATO members, and for a veto over military operations. In a pattern that continues to this day, Russian diplomats stubbornly refused to concede any more to a NATO that would not consider granting Moscow any decision-making capability. As a result of a very weak position and a habitus attuned to the external mode of pursuing security, the Russians used the only resources they had left – the military.

However, with the G8 summit upcoming in Cologne and the need to get the associated cultural-symbolic recognition, the Russians needed to reach an agreement with the Alliance. Although NATO's domination of Moscow may have been declining, it had certainly not disappeared by 1999. Russia's desire for Western recognition was still strong, particularly on the part of the country's president. In a phone call to Clinton, Yeltsin finally agreed that Russian troops would serve under the Bosnia model in Kosovo (with minor modifications). During a meeting between William Cohen (US Secretary of Defense), Madeleine Albright, Igor Sergeyev and Igor Ivanov in Helsinki a few days later, an agreement was reached to the effect that Russian troops would be scattered across four sectors and would share control of Pristina airport with NATO. Once again, despite weeks of unprecedented outcry, diplomatic brinkmanship and dangerous military moves, Moscow eventually had to largely cave in to NATO and accept a formula that gave it, in one insider's words, "only a paper-thin guise of military independence."[12] All was now in place for Yeltsin joining the G8 summit in Cologne in a celebration intended to symbolically demonstrate the importance of Russia in the world. Days after ordering a military stunt that could have degenerated into full-scale confrontation, Yeltsin hugged his "friends" from NATO more vigorously than ever.

---

[11] Quoted in Charodeyev (1999).   [12] Norris (2005, 290).

Tilting at windmills: the causes and consequences of hysteresis

Although the Kosovo crisis was solved peacefully, it also led to unprecedented brinkmanship and came close to provoking a military standoff at Pristina airport. In 1999 the Russian–Atlantic post-Cold War track record of non-violent settlement of disputes came close to an end, largely as a result of hysteresis and the quixotic practices that it sparked. In this section I explain how and why the Kosovo crisis further accentuated the mismatch between positions and dispositions in NATO–Russia diplomacy. By compounding hysteresis effects and weakening domination patterns in the relationship, the Kosovo episode also made security community development very unlikely. In its aftermath, Russia progressively turned into an insubordinate player in the international game defined by NATO-imposed rules.

Hysteresis grew because NATO's intervention in Kosovo catalyzed the resurgence of the Russian Great Power habitus while bringing no significant change to the field's structure. In his in-depth study of Russian identity in 1999, Hopf shows how the Kosovo crisis altered the balance between competing identity narratives in Moscow. Basically, the Westernizing discourse was discredited once and for all, giving way to a "liberal essentialist" discourse that remains the predominant Russian identity today. According to Hopf, this identity does not rest on any external others (such as the West or China, for instance) because its basic premise is that Russia is "unique and hence not comparable, or opposable, to any other state."[13] The Great Power habitus is at the forefront of this narrative. Viatcheslav Morozov similarly argues that the key factor in the rise of "romantic realism" in Moscow is "the interpretation of NATO's Kosovo campaign as a cynical geopolitical enterprise, the real aims of which had nothing in common with the proclaimed wish to protect the Albanian minority."[14] After Kosovo, the Alliance's campaign to show its peacefulness fell on deaf ears in Moscow. With the consolidation of Great Power dispositions, Russian officials became increasingly recalcitrant toward the Alliance-imposed rules of the international security game.

Despite all talk to the contrary, NATO's practices during the Kosovo crisis, apprehended from Moscow, appeared closer to realpolitik than

---

[13] Hopf (2002, 218).   [14] Morozov (2002, 411).

to the internal mode of pursuing security. As Gorbachev wrote: "the war provided evidence that the United States, which plays a commanding role in NATO, is willing not only to disregard the norms of international law but also to impose on the world its own agenda in international relations and, in fact, to be guided in these relations solely by its own 'national interests.'"[15] Consequently, Russian officials and experts concluded that NATO's discourse of democracy and human rights was in fact a convenient facade for cold-blooded, self-interested realpolitik. In this spirit, the air campaign was construed as a deliberate attempt to consolidate the Alliance's position at the very top of the hierarchy of the international security field. But the Alliance's authority over Russia, which had been so strong in the immediate aftermath of the Cold War, had almost vanished by 1999 – even in the eyes of traditionally pro-Western experts. As Tsygankov aptly concludes: "The irony of the Western intervention in Yugoslavia is that by trying to solidify the influence of the West in the world, it in fact undermined their influence."[16] Operation Allied Force permanently marginalized liberal elites in Moscow and their dispositions in favor of the internal mode of pursuing security. As Baranovsky explains, it basically reversed the burden of proof: "if the thesis of Russia's opponents to NATO about its 'aggressive character' had looked either like pure propaganda or something inherited from the cold war, the war against Yugoslavia became an impressive manifestation of its validity."[17] Starting in 1994, the double enlargement had sparked fears and aroused doubts in Moscow, gradually tipping the balance in favor of the Great Power habitus. The Kosovo intervention made any return to the obedient dispositions of the early post-Cold War years impossible. This time, virtually the entire Russian foreign policy elite reverted to the Great Power narrative, a dispositional evolution that lasts to this day.

On their side, however, NATO practitioners continued to expect Moscow to behave more or less in tune with Atlantic policies. Throughout the Kosovo crisis, Alliance officials construed the NATO stance as self-evident or naturally legitimate, prompting expectations that the Russians would "come to understand." In the words of a State Department official: "I feel that we overestimated Russia's strategic

---

[15] Gorbachev (1999).   [16] Tsygankov (2001, 142).
[17] Baranovsky (2003, 279).

competence. It was like playing chess with somebody who doesn't know the rules."[18] From the Alliance point of view, it was quite obvious that Russia's behavior during the conflict was out of place – so much so, in fact, that it was not even worthy of full consideration. As Deputy National Security Adviser James Steinberg put it, speaking of Kosovo: "The whole security of Europe would be thrown into question if Russia's sense of its interest precluded the international community addressing this serious question."[19] Since the Alliance embodied the international community in the post-Cold War field of international security – by occupying the hegemonic position of a dominant player able to impose the rules of the game – it "naturally" promoted the only vision that made sense. The Russians had to abide by it just like any other state.

For the Russians, however, NATO's actions in Kosovo exposed the legal fiction of the Founding Act agreed on two years earlier. In 1997, Alliance member states and Russia had pledged to "[refrain] from the threat or use of force against each other as well as against any other state, its sovereignty, territorial integrity or political independence in any manner inconsistent with the United Nations Charter." Parties had also declared: "If disagreements arise, NATO and Russia will endeavour to settle them on the basis of goodwill and mutual respect within the framework of political consultations." On both accounts, there was the feeling in Moscow that NATO practices had been duplicitous. In fact, the Kosovo crisis substantiated everything the Russians had feared about the doubly enlarged Alliance. It certainly showed up in a very stark light Moscow's powerlessness compared to the Alliance in the field of international security. As pundit Aleksei Pushkov put it: "What we see is a kind of standard arrangement for dealing with situations in which we disagree with the US and its NATO allies. First they admonish us, then they pretend they're going to compromise, making some pathetically symbolic concessions to us, and then they simply stop paying attention to us."[20] On the NATO side, many officials had counted precisely on Russia's weakness and impotence to contain and manage a possible backlash over Kosovo. For the Russians, however, this heavy-handed strategy was ignoring and in fact subverting Russia's claims to Great Power status.

---

[18] Quoted in Norris (2005, 308).
[19] Quoted in Goldgeier and McFaul (2003, 251).   [20] Pushkov (1999).

Because it was performed without a clear UN mandate, the NATO intervention in Kosovo also sparked fears in Moscow that Russia or its neighbors could be the next target. With violence gaining strength in Chechnya, many Russians speculated that the campaign against Serbia could soon be waged against their own country. The newly appointed Prime Minister Vladimir Putin commented in 1999: "I was convinced that if we didn't stop the extremists right away, we'd be facing a second Yugoslavia on the entire territory of the Russian Federation – the Yugoslavization of Russia."[21] As a result, new security dilemmas concerning an Atlantic intervention in or around Russia arose. Several practices, premised on positional agency and the availability of military capital, attest to the new fears sparked in Moscow. Most striking is the revived interest in nuclear deterrence. During a (Russian) Security Council meeting on April 27, 1999, Yeltsin agreed to accelerate a number of nuclear programs, including the development of tactical Iskander missiles up to an arsenal of 10,000, and the deployment of a new generation of strategic arms (SS-27). Emphasizing the need for an asymmetrical response to NATO's build-up, an October 1999 draft of Russia's military doctrine explicitly raised the possible use of nuclear weapons to deal with the potential threat of direct military aggression against Russia. In the official security doctrines that were adopted by Russia after the Kosovo crisis, three new threat perceptions surfaced that had never been mentioned in previous documents: attempts to ignore or infringe Russian interests in resolving international security problems; attempts to oppose the strengthening of Russia as one of the global centers of influence; and the introduction of foreign troops, without UN Security Council sanction, into the territory of contiguous states friendly with Russia. The new documents also listed destabilizing factors that were all connected to NATO's intervention in Kosovo: the dominance in the international community of developed Western states led by the US; the applying of military force as a means of humanitarian intervention without UN Security Council sanction; and unilateral actions. The Russian army put this new approach into practice shortly thereafter, in late June 1999, with military exercises codenamed Zapad-99 (*zapad* means West) – the largest ever organized since the breakup of the USSR. The scenario envisioned an aerial attack "from the West" on the

---

[21] Quoted in Evangelista (2002, 2).

Kaliningrad exclave to which Russian and Belarusian forces reacted with strikes on Poland, the Baltic states, Norway and Turkey. A land invasion of the Baltic states was also simulated, as well as a series of preventive nuclear strikes to deter the aggressor. Other smaller-scale but similar exercises were organized during the summer in the Baltic, Barents and North Pacific areas. These military rehearsals were a tangible demonstration of new security dilemmas in Moscow.

In confirming, and in fact worsening, Moscow's fears that its interests could not be accommodated in the NATO-dominated field of international security, the Kosovo crisis had one key effect that lasts to this day: it helped turn Russia into an insubordinate player of the post-Cold War rules of the game. In Chapter 5, I argued that Moscow had been a strong supporter of the internal mode of pursuing security in the immediate aftermath of the Cold War. This support decreased from 1994; by 1999 it had evaporated altogether. The Kosovo crisis confronted the Russians with the emergence of a "NATO-centric world" in which their country played only a minor role. In addition to being marginalized, Russia was also concerned about the attack on the sovereignty principle as embodied in the UN Charter. Viewed from Moscow, the Kosovo intervention endangered the international order built after the Second World War in which, contrary to the internal mode of pursuing security, the country had occupied a dominant position. In a striking rebuttal of the Kozyrev doctrine, the Russian elite began to argue in favor of non-intervention and sovereignty as the core institutions of an international security system based on the UN Security Council. In a speech given just after the Kosovo bombings had begun, Igor Ivanov expressed the notion that Russia had to actively defend the world against the hypocrisy of the internal mode of pursuing security: "while defending today Yugoslavia's right to sovereignty, we are also defending the future of the world and of Europe against the most recent form of colonialism – the so-called natocolonialism."[22] As a Great Power, Russia harked back to sovereignty, territorial integrity, and non-intervention as the key rules of the international security game.

Against this view was the new NATO Strategic Concept adopted at the Washington summit, which contained a number of revolutionary provisions in line with the internal mode of pursuing security,

[22] Quoted in Morozov (2002, 412).

including an emphasis on democracy, human rights and the rule of law; the characterization of Euro-Atlantic security as based on democratic institutions; a broad approach to security; and a call for wide-ranging partnerships. Even more shockingly for the Russians, the Concept opened the door to out-of-area missions. No geographical limits were placed on NATO's competence, and further waves of enlargement were called for. From the Kosovo crisis on, what the Alliance saw as a legitimate ground for intervention Moscow officials construed "as a flagrant violation of international law, as a heavy blow against the existing UN-based international system, as an attempt to establish a 'new world order' by force, allowing arbitrary interference in the internal affairs of states (on 'humanitarian' or any other grounds)."[23] In sum, for the Russians the Kosovo episode plainly exposed the extent to which NATO had come to dominate Russia and ignore its views in the post-Cold War era, especially by preaching the universal virtues of the internal mode of pursuing security in a self-interested manner. Until the end of 1999, the presence of Yeltsin at the helm seemed to partly hold in check Great Power dispositions and the related rejection of the NATO-imposed order. The turn of the century, however, brought with it a new political context for Russian–Atlantic relations.

Welcome to the twenty-first century: September 11, 2001 and its aftermath

The terrorist attack of September 11, 2001 caused a doxic change in the field of international security that also affected NATO–Russia relations. The events were socially and politically constructed in such a way that the internal and external modes of pursuing security were brought together: democratic peace remained key, but the use of force was deemed a legitimate means to achieve that end. This change in the rules of the game temporarily played to the advantage of Russia, whose status was upgraded by the creation of the NRC in 2002. The honeymoon was short-lived, however. From 2002 to 2006, the Alliance admitted seven new member states while simultaneously expanding its functional scope to the global scale. In a

---

[23] Baranovsky (2000, 454–5).

replay of the 1990s, NATO's double enlargement practices sparked further hysteresis effects in the relationship. All in all, but for the doxic shifts incurred by September 11, 2001, the political fabric of Russian–Atlantic relations remained much the same after the turn of the millennium.

NATO–Russia honeymoon, take two

The terrorist attacks that took place on September 11, 2001 led to a significant if temporary improvement in NATO–Russia relations, largely because dominant players interpreted the events in a way that transformed the rules of the international security game. As the agenda shifted toward "hard" security, the relative value of force increased as a means to reach "soft" ends. Most prominently, the American "war on terrorism" led to the revaluation of the military instrument. As a result, the field's doxa partly moved away from the security-from-the-inside-out paradigm. Of course, the democratization agenda remained prominent – witness Iraq. But dominant players in the field of international security imposed a new balance between the internal and the external mode of pursuing security. As Ivo Daalder and James Lindsay argue, the belief that the use of force could help bring about a new world order was at the core of the Bush Doctrine.[24] In this hybrid set of rules, the means of the external mode, especially military force, were privileged to achieve the goals of the internal mode, particularly regime change.

In this new set of rules of the international security game, NATO's role shifted accordingly. On September 12, 2001, the Alliance activated its collective defense clause (Article 5) for the very first time in its history. Since then, NATO has remained an alliance at war: for instance, the only Article 5 mission that was launched after the terrorist attacks, Operation Active Endeavour, was still ongoing eight years later. The Alliance's military operations in Afghanistan also flow directly from the September 11, 2001 attacks and the ensuing American invasion of the country. At the Prague summit in November 2002, NATO adopted a Military Concept for Defense against Terrorism that has become a cornerstone of its planning and strategy

---

[24] Daalder and Lindsay (2005, 12–14).

to defeat the terrorist enemy. While it is true that the Alliance plays only a supportive role in the US-led "war on terrorism," its focus has nonetheless switched significantly in the wake of September 11, 2001.[25] Issues that were central during the 1990s, such as peacekeeping in the Balkans, gave way to a new security agenda centered on terrorism and forceful democratization. This reorientation did not go entirely smoothly, however, as conflicting interpretations of the terrorist attacks emerged on each side of the Atlantic. Many continental European countries did not agree with the militarized response to the terrorist threat put forward by Washington: instead of preemption, deterrence and retribution, they preferred a softer approach based on regulations, legal and judicial means, and cooperation between the police and civil authorities. Despite this disagreement, however, in relative terms European and American security cultures remained closer to each other than to those of any other parts of the world. Moreover, even when confronted by a profound rift on the defense issue, NATO diplomats never stopped thinking *from* diplomacy in solving their disputes.[26] In the end, though, an Alliance inhabited by struggles over its own internal rules of the game certainly reveals a lower capacity to impose doxa in the field of international security.

On their side, the Russians came to embrace the post-September 11 rules of the game in the international security field imposed by the US, and to a lesser extent, by NATO. As Baranovsky noted: "Gradually, the fight against terrorism will become the priority task for states ... One can expect that the political and psychological barriers against using force will be lowered. Force will probably appear 'less unacceptable' than before."[27] This vision, widespread among Russian elites, happened to fit quite nicely with the American reaction to September 11, 2001. This homology between the new field's doxa and the ingrained Russian habitus constituted an unprecedented development. From the mid-1990s on, fast-amplifying hysteresis effects had erupted from the growing misalignment between the security-from-the-inside-out doxa and the Russian Great Power dispositions. In the year following Yeltsin's retirement, the new president Putin continued to characterize Russia as a Great Power[28] and publicly voiced his irritation with NATO – an "organization [that] often ignores the

[25] De Nevers (2007).   [26] Pouliot (2006).
[27] Baranovsky (2002, 14–15).   [28] Tsygankov (2005).

opinion of the international community and the provisions of international legal documents in its decision-making process."[29] The following question thus arises: if the new Moscow administration was so disposed toward Great Power status, why did it embrace the post-September 11 rules of the international security game imposed by the US and the Alliance?

Essentially, the new rules of the game after September 11, 2001 converged toward several dispositions that were already part and parcel of the Russian habitus as it had reemerged during the 1990s. In other words, thanks to this exogenous shock, dominant players met Moscow on its own ground. As Neumann correctly notes:

One of the reasons why Russia's visibility was so low during the 1990s was that the security agenda was to a high degree dominated by developments in sectors where Russia was peripheral. The "soft security" debate presupposed a way of framing questions to do with power, and particularly with appositeness of "soft power," that did not easily fit in with traditional Russian ways of framing these questions ... The Afghan campaign, on the other hand, meant that conventional warfare was back at the centre of the security agenda ... Russia has simply harvested what has come its way.[30]

Three main Russian dispositions appeared better attuned to the post-September 11 doxa. First, because the new order of things rested on a conservative understanding of national security, the Russians were better adapted than they used to be during the 1990s. Second and relatedly, the post-September 11 doxa revalued the form of capital that Moscow has traditionally preferred and possessed: military resources. Its positional agency – that is, its drive to act in certain ways due to the opportunity structure – was better attuned to the field's rules of the game. Third, the securitization of terrorism upon which the post-September 11 doxa came to rest replicated the extant political discourse inside Russia. In the preceding years, the Russians had repeatedly used Chechnya to raise the issue of international terrorism as a key new threat to international security. Yet NATO member states' reactions were skeptical. After September 11, 2001, Russian officials were able to portray themselves as being ahead of the twenty-first-century international security game. In this connection, NATO

[29] Quoted in President of Russia (2001).   [30] Neumann (2005b, 18–19).

officials quickly changed their discourse on the Russian operation in
the Caucasus, toning down their criticisms. In the new century, then,
the real shift in the security discourse came not from Russia but from
the US, and by extension NATO.[31]

As a result, in the post-September 11 rules of the game, by which
hard security was to take precedence over the soft agenda of security-
from-the-inside-out, Washington and Brussels became more inclined
to recognize Russia's improved position. Recall that because NATO
is the dominant player in the post-Cold War field of international
security, the Alliance habitus is "naturally" in tune with the order
of things (see Chapter 2). Compared to 1999, the dominant habitus
in Moscow was better adapted to the post-September 11 rules of
the international security game. In 2002, a new homology between
Russia's position in the field and its elites' dispositions seemed to be
emerging. It is particularly striking, for instance, that in the weeks
following September 11, 2001, the influential Council on Foreign and
Defense Policy – a loose network comprised of Moscow's most influential security elites – published a report in favor of Russia playing a
junior role in relation to the Alliance. Urging their country to accept
a NATO-based security system, the report argued that "multipolarity games, especially rhetorical ones, which are understood by most
of the world as resistance to the US and indeed to the West, are
too expensive and unpragmatic."[32] Note that this collective report
was signed by dozens of Kremlin-connected officials and specialists
including Primakov, Lukin, and Duma members Alexei Arbatov and
Dmitri Rogozin. Everything took place as if the Russian habitus could
better withstand a domination based on hard security rules than on
the internal mode of pursuing security.

The evolution toward the aligning of positions and dispositions in
Russian–Atlantic relations initiated a honeymoon almost as intense
as that of 1992. In its first ever extraordinary session on September
13, 2001, the PJC "expressed its anger and indignation at the bar-
baric acts committed against the people of the United States of
America ... NATO and Russia will intensify their cooperation under
the Founding Act to defeat this scourge."[33] Within a few weeks,
Moscow took several steps to implement this new agreement. First,

---

[31] See Pouliot (2003).   [32] Quoted in Ambrosio (2005, 140).
[33] NATO (2001a).

Russia voted in favor of UN Security Council Resolution 1373, which effectively endorsed American-led military action against the Taliban. Second, on national television Putin made a multipronged offer of assistance, including intelligence-sharing, the opening of Russian airspace for American planes supplying humanitarian assistance, help in search-and-rescue operations in Afghanistan, and enhanced military assistance to the anti-Taliban Northern Alliance. Third, Russia tacitly endorsed American requests to several Central Asian states for military basing rights. A few days after George W. Bush's September 20 speech announcing the invasion of Afghanistan, the US had secured flying and basing rights in all the Central Asian states. Despite much domestic criticism, the Kremlin's goodwill was later enlarged to Georgia, where American forces landed in 2002 without much protest.

NATO–Russia relations acquired a new meaning in the restruc-tured rules of the international security game. In the weeks following the attacks, under the leadership of British Prime Minister Tony Blair, the Alliance set about strengthening its institutional ties with Russia. Although the PJC had resumed its work in 2000, it was still widely considered to have failed to live up to expectations, especially in the wake of the Kosovo crisis. In October and November 2001, Putin and NATO Secretary-General Lord Robertson met twice. In Moscow, Robertson announced discussions of a new council between NATO and Russia that "would involve Russia having an equality with the NATO countries in terms of the subject matter and would be part of the same compromising trade-offs, give and take, that is involved in day-to-day NATO business. That is how we do business at 19."[34] In December, the NAC formally endorsed the proposal to give new impetus and substance to the NATO–Russia partnership. The pro-posal was also discussed at the PJC when the Foreign Affairs and Defense Ministers met later that same month.

At that time, however, a few member states started to air concerns about embracing Russia too quickly, and successfully voiced opposi-tion to the formula "NATO at twenty." In its early version, sponsored especially by the United Kingdom, Italy and Canada, the NRC would have given Russia a "right of equality." This proposal was considerably watered down in the early months of 2002, primarily under pressure

[34] NATO (2001c).

from Washington, with the support of Turkey, the Netherlands and the three new member states. Czech president Vaclav Havel, for instance, criticized the initiative as a "bureaucratic exercise" and warned that it could make the Alliance "just as spineless as the UN or the [OSCE]."[35] In a replay of the 1996–7 negotiations over the Founding Act, the main bone of contention was NATO's enlargement to the Baltic states.[36] In the end, at the May 2002 Rome summit, Russia and NATO adopted a declaration stating their "determination to build together a lasting and inclusive peace in the Euro-Atlantic area on the principles of democracy and cooperative security and the principle that the security of all states in the Euro-Atlantic community is indivisible ... [The NRC] will operate on the principle of consensus."[37] The British Foreign Minister went as far as to declare: "This is the last rites, the funeral of the cold war ... Fifteen years ago, Russia was the enemy, now Russia becomes our friend and ally."[38] Despite this optimistic language, however, the issue of enlargement had been brushed under the carpet while Russia's institutional association with NATO had been considerably diluted.

In terms of the NRC structure, the most important change from the original proposal was the addition of a retrieval or safeguard mechanism allowing participants to withdraw any issue from discussion. In practice, such a mechanism meant that Russia's inclusion in the settlement of a given security issue remained conditional on the goodwill of all NRC member states. Vilnius could then withdraw from the NRC agenda any discussion of NATO forces in Lithuania, for instance. This obviously poses serious limits on Russia being associated with NATO on contentious issues. Strikingly, Russian officials appeared quite happy with the results of the Rome summit nonetheless. For instance, Foreign Minister Igor Ivanov insisted the new Council was "not a consultative body, it's an executive body [in which] NATO and Russia must stand side by side."[39] But Danish Foreign Minister Per Stig Moeller held a different view: "the text of the agreement with Moscow includes a provision stating that all of the 19 NATO member

---

[35] Quoted in Yusin (2001).
[36] At the time, rumors that the Alliance would invite seven new members for admission (including the Baltic states) at its upcoming summit in Prague had already started to circulate.
[37] NATO (2002).   [38] Jack Straw quoted in Traynor (2002).
[39] Quoted in Traynor (2002).

countries have veto power. If a single country disagrees on some issue, the matter will be taken off the agenda for subsequent discussion."[40] Even after the structural shifts of September 11, 2001 and the window of opportunity that they opened, ambiguity remained in NATO–Russia institutional ties.

Moscow's enthusiasm over the watered-down NRC illustrates the fact that during the short-lived honeymoon that immediately followed September 11, 2001, Russia was ready to play a lesser role and let the Alliance take bolder steps to maintain its domination. Moscow took several initiatives to demonstrate its readiness to tone down Russia's Great Power quest. For instance, Putin did not blink when the US unilaterally withdrew from the Antiballistic Missile (ABM) treaty in December 2001; he shut down Russian military bases in Cuba and Vietnam; and he came to accept the American reluctance to consent to verification measures in the Strategic Offensive Reductions Treaty (SORT) signed in Moscow in spring 2002. Interestingly, Clifford Kupchan dubbed that meeting "the first asymmetrical summit ... the first time the Russians accepted they're not equal."[41] That was obviously a sea change from the obstructive approach that the Russians had come to adopt in the late 1990s. But when a few months later the Alliance returned to its double enlargement practices, as if September 11, 2001 had never happened, the same hysteresis effects that had plagued the relationship during the 1990s put an abrupt end to this period of renewed cooperation.

NATO goes global

The Russian–Atlantic honeymoon dissipated around 2003, in large part because NATO moved on with its double enlargement process pretty much as if nothing had changed after September 11, 2001. From the Russian perspective, Alliance officials went along with the heavy-handed approach of the 1990s in which no genuine consideration was given to Moscow's opinion. This forceful diplomacy shattered the fragile diplomatic momentum that had started to build in the immediate aftermath of September 11, 2001. At the geographical level, seven new member states entered the Alliance in 2004 after a process that appeared just as exclusionary to Moscow, if not more

---

[40] Quoted in Smirnov (2002).   [41] Quoted in Ambrosio (2005, 136).

so, than during the 1990s. In functional terms, NATO undertook an expansion toward a global role that generated growing suspicions among Russian officials in line with those sparked by the two Balkans interventions a few years earlier. These practices made little sense to the Russians, who had reacted to the doxic changes of September 11, 2001 with expectations of a closer integration with NATO. In a striking replay of the 1990s, Russian Great Power dispositions resurfaced again, provoking further hysteresis effects and stalling security community development once again.

A few months after taking office, President Bush firmly committed to a further wave of NATO enlargement, declaring in Warsaw:

Our goal is to erase the false lines that have divided Europe for too long ... The question of "when" may be still up for debate within NATO. The question of "whether" should not be. As we plan to enlarge NATO, no nation should be used as a pawn in the agendas of others. We will not trade away the fate of free European peoples. No more Munichs, no more Yaltas.[42]

The American determination to take in new members was not shaken by September 11, 2001, but rather bolstered. At the Prague summit in November 2002, the Russian–Atlantic honeymoon was not yet over when NATO announced its decision to accept seven new member states by 2004. Consistent with its reaction to the American withdrawal from the ABM treaty, at the time Moscow remained calm and circumspect. September 11, 2001 significantly contributed to this new Russian attitude: while in June 2001 Russia was still making clear its rigid opposition to enlargement, in October of the same year Putin confessed he could revise his opinion on the matter should NATO transform itself into a political organization. Prior to the Prague summit, Foreign Minister Ivanov similarly explained that although he considered expansion "a mistake," "Russia is not planning to get overly dramatic about the situation."[43] Though the policy was still opposed, everything took place as though the harsh resistance that had characterized the previous years had softened.

Similarly, in the immediate aftermath of September 11, 2001, NATO's functional enlargement was prudently tolerated in Moscow.

[42] Quoted in the *New York Times* (2001).
[43] Quoted in Kramer (2002, 748).

Recall that at the Washington summit in 1999, NATO had adopted a new Concept providing for out-of-area missions. That trend accelerated in the wake of the 2001 terrorist attacks. At the Prague summit in 2002, NATO created the Response Force, a body of approximately 20,000 troops available at short notice for deployment around the world and across the full spectrum of military operations. Then, at the 2004 Istanbul summit, the Alliance explicitly granted itself the right, and even the duty, to intervene anywhere on a global scale, stating its "determin[ation] to address effectively the threats our territory, forces and populations face *from wherever they may come*."[44] It was also in Istanbul that the Alliance took the decision to expand its International Security Assistance Force (ISAF) mission to the whole of Afghanistan, after it had taken control of the operation in August 2003. It created a dozen Provincial Reconstruction Teams and gradually expanded the mission beyond the confines of Kabul starting in 2004. Clearly the most militarily challenging mission ever undertaken by the Alliance, the NATO-led ISAF counted 31,000 troops in October 2006, coming in unequal proportions from the twenty-six member states as well as from ten partner countries. The significance of the Afghan mission for NATO's functional enlargement was not only that the country is located far away from the collective defense theatre (i.e. the North Atlantic area). It was also that the operation had a clear preventive dimension that was not historically characteristic of the Alliance's mandate. The largest deployment ever made by the Alliance was in line with its new, expanded function to combat threats wherever they surface in the world.

In this context, a new narrative emerged among Euro-Atlantic officials and experts to the effect that NATO was now "going global."[45] In the first few years of the new millennium, the Alliance lent logistical support to the African Union's mission in Darfur; assisted tsunami relief efforts in Indonesia; ferried supplies to victims of hurricane Katrina in the US; and airlifted food after a massive earthquake in Kashmir. For many experts, the next logical step would be to enlarge membership to any democratic state in the world. Not all countries and officials shared this conclusion, however. At the time of writing, the issue of the globalization of the

---

[44] NATO (2004b, emphasis added).   [45] Daalder and Goldgeier (2006).

Alliance remained one of the most hotly debated among its members. Nonetheless, since the Istanbul summit there exists a consensus that as transatlantic as the organization may be in membership, the issues it has to address now play themselves out on a global scale. In reality, NATO has already gone global, as the ISAF illustrates. This evolution was certainly not to Moscow's liking, where "a significant segment of the Russian policy-making elite appears to have concluded that there has been a direct correlation (and for many, a causal relationship) between NATO enlargement and the retreat of Russian influence."[46]

In addition to continuing its double enlargement, NATO undertook a number of policies that further alienated Russia. When selling its new round of enlargement to the Russians, the Alliance essentially used a similar line as during the 1990s: "Enlargement is not – as outdated perceptions have it – a zero-sum game where NATO wins and Russia loses ... We are aiming at including, not excluding Russia."[47] But this language was rejected as duplicitous by Moscow when, in early 2004, NATO began patrolling the Baltic states' airspace and policing the border with Russia. Even before these states formally entered the Alliance in late March 2004, Brussels had dispatched six F-16 fighters from Denmark, Belgium and the Netherlands. Moscow responded in kind by sending airplanes on similar reconnaissance missions along its borders with the Baltic states. This operation confirmed doubts about the alleged win-win, inclusive nature of NATO's expansion in Russia. Recall that in the aftermath of September 11, 2001 the Alliance subtly turned down offers from the Russian side for a deeper rapprochement. In March 2000, Putin had already surprised the world by responding "Why not?" to a British Broadcasting Corporation (BBC) journalist who was inquiring into the possibility of Russia one day entering NATO. At the time, the NATO Secretary-General had replied that Russian membership was not on the agenda. In late September 2001, Putin was reported as calling on NATO to admit his country, an offer that was received very coldly. In November, Putin reiterated to Washington his desire to go "as far as the North Atlantic Alliance itself is ready to go and as far as it will be able, of course, to take

---

[46] Braun (2008, 1).   [47] NATO (2001b).

into account the legitimate interests of Russia."[48] The offer again fell on deaf ears on the Atlantic side.[49]

Several other practices on the part of certain NATO member states contributed to resurging hysteresis in the following months. Obviously, the American invasion of Iraq was a case in point. The main problem for the Russians was the infringement of the principle of state sovereignty, which the Russians had come to interpret as the best safeguard against interference in the wake of the Kosovo crisis. In addition, in early 2002 the Pentagon's Nuclear Posture Review was leaked in the American media, counting Russia as one of seven states on which nuclear weapons could or should be targeted. During spring 2002, the Bush administration announced that the Transcaucasus and Central Asia had become areas of interest for the Alliance, while showing little inclination to remove its newly acquired facilities in Central Asia and Georgia. Finally, starting in early 2003, persistent rumors that the Pentagon was working on plans to deploy American forces in Bulgaria and Romania – in contravention of NATO's 1997 unilateral pledges – further alarmed the Russians.

The more cooperative tide post-September 11 definitely turned in the aftermath of the "color revolutions" in the post-Soviet space: the Rose Revolution in Georgia, in November 2003; the Orange Revolution in Ukraine, in December 2004; and the Yellow or Purple or Tulip Revolution in Kyrgyzstan, in October 2005. From the outset, Moscow suspected some shady involvement on the part of Western countries, particularly in financing opposition parties and in organizing demonstrations. Many high-level politicians denounced the meddling of the US and other Allied countries on behalf of democratization in the CIS area. Where the West applauded democratic revolutions, Moscow condemned the "continuation of the West's strategic line of staging a political takeover of the post-Soviet space."[50] To be

---

[48] Ministry of Foreign Affairs of the Russian Federation (2001).
[49] Another telling example is NATO's repeated refusal to establish ties with the Collective Security Treaty Organization (CSTO). Under Russia's initiative, this was proposed several times at NRC meetings and in high-level communications from 2004 through December 2006. Cooperation in drug trafficking and the establishment of a "security belt" around Afghanistan were proposed, among other things. The Alliance did not answer for a year, before declining the offer.
[50] Pushkov (2004).

sure, the new president of Ukraine, Viktor Yushchenko, had clearly stated his intention to move the country closer to, and eventually inside NATO prior to obtaining the West's support. In March 2004, NATO and Ukraine signed a memorandum by which Allied armed forces were granted the right of rapid access to the country's territory should the Alliance deem it necessary. A similar situation happened in Georgia with President Mikhail Saakashvili, who quickly opened the country's doors to American and NATO militaries after his rise to power. In May 2006, the GUAM, a loose group of post-Soviet states sponsored by the US, was enlarged and renamed the Organization for Democracy and Economic Development.

Faced with NATO's activism in its "near abroad," Russia reverted to a number of Great Power tactics, especially that of soft balancing. In October 2002, the CSTO was created, with a Russian general as its head, to institutionalize the alliance contracted back in 1992. In September 2003, Russia signed a deal with Kyrgyzstan to establish a new airbase in Kant, in the vicinity of an American contingent. A CSTO Rapid Deployment Force for Central Asia, funded by Moscow, was deployed there. Moscow also supported Uzbekistan in its decision to evict American forces from the Khanabad base during the summer of 2005. At the Minsk summit in June 2006, CSTO member states pledged to expand the collective forces' zone of operation beyond the member states' territories. In order to balance NATO's influence in the CIS, Russia also employed the Shanghai Cooperation Organization (SCO), which comprises China, Russia and the four Central Asian states. In August 2005, the SCO organized its first joint maneuvers intended to rout hypothetical terrorists, extremists and separatists entrenched in the Shandong peninsula. Since then, further exercises have been organized.

In sum, the NATO–Russia politics over the double enlargement that followed September 11, 2001 are in many respects reminiscent of the events that unfolded in the second half of the 1990s. In admitting seven more Eastern European countries and in expanding its collective-security mission from the European to the global stage, the Alliance pursued the same path it had set itself at the critical juncture of 1994. Unsurprisingly, this new wave of double enlargement pushed Russia further away from the internal mode of pursuing security. Once again, NATO's practices appeared to contradict the security-from-the-inside-out agenda that the Alliance had continued to advocate after September 11, 2001. From the Russian point of view, integrating seven more post-communist states in the Alliance meant not the consolidation of the democratic community, but the drawing of new divisions to Russia's exclusion. Similarly, the globalization of NATO's security mandate did not appear to yield more security for Moscow: given the Kosovo precedent, it rather seemed to undermine Russia's capacity to control its own fate and exert influence in world politics. In enlarging its security mandate as well as its membership, then, the Alliance played a game with Russia that smacked of real-politik instead of democracy promotion. As soon as the diplomatic momentum that immediately followed September 11, 2001 dissipated, deeply ingrained Great Power dispositions resurfaced among Russian elites. In a replay of the late twentieth century, the role of junior part-ner gave way to power balancing.

This time, however, Russia's insubordination went one step further with the public rejection of the democratization and human rights agenda advocated by Allied member states. Nothing better illustrates this change than mounting Russian criticisms of the OSCE over the last few years. In July 2004, CIS countries, under Russia's strong lead-ership, distributed a statement to the OSCE's Permanent Council in Vienna to the effect that the organization was "often failing to observe such fundamental Helsinki principles as noninterference in internal affairs and respect for the sovereignty of states."[51] For the first time in the post-Cold War era, a group of states led by Moscow mounted an objection opposing the very principles of the OSCE. By that time, Russia had become "a poster child of resistance to the democratic and human rights agenda."[52] Clearly, the pattern of domination that had given NATO so much authority over Moscow had changed; recent diplomatic interaction, including over Georgia, prove just that.

NATO–Russia diplomacy today: déjà vu all over again?

After 2006, NATO-Russia diplomacy continued on the same path of persistent symbolic power struggles. In this final section, I briefly survey key events that took place until the Georgia War of 2008. Since my historical narrative primarily intends to explain the origins of NRC practical sense as I recorded it in 2006, I do not go into

[51] Quoted in Lukyanov (2004).   [52] MacFarlane (2008, 41).

as much detail. Nonetheless, for the sake of policy relevance, it is important to understand how recent interactions and disputes fit the overall pattern of hysteresis and symbolic power struggles of the past fifteen years.

This pattern persisted in large part because NATO's double enlargement policy remained a central part of the Russian–Atlantic relationship. After the November 2006 Riga summit, the new name of the game for the Alliance became *functional* security – meaning that geography was no longer a constraint on its action. Russian officials feared that in becoming a global policeman, NATO could eventually meddle in conflicts that were of direct concern for, or in the close vicinity of, their country. Foreign Minister Lavrov expressed his concerns in the following way:

The parameters of our interaction largely depend on how the alliance's transformation will proceed. There are a number of aspects in this regard that evoke our concern. For example, it was agreed at the NATO Riga Summit in what cases military force could be used. The number of such hypothetical scenarios is increasing. But there is no clarity as to how this is going to correlate with the rules of international law, in particular, whether NATO will ask for permission from the United Nations, as it should be done under the Charter of the Organization. We cannot, of course, watch impartially the military structure of the alliance moving ever closer to our borders.[53]

Furthermore, the fact that Russia's material strength has developed considerably over the last couple of years has solidified the Great Power habitus in Moscow. Recent rearmament policies as well as warmer relations with certain post-Soviet neighbors clearly suggest that material-institutional capital remains the resource of choice for Russia.

As for geographical enlargement, the Bucharest summit of April 2008 saw two new countries (Albania and Croatia) enter into accession talks, while "NATO welcome[d] Ukraine's and Georgia's Euro-Atlantic aspirations for membership in NATO. We agreed today that these countries will become members of NATO."[54] Against the will of

---

[53] Quoted in Ministry of Foreign Affairs of the Russian Federation (2007b).
[54] NATO (2008a, para. 23).

President Bush and several East European states, a group of members including France, Germany, Hungary, Italy and the Benelux countries opposed granting a Membership Action Plan to these two countries, largely in response to Russia's staunch opposition. As French Prime Minister François Fillion declared: "We are opposed to the entry of Georgia and Ukraine because we think that it is not a good answer to the balance of power within Europe and between Europe and Russia."[55] Such circumspection was quite new in NATO–Russia relations.

It is essential to frame the Georgia War of summer 2008 within the issue of NATO's expansion. In 2006 a serious diplomatic row had already erupted after Tbilisi expelled several Russian officials on spying accusations. A few days earlier, the Alliance had offered an Intensified Dialogue preparing Georgia for membership. In the words of Russia's Foreign Minister: "The latest escapade involving the seizure of our officers occurred immediately after NATO's decision to adopt a plan for intensified cooperation with Georgia and after the visit that Mikhail Nikolayevich paid to the US ... Here's how it all unfolded in chronological order: the trip to Washington, the NATO decision, the taking of hostages."[56] As NATO's open-door policy reached the post-Soviet space up to its very borders, Moscow grew increasingly nervous.

This nervousness turned into outright aggressiveness during the summer of 2008, when Russia invaded Georgia and recognized South Ossetia and Abkhazia as independent countries. On August 7, Tbilisi launched an aerial bombardment and a ground attack on South Ossetia, killing civilians as well as a dozen Russian peacekeepers. In retaliation, in the following days Russian troops captured Tskhinvali, landed forces in Abkhazia, conducted airstrikes on military and industrial compounds near Tbilisi and bombed the Georgian seaport of Poti. Loud protests from the West fell on deaf ears in Moscow. When the Russians called an NRC meeting to discuss the conflict, the US blocked the initiative and instead convened a NAC meeting, which condemned Russia's use of "disproportionate" force.[57] Thereafter, the Alliance announced the suspension of NRC activities and barred a Russian ship from joining Operation Active Endeavour. In an attempt

---

[55] Quoted in Myers (2008).
[56] Lavrov quoted in Solovyov and Sidorov (2006).   [57] NATO (2008b).

to save face, Russia also halted cooperation with NATO indefinitely. Despite a ceasefire brokered by French president Nicolas Sarkozy on August 12, the Russian military remained deep into Georgian terri-tory for several weeks in order to create "buffer zones." At the end of the month, the new president Dmitri Medvedev formally recog-nized the new political entities, putting them under the "protection" of about 7,600 Russian soldiers.

The Georgia War gave way to very strong rhetoric on both the Russian and NATO sides. The new Russian president tried to downplay the importance of Western criticisms and retaliatory ges-tures: "We do not need illusions of partnership. When we are being surrounded by bases on all sides, and a growing number of states are being drawn into the North Atlantic bloc and we are being told, 'Don't worry, everything is all right,' naturally we do not like it. If they essentially wreck this [NRC] cooperation, it is nothing horrible for us. We are prepared to accept any decision, including the termination of relations."[58] The American Secretary of State, Condoleezza Rice, responded by putting Moscow on a "one-way path to self-imposed isolation and international irrelevance."[59] Tensions mounted particu-larly high when Georgia officially called on NATO to offer military assistance during the conflict. In the end, American planes and ships supplied aid to Georgia, combined with substantial financial assist-ance from the US, the EU and the IMF. One senior American offi-cial was quoted as saying: "Well, maybe we're learning to shut up now."[60]

Finally, another Russian–Atlantic row that illustrates particularly well how NATO's double enlargement has contributed to jeopardize even the strongest *acquis* of the end of the Cold War regards the CFE treaty, which was signed in late 1990 by NATO and Warsaw Pact countries and sets limits on armaments systems on the European con-tinent with solid verification and information exchange mechanisms. At Russia's request, an adapted version was agreed upon in 1999 in order to allow more flexibility in Moscow's deployments, notably in the Caucasus. In the 1999 OSCE Istanbul Final Act, Russia also agreed to withdraw its military from bases in Georgia and Moldova. In the ensuing weeks, NATO countries conditioned the ratification of

---

[58] Dmitri Medvedev quoted in Levy (2008).
[59] Quoted in BBC (2008).   [60] Quoted in Cooper (2008).

the Adapted CFE treaty on Moscow's fulfillment of what has come to be known as the "Istanbul commitments." For its part, the Russian Duma ratified the treaty in June 2004, while urging those new NATO member states not covered by the original CFE to sign it. In April 2004, at their very first NRC meeting, Slovenia and the Baltic states stated their intention to join the arms control regime. That was never done, however, and Moscow did not fully withdraw its forces from Georgia and Moldova either. In his presidential address in April 2007, President Putin proposed to suspend Russia's commitments under the CFE, a decision that came into effect in December that year.

From NATO's perspective, the failure of certain Allied member states to ratify the Adapted CFE treaty is a response to Moscow's refusal to fulfill its so-called Istanbul commitments. These commitments had been made in 1999 as President Yeltsin, on the verge of leaving office and eager to redeem his reputation in the West after Kosovo and a second invasion of Chechnya, had agreed to conditions that Russia was apparently not ready to fulfill. Under the Putin administration, Moscow openly contested NATO's conditioning of the Adapted CFE ratification to the 1999 pledge. As Lavrov put it in 2004: "There is no legal connection between these issues. From a legal standpoint, these demands are improper, since the agreements on resolving the situation with respect to the bases in Georgia and withdrawing military equipment from the Dnestr region were political, rather than legal, in nature; they are being fulfilled and are not bound by any strict deadlines."[61] Whatever reasons Russian officials may have given for their failure to withdraw on time, one must frame this policy within NATO's double enlargement. Georgia had become the main focus of NATO's and American political seduction in the preceding years and its possible membership was (and still is) a source of deep concern and irritation in Moscow.

In this context, for the Russians there is simply no incentive to continue to fulfill CFE provisions while several NATO member states either do not fall under its jurisdiction or do so in an outdated way. Recall that among the ten most recent allies in 2008, six were part of the Warsaw Pact in 1990 (Bulgaria, the Czech Republic, Hungary, Poland, Romania, Slovakia). The remaining four (the three Baltic states and Slovenia) were not independent states in 1990 and were

---

[61] Quoted in Sysoyev (2004).

thus not covered by the CFE arms limitations. General Baluyevsky expressed Moscow's exasperation quite clearly: "the expansion of NATO, the changed military and political status of six CFE signatory countries and the resulting changes in the structure and composition of the groupings – all these things supposedly have nothing to do with the CFE Treaty, while Russia's bilateral relations with Moldova and Georgia have a direct bearing on the treaty and are preventing its ratification!"[62] With a new phase of enlargement looming, Russia sees no interest in maintaining the CFE regime. The link between the moratorium and NATO's double enlargement was explicitly made by Putin in early 2007: "It turns out that NATO has put its frontline forces on our borders, and we continue to strictly fulfil the [CFE] treaty obligations and do not react to these actions at all ... And now they are trying to impose new dividing lines and walls on us – these walls may be virtual but they are nevertheless dividing, ones that cut through our continent."[63]

Russia's suspension of its CFE commitments, which seemed to take NATO by surprise although the idea had been publicly floated many times since 2004, illustrates very clearly the loss of symbolic authority in NATO–Russia diplomacy. In another fascinating hysteresis effect, Alliance officials greatly overestimated their capacity to force Russia into complying with the Istanbul agreement by withholding ratification of the amended CFE treaty. Even after Russia's suspension, NATO countries refused to compromise during ensuing negotiations, and the Alliance's calls for more talks did not succeed in getting the Russians to budge either. For its part, in June 2008 Moscow proposed a new treaty on European security premised on "the essential principles of interstate relations" inherited from the Helsinki Accords, including "the inviolability of borders, the indivisibility of security and the illegitimacy of ensuring [one's] security at the expense of the security of other participants in international relations." As Medvedev optimistically added: "The first reaction that we received was at least neutral, and this is in some ways encouraging."[64] The quixotic aspect of this proposal, confirmed by NATO's very reserved reaction, illustrates quite well the larger hysteresis pattern that plagues NATO–Russia diplomacy today.

---

[62] Quoted in Izvestia (2004).   [63] President of Russia (2007).
[64] Quoted in President of Russia (2008).

Conclusion: drawing a lesson

The story I have told in this and the preceding chapters is the story of a missed opportunity. With the collapse of the USSR in the early 1990s, many new paths opened for Moscow and its former Atlantic enemy to build peace in and through practice. In 1992–3, everything was taking place as though a new security community was in the making. All the necessary conditions were in place, including NATO's strong domination of the field of international security, to make diplomacy the self-evident practice of Russian–Atlantic relations.[65] That window of opportunity started to shrink in 1994, when the Alliance decided to accept new members and to implement its functional expansion in Bosnia despite Moscow's objections. Since then, the exclusionary consequences of the double enlargement have led to the reemergence of Great Power dispositions among Russian officials. This Great Power habitus later hardened over the Kosovo crisis, the globalization of NATO and a new wave of enlargement. Today, as the CFE controversy and the Georgia War demonstrate, the Russian–Atlantic relationship has embarked upon a path of mild rivalry that, as non-violent as it may remain, appears to be conducive to security dilemmas more than to a security community. The relationship is mired in symbolic power struggles between two masters in search of an apprentice. One generation later, not only have the promises of the end of the Cold War failed to materialize – they now seem on the way to oblivion.

Of course, one should not overlook the considerable changes in Russian–Atlantic relations after the end of the Cold War. Except for a few exceptions, scenarios of mutual military confrontation have mostly faded from the intersubjective background. I showed in Chapter 4 that in 2006 the practice of diplomacy was normalized at the NRC, although it stopped short of self-evidence. In and through practice, Russia and NATO cannot be said to form a security community, yet they have certainly moved away from the insecurity community of the Cold War. Critics may retort that two former enemies who pointed nuclear missiles at one another for decades should not be expected to overcome their mutual animosity in just one generation. One should indeed not hope for miracles in such a short time span. But even with this caveat in mind, the pace of Russian–Atlantic pacification pales in

---

[65] See Pouliot (2007).

comparison to other historical cases, such as Franco-German reconciliation. Of course, Russia was neither defeated nor occupied the way Germany was. The political contexts were surely different. However imperfect, this analogy nonetheless suggests that an opportunity was missed in the 1990s to construct a durable peace, in and through practice, between the Alliance and Russia. That this possibility now appears more and more remote only stresses the pressing need for IR scholars to understand what went wrong so as to avoid replicating the same mistakes in the future.

But for NATO's double enlargement, would the development of a Russian–Atlantic security community have stalled? Asking counterfactual questions is always a bit tricky because social life is non-linear, path-dependent and multiply realizable. A macro-pattern such as NATO–Russia relations may be realized, alternatively, through several different factors and various processes but with the same effect. Similarly, a slight and apparently unrelated change in the early conditions – for instance, higher oil prices in the early 1990s – might have changed the whole story of post-Cold War Russian–Atlantic relations. In this context my counterfactual strategy is twofold. On the one hand, I assert that the development of a Russian–Atlantic security community would not have slowed down *as early and to the same extent* had NATO not decided to enlarge in the mid-1990s. In Chapter 5, I showed that the Alliance took its crucial decisions *before* Moscow reverted to a more assertive foreign policy. In addition, the double enlargement quickly led to a new consensus among Russian security elites and the disempowerment of Westernizing elites *à la* Kozyrev. But, on the other hand, I acknowledge that the historical roots of Great Power dispositions, as well as the upheaval of Russian transition, both of which have nothing to do with the double enlargement, constituted particularly fertile soil for Moscow to lapse into quixotic practices in relation to NATO. In the face of their sharp decline, the Russians failed to adjust their expectations to the international hierarchy of the post-Cold War era. Positional agency also directed Russia toward quixotic practices based on military capital. Even without the double enlargement, then, it is conceivable that many of the policies of the Bush administration, for example, would have been just as badly received in Russia.

How did the relationship move from the strong alignment of 1992–3 and later of 2001–2 to today's growing mismatch? While the historical roots of the Great Power habitus and the troubles of domestic transition certainly played a role, this and the previous chapter demonstrated that the NATO policy of double enlargement was profoundly self-defeating and shortsighted as far as pacification with Russia was concerned. Of course, keeping alive the "most successful military alliance in history" or "welcoming back to the European family" countries that had been brutally occupied for decades cannot be said to be wrong in intent. Nor can Alliance officials be completely blamed for being prudent with their former enemies in Moscow, who remained particularly difficult partners and failed to change their expectations after the implosion of the USSR. Instead, NATO's fault rests with its failure to realize that Russia would not, and in fact could not, understand the double enlargement in the same way as Westerners. As much as expansion made sense from the NATO point of view, it made no sense to Moscow: exclusionary and delusionary, the policy fitted better with the old realpolitik of Cold War containment than with the new rules of security-from-the-inside-out professed by the Alliance.

Worse, NATO officials also failed to come to terms with the fact that by contributing to the strengthening of Great Power dispositions in the Kremlin, they were undermining their own dominant position at the symbolic level. There seemed to be a naïve but widespread conviction that whatever policies NATO could impose, ultimately Moscow officials would always back down without hard feelings. The pervasive feeling that the Alliance was right and that Russia would come to realize it precluded compromise and genuine diplomacy, to Russia's growing alienation. Everything took place as if the Alliance was systematically justified in imposing its decisions on its former Russian enemy. Things happened quite differently, though, as resentment steadily and cumulatively built up in Moscow. The seeds of today's aggravating problems were planted back in 1994; since then they have continued to grow, as habitus is a durable matrix of action. NATO's own practices, in many ways, played a key role in consolidating Great Power dispositions among Russian officials, who were unable to adjust to the new structure of the post-Cold War field of international security.

At the end of the day, the main brake on security community development was not individual but relational. The unremitting bickering over the terms of interaction that has been plaguing NATO–Russia relations for the last fifteen years feeds on the growing mismatch between Russia's ingrained dispositions and the country's position in the field as defined by the dominant Atlantic players. NATO officials consistently behave as if all their policies are inherently right while the Russians keep asking for a status that the dominant player feels is out of place. As a result, there are two masters but no apprentice in NATO–Russia diplomacy, a symbolic stalemate that considerably undermines security community development in and through practice.

The tragedy of hysteresis is that there are no absolute grounds from which to assess who is right and who is wrong in a symbolic power struggle. From the dominant perspective, it is obviously the dominated players who need to take note of the tough reality and adjust their practices accordingly. Yet Don Quixote happens to live in a different world, where the imposed order of things makes no sense compared to tilting at windmills. There is no obvious way to reconcile hysteretic practices and move beyond symbolic stalemate. Argument and persuasion will probably not do the trick, as players are positionally opposed in a struggle that can produce no winners: the dominant are unable to impose the rules of the game on the dominated, who in turn are combating a structure which they cannot defeat. And the struggle goes on and on.

7 | Conclusion

The world of international security works quite differently from the point of view of its practitioners than from that of the distant observer. As this book has shown, interstate pacification is less about people representing one another as part of the same "we," than it is about joining together in the increasingly commonsense enactment of diplomacy. Practices always rest on an engagement with the world inherited from past interactions and framed by social configurations. By emphasizing practical logics, I certainly do not deny that the theoretical point of view also sheds crucial light on political processes, not least by making sense of practicality in a larger historical and contextual perspective. But this analytical incisiveness requires that social scientists, and more specifically IR scholars, pay equal attention to the logic of practicality in world politics.

In this concluding chapter I want to do three main things. First, I shall wrap up the book's key arguments and highlight in particular how my theory of practice of security communities helps understand the fundamentally hysteretic nature of NATO–Russia diplomacy in the post-Cold War era. Second, I shall briefly return one last time to my case study in order to glean a few policy-relevant insights from my Bourdieu-inspired analytical framework. Third, and finally, I shall address the implications that practice theory raises for IR theory in general. Far from a competing paradigm, practice theory actually overlaps in innovative ways with some essential parts of existing theories. In this spirit, I treat other IR theories less as alternative explanations than as pieces of a larger puzzle that practice theory may help assemble.

The incisiveness of the theory of practice of security communities

This book intends to make two main contributions to IR scholarship. First, I have developed a theory of practice of security communities

that defines self-evident diplomacy as the constitutive practice of
security communities. This framework not only restores the practical logic of peace as a particular way to engage with the world of
diplomacy, it also sheds new light on its ordering mechanisms at both
the micro and macro levels. Second, I develop a sobjective narrative
of post-Cold War NATO–Russia relations that combines practicality,
intersubjectivity and historicity in order to explain and understand
the symbolic power politics of a fundamental axis of contemporary
world politics. In Russian–Atlantic relations, the diplomatic order
remains fragile, largely because of the growing mismatch between
players' dispositions and their positions in the game of international
security.

Bringing practice theory *à la* Bourdieu to the study of security communities yields two main theoretical and conceptual gains. First, it
directs attention toward what practitioners do differently, in the field
of diplomacy, when they are at peace. Inside mature security communities, diplomacy – the non-violent settlement of disputes – is the
practical starting point of any and all interaction. When they tackle
their disagreements, practitioners who belong to a security community think (talk, judge, reason, act) *from* diplomacy instead of *about*
its opportunity. Practitioners do not necessarily start seeing each
other as "one," nor do they inevitably quibble less or agree more.
What changes is the background knowledge that tacitly informs their
practices: the self-evidence of diplomacy is what differentiates, in a
positive way, a security community from other interstate configurations. By comparison, a non-war community is characterized by
normal diplomacy, a practical relationship with far less immediate
adherence to the non-violent settlement of disputes as the "natural"
order of things.

Second, for a practice to be self-evident – that is, for it to belong to
the doxic and unthought order of things – it must be part of a social
pattern of domination. Therefore, my Bourdieu-inspired theory of
practice of security communities brings symbolic power struggles to
the fore. Doxa stems from the alignment between the dispositions that
are embodied by agents in their habitus and the positions that they
occupy in the field. Under circumstances of homology, the orchestra
can play without a conductor: both dominant and dominated players
behave in tune with commonsense. When habitus loses touch with the
structure of the field, however, hysteresis effects emerge and agents

appear to forget the sense of their place. Quixotic practices weaken the doxic pattern of domination and action, calling its self-evidence into question. Because of hysteresis, the practical sense of different agents clash. In sum, the theory of practice of security communities suggests that, all other things being equal, the stronger the security community members' sense of place, the better the chances that the diplomatic practice may become axiomatic.

The incisiveness of the theory of practice of security communities can be illustrated by the rift that opened inside the transatlantic security community in the wake of the Iraq War.[1] Despite very intense disputes over sensitive matters of defense, security practitioners inside the transatlantic security community never stopped using diplomacy as the axiomatic practice for solving mutual disputes. The profound identity crisis did not seem to shake the practical foundation of the security community. Indeed, the background knowledge that gives birth to the diplomatic practical sense inside the transatlantic security community is part of a deeper social pattern of order by which "things fall in their place," even in case of an identity struggle. That said, the transatlantic rift also provoked fairly strong hysteresis effects in the relationship between the USA and a number of European countries. Jacques Chirac's admonition of some new NATO members that they had "missed a great opportunity to shut up"[2] was a stark reminder of the pattern of domination that usually structures inter-Allied relations. To many Europeans, the United States lost the sense of its place in the run-up to the Iraq crisis: perceived as arrogant and bullying, Washington went further than its own dominant position within the security community warranted. Conversely, most Americans construed the actions of several of their European allies as out of touch with the structure of the transatlantic security community. With Eastern European apprentices acquiescing to their new master, it seemed to Washington that Paris, Berlin, and others were unduly trying to punch above their weight. In the end, though, while the deleterious effects of hysteresis on peace dynamics were very clear, in the transatlantic case they never gathered enough intensity to jeopardize the long-embodied diplomatic practical sense upon which the security community thrives in and through practice.

[1] See Pouliot (2006).   [2] CNN (2003).

How about NATO–Russia diplomacy in the post-Cold War era?
Applying my theory of practice of security communities to this case
helps make sense of the limited pacification of the last twenty years.
In Chapter 4, I used three practical indicators of the self-evidence
of diplomacy to reach a nuanced conclusion: diplomacy is a normal
though not a self-evident practice in NRC dealings. As practitioners
embody somewhat contradictory dispositions with regard to diplomatic interaction, it is hard to determine the net effects of background
knowledge on interstate relations. This ambiguity, I concluded, suggests that contemporary Russian–Atlantic diplomatic relations stop
short of a security community in and through practice: normal diplomacy rather indicates a non-war community.[3]

In order to explain the political origins of this limited diplomatic
commonsense, in Chapters 5 and 6 I went back into post-Cold War
history and revealed an intriguing paradox in the Russian–Atlantic
relationship. On the one hand, since 1992 Russia and NATO member states have solved each and every one of their disputes, including
fierce ones over the double enlargement, by non-violent means. Such
a track record of peaceful change is a reversal of the situation during the Cold War, when force and threats of force were consistently
looming over East–West interactions. By contrast, the post-Cold
War era has been characterized by a handful of "non-wars" –
"conflicts about issues that would typically lead to war, but [that]
were peacefully resolved."[4] Under the conditions that prevailed for
four decades, with thousands of nuclear missiles on high alert and
scores of soldiers standing on both sides of the Iron Curtain or in
proxy theatres, chances are that the Kosovo intervention, Ukraine's
Orange Revolution or the Georgia War might have led to threats of
force by one side or the other. On the other hand, I have also shown
how NATO's practices of double enlargement have contributed to
the resurgence of the Russian Great Power habitus and weakened
the symbolic pattern of domination necessary for the diplomatic
commonsense to surface. Disconnected from the field's structure as
defined by NATO, resurging Russian dispositions created growing
hysteresis in the relationship, to the point of inconclusive symbolic

---

[3] On overlapping regional mechanisms of security governance in NATO–Russia
relations, see Adler and Grieve (2009); and Pouliot (n.d.).
[4] Wiberg quoted in Wæver (1998, 72).

power struggles over the rules of the international security game and the role of each player. As Table 7.1 shows, the post-Cold War history of NATO–Russia diplomacy is one of limited security community development caused by an increasing mismatch between players' dispositions and their positions in the game.

Chapter 4 supplied evidence of the deleterious effects that hysteretic symbolic stalemate can have on the non-violent settlement of disputes and the normalization of diplomacy. When it comes to organizing joint peacekeeping operations, for instance, Russian and Alliance practitioners have a very hard time finding a working compromise on standards and rules of interaction. As the dominant player in the field, NATO cannot imagine having to negotiate with anybody over its ways of doing things and especially not with the Russians. On their side, Russian practitioners take for granted that as a Great Power they ought not to adopt others' procedures without a minimal amount of negotiation and compromise. The concrete result is that the prospects of a NATO–Russia peacekeeping operation are increasingly remote. In fact, the last time it happened, during the 1990s, it left wounds that have yet to heal. During the extremely tense negotiations over the Kosovo peacekeeping operation, Russia would not sign up to anything short of a sector under its own command, which NATO was unwilling to grant. The symbolic struggle, which lasted several days, reached unprecedented levels of intensity and even led to one of the most dramatic episodes of the post-Cold War Russian–Atlantic relationship: the Pristina airport incident. Under such acute conditions of hysteresis, it is doubtful that any pattern of social order can emerge and turn diplomacy into a self-evident, doxic practice.

A mismatch between dispositions in habitus and positions in the field, hysteresis trumps practical sense. People cannot behave in tune with commonsense if they do not agree on what commonsense is in the first place. In the process of security community development, hysteresis considerably weakens the diplomatic order. Because it conceived of itself as the undisputed ruler of the field of international security, NATO felt that it was normal for it to impose its double enlargement despite Russia's loud objections. Seen from Moscow, Alliance practices appeared heavy-handed and uncompromising. Starting in late 1994, Russian practitioners increasingly felt that their NATO counterparts were consistently failing to show the kind of consideration that Russia deserved given its Great Power status. To

Table 7.1 *Evolving (mis)match of positions and dispositions in NATO–Russia relations*

Dates	Degree of (mis)match	Sources of (mis)match between positions and dispositions	Effect on security community development
1992–late 1994	Very strong match (homology)	Empowered habitus in Moscow fits the NATO-imposed rules of the international security game; positional agency leads to a strong sense of one's place	Strong dynamics of security community development
Late 1994– 1998	Growing mismatch (low hysteresis)	Gradual resurfacing of the Great Power habitus in Moscow as double enlargement kicks off; Russia's positional agency overlooked by a triumphant NATO	Security community development undermined
1999–late 2001	Strong mismatch (high hysteresis)	Great Power habitus becomes dominant in Moscow; hysteresis grows as Russian dispositions are out of touch with Russia's position as defined by dominant NATO	Security community development stalled
Late 2001– 2003	Restored match (receding hysteresis)	Post September 11 rules of international security defined by NATO improves Russian position, which is better in tune with toned-down Great Power habitus in Moscow	Security community development a possibility once again
2003– 2007	Growing mismatch (high hysteresis)	Hysteresis returns in force as Great Power habitus prevails in Moscow, clashing with NATO's position and dispositions as dominant player in the field	Security community development stalled

this day, as Russia and NATO do not cast each other in the roles that they actually play together, each side perceives the other as trying to punch above its weight. This obviously makes for difficult and tense diplomacy and it makes the possibility of the development of a security community in and through practice seem remote.

A key thread of this book is that in order to understand security community development and its false starts, it is more productive to start with practice than with collective identity. Rather than conceiving we-ness as the *driver* of practice (that is, as a representation that precedes action), I proposed to construe collective identity as the *result* of practice. Collective identification is embedded in practice, as Adler aptly argues about self-restraint in the spread of security communities: "their engagement in a common practice makes them share an identity and feel they are a 'we.' "[5] As this book's case study has demonstrated, for interstate pacification to thrive we-ness must not only be represented but also enacted in and through practice. This is certainly one of the key contributions that practice theory can make to social and IR theories. There are several others, which I will discuss below. Meanwhile, I want to return to my case study one last time in order to derive a couple of policy recommendations about the politics of NATO–Russia diplomacy today.

Shto Delat'?: the practice of NATO–Russia diplomacy today

Faced with growing hysteresis in Russian–Atlantic relations, the old Russian question arises: *shto delat'?* – what is to be done? My point of departure is a simple one: both the Russian Great Power habitus and the Alliance's tendency to speak in the name of the "international community" are here to stay. These dispositions constitute a deeply ingrained, historically inherited background that cannot, and will not, change overnight. As I have demonstrated in this book, practices and interactions in the first post-Cold War generation hardened this habitus even further. The coming to power of new presidents in Washington and Moscow might help push the "reset button" at the highest level, but in and of itself it will not terminate the powerful influence that pervasive dispositions exert on each side's foreign policy. Thus it is more productive to start from the assumption that

[5] Adler (2008, 201); see Wenger (1998).

habitus will not change in the short or medium term; the challenge is to craft sound policy based on that social reality.

In order to genuinely pacify its relationship with Russia, NATO must alter its course. My point is *not* that the Alliance should give in to the many whims of Moscow's Great Power habitus. As symbolic interactionism indicates, treating somebody as if she were an *X* generally reinforces, in and through practice, the *X* identity.[6] Caving in to Moscow's self-understanding as a Great Power could potentially amount to reinforcing this narrative. The problem rather stems from the fact that over the last twenty years the Alliance has adopted a very ambivalent, and in fact incoherent, policy on the matter. As I have demonstrated above, at specific points in time NATO has shown some willingness to grant the symbolic pomp of equality to Russia in order to obtain its cooperation. But when the time came to also recognize the power and influence that generally comes with that status, the Alliance proved immovable. In the end, this disjointed approach created enormous frustrations for the Russians, reinforcing their quest for Great Power status while making the objective more and more inaccessible.

Of course, sooner or later Russian practitioners will have to face the fact of their country's decline in the new rules of the international security game – something they have consistently proved incapable of doing hitherto. French and British diplomats, whose countries went through a similar pattern of decline in the twentieth century, can tell what a difficult process that is. Time will tell whether the Russians can successfully go through this experience in the twenty-first century. At the moment, the only certainty that we can have is that the Great Power habitus will not disappear in the near future. From the NATO point of view, Russia will continue to be a particularly vexing partner, one of the few that openly contests the order of international security. As the Georgia War manifestly showed, the Alliance's influence over Moscow has become very limited. Based on this observation, what can be done to gradually rein in hysteresis in NATO–Russia diplomacy?

I infer from my theory of practice of security communities two related policy recommendations. First, if NATO wants Russia to play by the rules of the security-from-the-inside-out game, it should

[6] See Wendt (1999).

provide it with enough cultural-symbolic resources to have a minimally successful hand in the game. Positional field analysis teaches us that where you sit is what you do: practices tend to derive in large part from the resources that players possess and can use in their doxic struggle in the field. The drive to act is strongly determined by the opportunity structure. It is not only ingrained dispositions that produce the diplomatic practical sense but also the countries' positions in the hierarchy, as determined by their various stocks of capital. So long as Russia possesses no recognized stock of cultural-symbolic capital, it has no means with which to play by the rules of the internal mode of pursuing security. As the post-Cold War era showed, under the current doxa all that Moscow could do was play a losing hand; and when it became impossible for the Russians to abide by a security-from-the-inside-out doxa that had so little to offer them, they called it quits and turned against the NATO-imposed rules. By comparison, Russia's hand was stronger in the old game of power-balancing and nuclear deterrence, and the country increasingly resorted to similar practices. Enlightened self-interest suggests that in order to prolong a game that is to its own benefit, NATO should ensure that enough players are able to join – even if that means deliberately changing the distribution of resources to their advantage. Given the dominant position it still enjoys, NATO might have the authority to attribute more cultural-symbolic capital to the Russians and seduce them back into the internal mode of pursuing security.

Second, the relationship between NATO member states and Russia should be refocused on the domains where dispositions do not clash as easily as in the field of international security. Because of past interactions both during and after the Cold War, the field of international security has become the locus par excellence where the Russian Great Power habitus and NATO's embodiment of the "international community" are expressed. This source of tension can be partly defused by moving the diplomatic action into different contexts. For example, when it comes to the field of international trade organized around the WTO doxa, the Russians tend to tone down their quest for Great Power status. With a gross domestic product equivalent to only twice that of the Netherlands, the tough reality of Russia's commercial marginality provides an indomitable check to quixotic practices. With fast-growing powerhouses such as China, India, Brazil and others around the WTO table, Moscow does not need the West to be put back in its place. NATO member states would thus have a clear advantage in multiplying interactions with Russia in those forums where its quest for status cannot be expressed as strongly as in the realm of nuclear warheads and geostrategy. This logic works for the Russians as well. Again, the field of international trade is one in which Western diplomats have recently had to learn the hard way that the "international community" is not always coterminous with the Quad (made up of Canada, the EU, Japan and the US). The latter's incapability to move the Doha Round forward, in part because of Indian and Chinese reservations, could be the eye-opener required for the West to finally lose the illusion of being the center of the world. The NATO–Russia relationship would probably benefit from more interactions in multilateral forums where each side's posturing would be constrained as much as possible.

As far as NATO–Russia diplomacy per se is concerned, I doubt that either side would be ready for Moscow's formal integration in the Alliance for the time being. The clash of habitus is simply too strong as things currently stand. That said, I believe that the Alliance should state openly and unambiguously that it is ready to examine Russia's candidacy in due time. While this strategy entails some risks – for instance, legitimating a troublesome player – it would engage Russia as a potential member of the club, something that has cruelly been lacking in the post-Cold War era. This, again, would likely improve the chances of Moscow being seduced into playing NATO's game of security-from-the-inside-out (although probably inelegantly for a time). The main tradeoff for opening the Alliance's door to Moscow's membership is the potential weakening of the "transatlantic consensus"; but the risk is well worth taking in the currently deteriorating situation. Preserving the transatlantic consensus at all costs would be profoundly misguided: in the post-Cold War era, leaving Russia on the margins of Alliance diplomacy turned out to be a self-reinforcing dynamic. The transatlantic consensus is useless, and in fact harmful, if it leads the Alliance to exclude certain states outright and precludes it from meaningfully engaging with its former enemies. Furthermore, the risk is all the more worthy of taking because NATO has historically been a coalition of former enemies.[7] A security community comprised of France, Germany, Italy, the United Kingdom and the US

---

[7] Baker (2002).

would have sounded unlikely in 1945. It is time for NATO countries to pluck up the courage to sacrifice certainties in order to turn the page on Russian–Atlantic rivalry once and for all.

Even in the longer run, though, I seriously doubt that NATO members, especially those that have suffered from decades of Soviet occupation, would ever agree to inviting Russia into their ranks. I would not bet on Moscow begging for membership either. In the meantime, the choice is not between a NATO that backs down every time that the Russians express dissent or one that wholly disregards Moscow's objections. In the wake of the Georgia War, some Alliance members have brought back to the fore a seemingly irrefutable yet fallacious argument: if Russia were to remain cooperative despite NATO's expansion, then NATO could overlook Moscow's objections without consequences; if, however, Moscow were to revert to praetorian tactics in response, then enlargement makes sense to guard former satellites against Moscow's wrath. I believe that this is a false alternative, not least because NATO has fabricated it through its own practices over the past fifteen years. In a way reminiscent of Charles Tilly's "protection racketeer,"[8] the Alliance has come to create insecurity in order to justify the provision of security. Take Georgia: but for the Alliance's proactive and sustained courtship of Tbilisi, the tensions with Moscow would have probably not risen to the level that they reached in 2006. The vicious circle is clear: NATO must enlarge because Georgia needs more security; Georgia needs more security because NATO must enlarge. This is the type of self-fulfilling prophecy that so often spirals out of control, feeding unnecessary rivalries. The time is ripe for practitioners to learn their way out of that, and NATO–Russia diplomacy is the right place to start.

Practice theory and IR theories

Bourdieu-inspired practice theory shares a number of assumptions with existing IR theories yet it also brings much value added to the current theoretical landscape. Contrary to the usual take on the matter, in this final section of the book I conceive of competing frameworks less as alternative explanations than as different pieces

[8] Tilly (1985).

of a larger puzzle that practice theory helps assemble. I want to show that my analysis of NATO–Russia politics in the post-Cold War era shares common ground with most IR theories, while also revisiting some of their assumptions. The goal is neither eclecticism nor synthesis, but the demonstration that practice theory boasts the potential to move beyond theoretical atomization in IR.[9] For demonstration purposes, I pick one central proposition from six major IR theoretical frameworks and show how Bourdieu-inspired practice theory not only builds but also improves on them.

(1) A core assumption of rational choice theory is that people act rationally on the basis of their interests. As Jon Elster argues: "To act rationally is to do as well for oneself as one can."[10] Bourdieu-inspired practice theory is fully compatible with this insight: of course people seek to foster their interests in and through practice. NATO enlarged its membership and mandate because it believed this to be in its interests; Russia opposed the policy for the same reason. However, because it exogenously assumes preferences, from a practice perspective the rational choice argument is insufficient. If interests drive the world, then social scientific theories need to explain not only their enactment but also their content and origin: why do people want what they want and why do they pursue their ends the way they do? Constructivists have long voiced this criticism of rational choice theory; yet by systematically emphasizing structural ideations as constitutive of interests, I believe that several authors have thrown out the baby of strategic action with the constructivist bathwater.

Practice theory *à la* Bourdieu reminds us that both interests and strategies, as pervasive features of political life, have social origins. Strategic action is not given by human nature; it inheres in a number of fields and habitus because of history. Instrumental rationality is an evolutionary disposition that reproduces itself in bodies and things, becoming increasingly pervasive in our iron-caged world, as Weber would have it. In Williams's words: "The universe of potential strategies (and indeed of potential interests) of a given actor is circumscribed – though not mechanistically determined – by the structure of the game and operation of the habitus."[11] Thus the issue is not

---

[9] See Adler and Pouliot (n.d.).   [10] Elster (1989, 28).

[11] Williams (2007, 36). Again, the best explanation for the origins of "focal points," for instance, is the logic of practicality – a socially inherited, context-dependent and intuitive feel that inclines agents toward common practices.

whether people act on the basis of their interest (instrumentality) *or* their identity (legitimacy), as many social theorists now have it; it is always and by necessity both. From a Bourdieu perspective, interests are constituted in large part by field dynamics in the form of an inarticulate investment in the game or *illusio*. To the traditional view of agents investing in a game to foster their interests, Bourdieu adds a recursive loop whereby agents become invested *by* the game: "no one can take advantage of the game, not even those who dominate it, without being taken up and taken in by it. Thus there would be no game without belief in the game and without the wills, intentions and aspirations which actuate the agents; these impulses, produced by the game, depend on the agents' positions in the game."[12] Interests and strategies find their roots in social games, not in individual agents.

(2) A similar point could be made about IR theories informed by social psychology. For instance, David Welch argues that "foreign policy change is most likely when decision-makers perceive that their current policies are incurring painful costs."[13] This valuable insight reminds us that practitioners daily go through a series of cognitive processes that shape their decisions and, by consequence, international politics. From a practice theory perspective, however, cognition is not a purely individual process: the dispositions that comprise habitus and incline actors toward certain ends and strategies are social in origins. They are the accumulated deposit of collective experiences and history. To return to Welch's quote, the reasons why leaders "perceive the costs" of their policy the way they do has less to do with individual cognition (even though it constitutes a necessary transmission belt) than with the embodiment of intersubjective knowledge. The inclinations that render individual practices possible are socially constituted: for instance, Russia's Great Power habitus is triggered particularly strongly in the context of international security, where Moscow has a history of interacting with other dominant powers such as NATO. Although it also has domestic origins, the habitus is challenged or reinforced at the relational level.[14] In order to

---

[12] Bourdieu (1981, 307–8).
[13] Welch (2005, 46).
[14] On this point, see Hopf (2002, 290). I agree with Hopf that identities, and more especially habitus, are shaped first and foremost at the domestic level where a number of mimesis mechanisms are in place. As he also notes, some of these dispositions, for instance the Great Power habitus, are then challenged or reinforced in and through relations at the systemic level.

understand the specific direction that cognitive processes take, one needs to look at social relations.

(3) Structural realism rests on the systemic assumption that what units do is determined by their position in the distribution of material power. As Kenneth Waltz notes: "The concept of structure is based on the fact that units differently juxtaposed and combined behave differently."[15] There are two parts to this neorealist insight: a positional logic, with which practice theory fully concurs, and a materialistic assumption, which I want to amend. Earlier in the book I gave numerous illustrations of the operation of positional agency: the drive to act in certain ways due to the opportunity structure. Russia's quixotic practices in response to the double enlargement were largely due to its low position in the hierarchy of international security, and more specifically its reliance on a devalued form of military capital. Likewise, many of NATO's actions, including the drive to enlarge, derive from the organization's dominant position. Bourdieu's structural constructivism paves the way to "topological analysis": "The political field constitutes a space that is structured such that the value of each constituent element is formed through the network of relationships this element entertains with the other elements in the field."[16] Positional agency implies that where you sit is what you do, an insight that structural realists also share.

That said, there is no valid justification for presuming that the only positional logic that prevails in international security is a material one. This is not to say that economic riches or military force do not matter; they clearly do – for instance in explaining one key dimension of NATO's domination over Russia in the post-Cold War period. I explained Moscow's recourse to its military capital by the fact that this was pretty much the only resource available to pursue Great Power status. Material conditions do matter, but as part of a game that is fundamentally social. The basic issue, in this revised positional logic, is not only how much power one *has*, but also what power *is* in the first place. Bourdieu's sociology has an edge over a materialistic take on structures because it can account for the historical and interactional processes that make certain resources valuable (i.e. powerful) in certain contexts but not in others. In this spirit, Reus-Smit shows that Florence's superior status (and success) in Italian Renaissance

[15] Waltz (1979, 81).   [16] Kauppi (2005, 29).

diplomacy was due not to military superiority, which it did not have, but to its unparalleled competence in ornamental diplomacy premised on cultural mores and practices.[17] The yardstick of power varies over time and space because the players that occupy any given field define and struggle over its meaning. The concept of capital, together with the recovery of the practical point of view, reminds us that resources have to be recognized as such in order to establish the basis of a power relation. Not only do players employ capital to get the upper hand in the field, they also struggle over the meaning and value of resources.

There are a few realists who recognize the importance of "prestige" or "status competition" in international politics; yet ultimately they too reduce these symbolic power struggles to a material basis.[18] Alternatively, Barry O'Neill puts the pursuit of honor, face and prestige at the center of his theory but finally concludes that "they are fought over for the benefits they yield"[19] – presumably material. Again, I do not quibble that material resources have often been highly prized in human societies, including in international politics; but this is an empirical observation that cannot be theoretically assumed away. To reify a contingent observation into a timeless assumption actually reveals more about the theorist's own habitus than anything else. Moreover, the premise that material power is always preponderant is unwarranted in an increasingly institutionalized world where survival is only very rarely at stake. As we enter the twenty-first century, belonging to the club of liberal democracies is often more powerful a resource than owning a large army. From a Bourdieu-inspired perspective, the yardsticks that structure positions in a field are socially constructed, culturally specific and historically contingent. Structure too has a practical logic; and its causal efficacy rests with practice.

(4) A similar point applies to the English School, whose greatest insight probably consists of showing the weight of history on international practices. Practices evolve over time through patterns of reproduction and contestation, as is the case with diplomacy, for instance.[20] But while the English School is very apt in showing how institutions

---

[17] Reus-Smit (1997, 63–86).
[18] Gilpin (1981, 28–31); Wohlforth (2009, 55). The relational competitiveness for status is generally inspired from Weber's path-breaking works on status groups; more recently it has found solid empirical backing in social identity theory. In IR, see e.g. Mercer (1995); and Lebow (2008).
[19] O'Neill (1999, 244).   [20] Watson (1991).

are historically emergent, it fails to capture the agent-level processes that carry the past over into the present and the future. Bourdieu-inspired practice theory palliates this weakness thanks to the concept of habitus. As Bourdieu contends:

> every historical action brings together two states of history: objectified history, i.e. the history which has accumulated over the passage of time in things, machines, buildings, monuments, books, theories, customs, law, etc.; and embodied history, in the form of habitus ... The relationship to the social world is not the mechanical causality that is often assumed between a "milieu" and a consciousness, but rather a sort of ontological complicity. When the same history inhabits both habitus and habitat, both dispositions and position, the king and his court, the employer and his firm, the bishop and his see, history in a sense communicates with itself, is reflected in its own image ... The doxic relation to the native world, a quasi-ontological commitment flowing from practical experience, is a relationship of belonging and owning in which a body, appropriated by history, absolutely and immediately appropriates things inhabited by the same history.[21]

In other words, Bourdieu-inspired practice theory reminds us that as important as historical processes may be, they require a micro-mechanism in order to carry on to the present. The embodied dispositions that comprise habitus help make sense of the weight of history on practices, as my discussion of resurging Great Power dispositions in Russia has shown.

(5) The pervasiveness of power, competition and struggle is a key Marxian premise, which also informs brands of realism as well as poststructuralism. John Mearsheimer writes, in a way reminiscent of classical figures such as Hans Morgenthau, that in world politics the "ultimate aim is to gain a position of dominant power over others."[22] While poststructuralism rejects the realist and Marxist focus on material conditions, it also centers on power and explores the nexus with knowledge in establishing the boundaries of discourse.[23] The assumption that power cannot be transcended also deeply influenced Bourdieu. Social struggles and domination are endemic; solving one conflict will inevitably spark new ones; redressing one imbalance creates another elsewhere. As such, a Bourdieu-inspired theory

---

[21] Bourdieu (1981, 305–6).   [22] Mearsheimer (2001, xi).
[23] Barnett and Duvall (2005).

of practice sharply disagrees with liberalism and the possibility of "win-win compromises," even under conditions of peace. As Edward Hallett Carr once noted: "The common interest in peace masks the fact that some nations desire to maintain the *status quo* without having to fight for it, and others to change the *status quo* without having to fight in order to do so."[24] In this spirit, a practice framework is more akin to "realist constructivism" and the view that "power inheres in social practices."[25] Competition and power struggles are endless features of social relations, including the most peaceful ones. As this book showed, NATO–Russia diplomacy is plagued with symbolic conflicts; but the particularly mature transatlantic security community is just as well.

(6) Finally, the dominant constructivist take on structure defines it as the distribution of knowledge.[26] As a result, structure and culture are coterminous. This analytical focus on ideational structures is certainly warranted given the traditional bias toward materialism in IR theory. In terms of Bourdieu's theoretical apparatus, understanding intersubjectivity is absolutely crucial in order to grasp, on the one hand, the dispositions (habitus) on the basis of which agents act and, on the other hand, the rules of the game (field) under which social action takes place. That said, dispositional and intersubjective-contextual processes are not the sole drivers of social action. My account of security community development points toward a structural form of constructivism by which the social construction of reality is carried out under structural and historical constraints that primarily have to do with *positions*, that is, with agents' relative location in a social structure.

Constructivism teaches us that the link between resource and power is intersubjectivity – what power *is* in a given context. Dispositions and rules of the game are fundamental determinants of the structure of positions; yet constructivists need to appreciate that the reverse is also true. For instance, while it is through social construction that, in our banking system, people come to attach the value of twenty dollars to certain bits of paper with specific engravings, the distribution of those

---

[24] Carr (1958, 52–3).   [25] Jackson and Nexon (2004, 340).
[26] Wendt (1999, 141). Wendt does allow for other structures (e.g. material, interest) but his "primary focus is on a subset of social structure, socially *shared* knowledge or '*culture*.'"

socially constructed money bills across agents is still very important
to understand the workings of society. Social constructs create structures of positions, which in turn help determine meaning. In this sense,
Jennifer Sterling-Folker is right that "[t]he proposition that there may
be limitations on how human beings construct their social realities
opens the theoretical space necessary for a potential dialogue with
realists."[27] Positions correlate with position-taking: one's location in
a field partly determines one's representations of the world.[28] It is
only by integrating dispositional and positional analysis that we can
develop genuinely relational theories that can account for both the
social construction of resources as powerful (dispositions and doxa)
and their distribution across a social configuration (positions).

As Bourdieu argues: "Sociology, in its objectivist moment, is a
social topology ... an analysis of relative positions and of the objective relations between these positions."[29] In this book I have shown
how NATO's and Russia's relative stocks of material-institutional
and cultural-symbolic capital explain several of their practices in the
post-Cold War era. Throughout that period, practitioners attempted
to make sense of the world and in so doing participated in its social
construction; yet they did so from a particular position in the field of
international security. Nexon's "relational institutionalism" presents
a similar combination of structural and constructivist arguments.
His book argues that the Reformations, although intersubjective
in nature, had profound impacts on the institutional structure of
the European composite states of the early modern era. As Nexon
explains in a Tillyesque fashion: "Once we treat structures as networks composed of social transactions, it follows that structures exist
by virtue of ongoing processes of interaction but simultaneously position actors in various structurally consequential positions relative to
one another."[30] In this framework, international change is not only
intersubjective evolution, but also (primarily) change in patterns of
collective mobilization.

In sum, practice theory combines together, in a refreshing way,
insights from a number of IR theories (see Table 7.2). From rational
choice theory, it accepts the focus on interests and strategies; with
political psychology, it looks into cognitive processes that operate

---

[27] Sterling-Folker (2002, 76).   [28] Bourdieu (2003, 190).
[29] Bourdieu (1989, 16).   [30] Nexon (2009, 14).

Table 7.2 *Practice theory and IR theories*

	Common ground	Practice theory's added value
Rational choice	People act rationally on the basis of their interests	Interests and strategies have social origins
Political psychology	Cognitive biases operate in individual decisionmaking	Cognition is rooted in culturally and historically inherited habitus
Neorealism	Position in structure determines behavior	Structure is defined along field-dependent axes
Marxism	Power and domination cannot be transcended	Power and domination are primarily symbolic in nature
English School	History matters	History carries over into the present through field and habitus
Constructivism	People attach meanings to objects and act on their basis	Meaning-making depends in part on position in the field

through individuals; practice theory agrees with the neorealist positional logic as well as with the English School's appreciation of historical processes; it also shares the Marxian (and derivatively realist and poststructuralist) premise that power and domination cannot be transcended; and, finally, a Bourdieu-inspired framework follows constructivism in giving the central position to meaning-making in politics. Beyond this common ground, however, practice theory emphasizes the social roots of interests, strategies and cognitive processes; it revisits materialistic assumptions; and it recalls that although people socially construct their world, they do so from a specific social location and under structural constraints. The common thread across these contributions, which also runs throughout this book, is a concern for practical logics, without which one cannot make sense of interests, positionality and symbolic struggles as they play themselves out in and through practice.

A practical ontology that is both positional and dispositional suggests that there can be no end to social struggles over the meaning of the world, because agents always stand in relation to others as they engage in practices. This relational dynamic perpetuates symbolic fights and domination patterns, as the case of NATO–Russia diplomacy has demonstrated. Although there may be more peaceful means to settle conflicts than others, these fundamental features of social life will not go away, despite technological prowess or increasing communications. As Neumann insightfully argues about Self–Other dynamics, "since what is at issue in delineation is not 'objective' cultural differences, but the way symbols are activated to become part of the capital of the identity of a given human collective, it is simply wrong that global homogenizing trends make it less easy to uphold delineation. Any difference, no matter how minuscule, may be inscribed by political importance and serve to delineate identities."[31] That we are stuck reinstantiating and sometimes even fighting for arbitrary fault lines is as fatalistic an observation as it is an eye-opener for the theory and practice of international politics.

[31] Neumann (1996, 166).

Bibliography

Adler, Emanuel (1997), "Seizing the Middle Ground: Constructivism in World Politics," *European Journal of International Relations* 3(3): 319–63.

(1998), "Seeds of Peaceful Change: The OSCE's Security Community-Building Model," in Emanuel Adler and Michael Barnett, eds., *Security Communities*, 119–60. New York: Cambridge University Press.

(2002), "Constructivism and International Relations," in Walter Carlsnaes, Thomas Risse and Beth A. Simmons, eds., *Handbook of International Relations*, 95–118. Thousand Oaks, CA: Sage.

(2005), *Communitarian International Relations: The Epistemic Foundations of International Relations.* New York: Routledge.

(2008), "The Spread of Security Communities: Communities of Practice, Self-Restraint, and NATO's Post Cold War Transformation," *European Journal of International Relations* 14(2): 195–230.

Adler, Emanuel and Michael Barnett (1998), "A Framework for the Study of Security Communities," in Emanuel Adler and Michael Barnett, eds., *Security Communities*, 29–65. New York: Cambridge University Press.

Adler, Emanuel and Patricia Grieve (2009), "When Security Community Meets Balance of Power: Overlapping Regional Mechanisms of Security Governance," *Review of International Studies* 35(1): 59–84.

Adler, Emanuel and Vincent Pouliot (n.d.), "The Practice Turn: Introduction and Framework," mimeo, August 2008.

Adler-Nissen, Rebecca (2008), "The Diplomacy of Opting Out: A Bourdieudian Approach to National Integration Strategies," *Journal of Common Market Studies* 46(3): 663–84.

Allison, Roy (2006), "Russian Security Engagement with NATO," in Roy Allison, Margot Light and Stephen White, *Putin's Russia and the Enlarged Europe*, 94–129. Oxford: Blackwell.

Ambrosio, Thomas (2005), *Challenging America's Global Preeminence: Russia's Quest for Multipolarity.* Burlington, VT: Ashgate.

Antonenko, Oksana (2007), "Russia and the Deadlock over Kosovo," *Survival* 49(3): 91–106.

Arbatov, Alexei and Vladimir Dvorkin (2006), *Beyond Nuclear Deterrence: Transforming the U.S.– Russian Equation.* Washington, DC: Carnegie Endowment for International Peace.

Ashley, Richard (1987), "The Geopolitics of Geopolitical Space: Toward a Critical Social Theory of International Politics," *Alternatives* 12(4): 403–34.

Asmus, Ronald D. (2002), *Opening NATO's Door: How the Alliance Remade Itself for a New Era.* New York: Columbia University Press.

Asmus, Ronald D., Richard L. Kugler and F. Stephen Larrabee (1993), "Building a New NATO," *Foreign Affairs* 72(4): 28–40.

Baker, James A. III (2002), "Russia in NATO?" *Washington Quarterly* 25(1): 95–103.

Baranovsky, Vladimir (2000), "Russia: A Part of Europe or Apart from Europe?" *International Affairs* 76(3): 443–58.

(2002), "11 septembre: une vision russe" (11 September: A Russian View") *Politique étrangère* 67(1): 9–20.

(2003), "Russian Views on NATO and the EU," in Anatol Lieven and Dmitri Trenin, eds., *Ambivalent Neighbors: The EU, NATO and the Price of Membership,* 269–94. Washington, DC: Carnegie Endowment for International Peace.

Barnes, Barry (2001), "Practice as Collective Action," in Theodore R. Schatzki, Karin Knorr Cetina and Eike von Savigny, eds., *The Practice Turn in Contemporary Theory,* 17–28. New York: Routledge.

Barnett, Michael (2002), *Eyewitness to a Genocide: The United Nations and Rwanda.* Ithaca, NY: Cornell University Press.

Barnett, Michael and Emanuel Adler (1998), "Studying Security Communities in Theory, Comparison, and History," in Emanuel Adler and Michael Barnett, eds., *Security Communities,* 413–41. New York: Cambridge University Press.

Barnett, Michael and Raymond Duvall (2005), "Power in International Politics," *International Organization* 59(1): 39–75.

Barnett, Michael and Martha Finnemore (2004), *Rules for the World: International Organizations in Global Politics.* Ithaca, NY: Cornell University Press.

Bartelson, Jens (1995), *A Genealogy of Sovereignty.* New York: Cambridge University Press.

BBC (2008), "Rice Criticises 'Isolated' Russia," September 19 (http://newsvote.bbc.co.uk/mpapps/pagetools/print/news.bbc.co.uk/2/hi/americas/7623555.stm, accessed September 19, 2008).

Berridge, G. R., ed. (2004), *Diplomatic Classics: Selected Texts from Commynes to Vattel.* New York: Palgrave Macmillan.

Bigo, Didier (1996), *Polices en réseaux. L'expérience européenne* (Networked Police: The European Experience). Paris: Presses de Sciences Po.

(2000), "When Two Become One: Internal and External Securitisations in Europe," in Morten Kelstrup and Michael C. Williams, eds., *International Relations Theory and the Politics of European Integration: Power, Security and Community*, 171–204. New York: Routledge.

Bjola, Corneliu and Markus Kornprobst (2007), "Security Communities and the Habitus of Restraint: Germany and the United States on Iraq," *Review of International Studies* 33(2): 285–305.

Black, Ian (1997), "Albright to Offer Arms Cuts as Russia Digs in on NATO," *Guardian*, February 20.

Blacker, Coit D. (1998), "Russia and the West," in Michael Mandelbaum, ed., *The New Russian Foreign Policy*, 167–93. New York: Council on Foreign Relations.

Bourdieu, Pierre (1980), *Questions de sociologie* (Questions of Sociology). Paris: Minuit.

(1981), "Men and Machines," in Karin Knorr-Cetina and Aaron V. Cicourel, eds., *Advances in Social Theory and Methodology: Toward an Integration of Micro- and Macro-Sociologies*, 304–17. New York: Routledge and Kegan Paul.

(1986), "The Forms of Capital," in J. G. Richardson, ed., *Handbook of Theory and Research for the Sociology of Education*, 241–58. New York: Greenwood.

(1987), *Choses dites* (Things Said). Paris: Minuit.

(1989), "Social Space and Symbolic Power," *Sociological Theory* 7(1):14–25.

(1990a [1980]), *The Logic of Practice*. Stanford, CA: Stanford University Press.

(1990b), "The Scholastic Point of View," *Cultural Anthropology* 5(4):380–91.

(1994), "Rethinking the State: Genesis and Structure of the Bureaucratic Field," *Sociological Theory* 12(1): 1–18.

(2000 [1972]), *Esquisse d'une théorie de la pratique, précédé de trois études d'ethnologie kabyle* (Outline of a Theory of Practice, Preceded with Three Studies in Kabylian Ethnology). Paris: Seuil.

(2001a [1982]), *Langage et pouvoir symbolique* (Language and Symbolic Power). Paris: Seuil.

(2001b), *Science de la science et réflexivité* (Science of Science and Reflexivity). Paris: Raison d'agir.

(2003 [1997]), *Méditations pascaliennes* (Pascalian Meditations). Paris: Seuil.

Bourdieu, Pierre, ed. (1993), *La misère du monde* (The World's Misery). Paris: Seuil.

Bourdieu, Pierre and Loïc J. D. Wacquant (1992), "The Purpose of Reflexive Sociology (The Chicago Workshop)," in Pierre Bourdieu and Loïc J. D. Wacquant, *An Invitation to Reflexive Sociology*, 60–215. Chicago: University of Chicago Press.

Braun, Aurel (2008), "Introduction: Thinking about Security and Democracy," in Aurel Braun, ed., *NATO–Russia Relations in the Twenty-First Century*, 1–8. New York: Routledge.

Bull, Hedley (1995 [1977]), *The Anarchical Society: A Study of Order in World Politics*, 2nd edition. New York: Columbia University Press.

Buzan, Barry, Ole Wæver and Jaap de Wilde (1998), *Security: A New Framework for Analysis*. Boulder, CO: Lynne Rienner.

Carr, Edward Hallett (1958 [1939]), *The Twenty Years' Crisis 1919–1939: An Introduction to the Study of International Relations*, 2nd edition. London: MacMillan.

Cederman, Lars-Erik (1997), *Emergent Actors in World Politics: How States and Nations Develop and Dissolve*. Princeton, NJ: Princeton University Press.

Charodeyev, Gennady (1999), "There's Only One Person Who Could Have Given the Order: The President," *Izvestia*, June 15, translated in *Current Digest of the Post-Soviet Press* 51(24).

Checkel, Jeffrey T. (1997), *Ideas and International Political Change: Soviet/Russian Behavior and the End of the Cold War*. New Haven, CT: Yale University Press.

(2001), "Why Comply? Social Learning and European Identity Change," *International Organization* 55(3): 553–88.

(2004), "Social Constructivisms in Global and European Politics: A Review Essay," *Review of International Studies* 30(2): 229–44.

(2005), "International Institutions and Socialization in Europe: Introduction and Framework," *International Organization* 59(4): 801–26.

(2008), "Process Tracing," in Audie Klotz and Deepa Prakash, eds., *Qualitative Methods in International Relations: A Pluralist Guide*, 114–27. New York: Palgrave Macmillan.

CNN (2003), "Chirac Lashes Out at 'New Europe,'" February 18 (www.cnn.com/2003/WORLD/europe/02/18/sprj.irq.chirac, accessed May 31, 2008).

Colton, Timothy J. (2008), "Post-postcommunist Russia, the International Environment and NATO," in Aurel Braun, ed., *NATO–Russia Relations in the Twenty-First Century*, 25–38. New York: Routledge.

Cooper, Helene (2008), "In Georgia Clash, a Lesson on U.S. Need for Russia," *New York Times*, August 9.

Council of the EU (2003), "A Secure Europe in a Better World," European Security Strategy, December 12.

Cox, Michael (1992), "Western Intelligence, the Soviet Threat and NSC-68: A Reply to Beatrice Heuser," *Review of International Studies* 18(1): 75–86.

Crawford, Neta C. (2002), *Argument and Change in World Politics: Ethics, Decolonization, and Humanitarian Intervention*. New York: Cambridge University Press.

Cross, Mai'a K. Davis (2006), *The European Diplomatic Corps: Diplomats and International Cooperation from Westphalia to Maastricht*. New York: Palgrave Macmillan.

Daalder, Ivo and James Goldgeier (2006), "Global NATO," *Foreign Affairs* 85(5): 105–13.

Daalder, Ivo H. and James M. Lindsay (2005 [2003]), *American Unbound: The Bush Revolution in Foreign Policy*, 2nd edition. Hoboken, NJ: John Wiley and Sons.

D'Andrade, Roy (1995), *The Development of Cognitive Anthropology*. New York: Cambridge University Press.

Dannreuther, Roland (1999–2000), "Escaping the Enlargement Trap in NATO–Russian Relations," *Survival* 41(4): 145–64.

De Certeau, Michel (1990 [1980]), *L'invention du quotidien 1. Arts de faire* (The Invention of the Everyday: Ways of Doing). Paris: Gallimard.

De Nevers, Renée (2007), "NATO's International Security Role in the Terrorist Era," *International Security* 31(4): 34–66.

Der Derian, James (1987), *On Diplomacy: A Genealogy of Western Estrangement*. Oxford: Blackwell.

Deutsch, Karl W., Sidney A. Burrell, Robert A. Kann, Maurice Lee Jr., Martin Lichterman, Raymond E. Lindgren, Francis L. Loewenheim and Richard W. Van Wagenen (1957), *Political Community and the North Atlantic Area: International Organization in the Light of Historical Experience*. Princeton, NJ: Princeton University Press.

Dezalay, Yves and Bryant Garth (2002), *The Internationalization of Palace Wars: Lawyers, Economists, and the Contest to Transform Latin American States*. Chicago: University of Chicago Press.

Doty, Roxanne Lynn (1996), *Imperial Encounters: The Politics of Representation in North–South Relations*. Minneapolis: University of Minnesota Press.

Duffy, Gavan, Brian K. Frederking and Seth A. Tucker (1998), "Language Games: Dialogical Analysis of INF Negotiations," *International Studies Quarterly* 42(2): 271–94.

Eckstein, Harry (1975), "Case Studies and Theory in Political Science," in Fred I. Greenstein and Nelson W. Polsby, eds., *Handbook of Political Science*, vol. VII, 94–137. Berkeley, CA: University of California Press.

Elster, Jon (1989), *Nuts and Bolts for the Social Sciences*. New York: Cambridge University Press.

English, Robert D. (2000), *Russia and the Idea of the West: Gorbachev, Intellectuals, and the End of the Cold War*. New York: Columbia University Press.

Epstein, Seymour (1994), "Integration of the Cognitive and the Psychodynamic Unconscious," *American Psychologist* 49(8): 709–24.

Evangelista, Matthew (1999), *Unarmed Forces: The Transnational Movement to End the Cold War*. Ithaca, NY: Cornell University Press.

(2002), *The Chechen Wars: Will Russia Go the Way of the Soviet Union?* Washington, DC: Brookings Institution Press.

Fierke, Karin M. (1998), *Changing Games, Changing Strategies: Critical Investigations in Security*. New York: Manchester University Press.

(2004), "World or Worlds? The Analysis of Content and Discourse," *Qualitative Methods* 2(1): 36–9.

(2005), *Diplomatic Interventions: Conflict and Change in a Globalizing World*. New York: Palgrave Macmillan.

Finnemore, Martha (2003), *The Purpose of Intervention: Changing Beliefs about the Use of Force*. Ithaca, NY: Cornell University Press.

Finnemore, Martha and Kathryn Sikkink (2001), "Taking Stock: The Constructivist Research Programme in International Relations and Comparative Politics," *Annual Review of Political Science* 4: 391–416.

Fiske, Alan Page, Shinobu Kitayama, Hazel Rose Markus and Richard E. Nisbett (1999), "The Cultural Matrix of Social Psychology," in D. T. Gilbert, S. T. Fiske and G. Lindzey, eds., *The Handbook of Social Psychology*, 3rd edition, volume II, 915–81. Boston: McGraw-Hill.

Flynn, Gregory and Henry Farrell (1999), "Piecing Together the Democratic Peace: The CSCE, Norms, and the 'Construction' of Security in Post-Cold War Europe," *International Organization* 53(3): 505–35.

Foucault, Michel (1980), *Power/Knowledge: Selected Interviews and Other Writings 1972–1977*, edited by Colin Gordon. New York: Pantheon.

Fourcade, Marion (2006), "The Construction of a Global Profession: The Transnationalization of Economics," *American Journal of Sociology* 112(1): 145–94.

Fritch, Paul (2007), "The NATO–Russia Partnership: More than Meets the Eye," *NATO Review* 2.

Garfinkel, Harold (1967), *Studies in Ethnomethodology*. Englewood Cliffs, NJ: Prentice-Hall.

Geertz, Clifford (1973), *The Interpretation of Cultures: Selected Essays*. New York: Basic Books.

(1987), "'From the Native's Point of View': On the Nature of Anthropological Understanding," in Michael. T. Gibbons, ed., *Interpreting Politics*, 133–47. Oxford: Blackwell.

George, Alexander L. (1993), *Bridging the Gap: Theory and Practice in Foreign Policy*. Washington, DC: United States Institute of Peace Press.

George, Alexander L. and Andrew Bennett (2005), *Case Studies and Theory Development in the Social Sciences*. Cambridge, MA: MIT Press.

Ghebali, Victor-Yves (1996), *L'OSCE dans l'Europe post-communiste, 1990–1996. Vers une identité paneuropéenne de sécurité* (The OSCE in Post-Communist Europe, 1990–1996: Toward a Paneuropean Security Identity). Brussels: Bruylant.

Gheciu, Alexandra (2005), *NATO in the "New Europe": The Politics of International Socialization after the Cold War*. Stanford, CA: Stanford University Press.

Giddens, Anthony (1984), *The Constitution of Society: Outline of the Theory of Structuration*. Berkeley, CA: University of California Press.

Gilpin, Robert (1981), *War and Change in World Politics*. New York: Cambridge University Press.

Glaser, Barney G. and Anselm L. Strauss (1967), *The Discovery of Grounded Theory: Strategies for Qualitative Research*. New Brunswick, NJ: Aldine Transaction.

Goffman, Erving (1959), *The Presentation of Self in Everyday Life*. New York: Doubleday.

Goldgeier, James M. and Michael McFaul (2003), *Power and Purpose: U.S. Policy Toward Russia after the Cold War*. Washington, DC: Brookings Institution Press.

Gorbachev, Mikhail (1994), "The NATO Ultimatum Was the Worst Possible Way of Handling the Bosnian Crisis," *Nezavisimaya Gazeta*, February 22, translated in *Current Digest of the Post-Soviet Press* 46(7).

(1999), "No, No, NATO," *Boston Globe*, July 16.

Gornostayev, Dimitri and Vladimir Katin (1998), "'We Shouldn't Set a Precedent for NATO,'" *Nezavisimaya Gazeta*, May 30, translated in *Current Digest of the Post-Soviet Press* 50(22).

Guk, Sergei (1992), "NATO Could Become Guarantor of Russia's Security," *Izvestia*, January 22, translated in *Current Digest of the Post-Soviet Press* 44(3).

Gusterson, Hugh (1993), "Exploding Anthropology's Canon in the World of the Bomb: Ethnographic Writing on Militarism," *Journal of Contemporary Ethnography* 22(1): 59–79.

(2008), "Ethnographic Research," in Audie Klotz and Deepa Prakash, eds., *Qualitative Methods in International Relations: A Pluralist Guide*, 93–113. New York: Palgrave Macmillan.

Guzzini, Stefano (2000), "A Reconstruction of Constructivism in International Relations," *European Journal of International Relations* 6(2): 147–82.

(2005), "The Concept of Power: A Constructivist Analysis," *Millennium: Journal of International Studies* 33(3): 495–521.

Haas, Peter M. and Ernst B. Haas (2002), "Pragmatic Constructivism and the Study of International Institutions," *Millennium* 31(3): 573–601.

Hacking, Ian (1982), "Language, Truth and Reason," in Martin Hollis and Steven Lukes, eds., *Rationality and Relativism*, 48–66. Oxford: Blackwell.

(1999), *The Social Construction of What?* Cambridge, MA: Harvard University Press.

(2002a), *Historical Ontology*. Cambridge, MA: Harvard University Press.

(2002b), "Inaugural Lecture: Chair of Philosophy and History of Scientific Concepts at the Collège de France, 16 January 2001," *Economy and Society* 31(1): 1–14.

Hafner-Burton, Emilie M. and Alexander H. Montgomery (2006), "Power Positions: International Organizations, Social Networks, and Conflicts," *Journal of Conflict Resolution* 50(1): 3–27.

Hall, Peter A. (2003), "Aligning Ontology and Methodology in Comparative Research," in James Mahoney and Dietrich Rueschemeyer, eds., *Comparative Historical Analysis in the Social Sciences*, 373–404. New York: Cambridge University Press.

Hamilton, Keith and Richard Langhorne (1995), *The Practice of Diplomacy: Its Evolution, Theory and Administration*. New York: Routledge.

Hansen, Lene (2006), *Security as Practice: Discourse Analysis and the Bosnian War*. New York: Routledge.

Headley, Jim (2003), "Sarajevo, February 1994: The First Russia–NATO Crisis of the Post-Cold War Era," *Review of International Studies* 29(2): 209–27.

Heider, Karl G. (1988), "The Rashomon Effect: When Ethnographers Disagree," *American Anthropologist* 90(1): 73–81.

Heuser, Beatrice (1991), "NSC 68 and the Soviet Threat: A New Perspective on Western Threat Perception and Policy Making," *Review of International Studies* 17(1): 17–40.

Hollis, Martin and Steve Smith (1990), *Explaining and Understanding International Relations*. Oxford: Oxford University Press.

Hopf, Ted (2002) *Social Construction of International Politics: Identities and Foreign Policies, Moscow, 1955 and 1999*. Ithaca, NY: Cornell University Press.

(n.d.), "The Logic of Habit in International Relations," mimeo, May 2008.

Huysmans, Jef (2002), "Shape-shifting NATO: Humanitarian Action and the Kosovo Refugee Crisis," *Review of International Studies* 28(3): 599–618.

Ivanov, Sergey B. (2004), "International Security in the Context of the Russia–NATO Relationship," Munich, February 7 (www.securityconference.de/konferenzen/rede.php?menu_2005=&menu_konferenz, accessed July 27, 2007).

Izvestia (2004), "Yury Baluyevsky, First Deputy Chief of the Russian General Staff: 'NATO Expansion Will Strike a Fatal Blow to the Treaty on Conventional Armed Forces in Europe," *Izvestia*, March 3, translated in *Current Digest of the Post-Soviet Press* 56(9).

Jackson, Patrick Thaddeus (2004), "Hegel's House, or 'People Are States Too,'" *Review of International Studies* 30(2): 281–7.

(2006a), *Civilizing the Enemy: German Reconstruction and the Invention of the West*. Ann Arbor, MI: University of Michigan Press.

(2006b), "Making Sense of Making Sense: Configurational Analysis and the Double Hermeneutic," in Dvora Yanow and Peregrine Schwartz-Shea, eds., *Interpretation and Method: Empirical Research Methods and the Interpretive Turn*, 264–80. New York: M. E. Sharpe.

(2008), "Foregrounding Ontology: Dualism, Monism, and IR Theory," *Review of International Studies* 34(1): 129–53.

Jackson, Patrick Thaddeus and Daniel H. Nexon (1999), "Relations before States: Substance, Process and the Study of World Politics," *European Journal of International Relations* 5(3): 291–332.

(2004), "Constructivist Realism or Realist-Constructivism?" *International Studies Review* 6(2): 337–41.

Jackson, Peter (2008), "Pierre Bourdieu, the 'Cultural Turn' and the Practice of International History," *Review of International Studies* 34(1): 155–81.

Johnston, Alastair Iain (2001), "Treating International Institutions as Social Environments," *International Studies Quarterly* 45(4): 487–515.

Jönsson, Christer and Martin Hall (2005), *Essence of Diplomacy.* New York: Palgrave Macmillan.

Kagan, Robert (2003), *Paradise and Power: America and Europe in the New World Order.* London: Atlantic Books.

Kahneman, Daniel (2002), "Maps of Bounded Rationality: A Perspective on Intuitive Judgment and Choice" (nobelprize.org/nobel_prizes/economics/laureates/2002/kahnemann-lecture.pdf, accessed April 15, 2009).

Kassianova, Alla (2001), "Russia: Still Open to the West? Evolution of the State Identity in the Foreign Policy and Security Discourse," *Europe–Asia Studies* 53(6): 821–39.

Katzenstein, Peter J., Robert O. Keohane and Stephen D. Krasner (1998), "International Organization and the Study of World Politics," *International Organization* 52(4): 645–85.

Katzner, Donald W. (1999), "Hysteresis and the Modeling of Economic Phenomena," *Review of Political Economy* 11(2): 171–81.

Kauppi, Niilo (2005), *Democracy, Social Resources and Political Power in the European Union.* New York: Manchester University Press.

Keck, Margaret E. and Kathryn Sikkink (1998), *Activists beyond Borders: Advocacy Networks in International Politics.* Ithaca, NY: Cornell University Press.

Kipp, Jacob W., Timothy L. Thomas, Lester W. Grau *et al.* (2000), "Lessons and Conclusions on the Execution of IFOR Operations and Prospects for a Future Combined Security System: The Peace and Stability of Europe after IFOR," 2nd edition. Fort Leavenworth, KS: US Army Combined Arms Center.

Kissinger, Henry A. (1973), *A World Restored: Metternich, Castlereagh and the Problem of Peace 1812–1822.* Gloucester, MA: Peter Smith.

(1994), *Diplomacy.* New York: Simon and Schuster.

Kitchen, Veronica (2009), "Argument and Identity Change in the Atlantic Security Community," *Security Dialogue* 40(1): 95–114.

Kondrashov, Stanislav (1996), "The Diplomatic Gospel according to Yevgeny on the Eve of the Second Coronation of Boris," *Izvestia,* August 9, translated in *Current Digest of the Post-Soviet Press* 48(32).

Koremenos, Barbara, Charles Lipson, and Duncan Snidal (2001), "The Rational Design of International Institutions," *International Organization* 55(4): 761–99.

Kornprobst, Markus, Vincent Pouliot, Nisha Shah and Ruben Zaiotti, eds. (2008), *Metaphors of Globalization: Mirrors, Magicians, and Mutinies.* New York: Palgrave Macmillan.

Kozyrev, Andrei V. (1992), "Russia and Human Rights," *Slavic Review* 51(2): 287–93.

(1993), "The New Russia and the Atlantic Alliance," *NATO Review* 1 (www.nato.int/docu/review/1993/9301-1.htm) accessed August 27, 2007).

(1994a), "The Lagging Partnership," *Foreign Affairs* 73(3): 59–71.

(1994b), "Russia and the U.S.: Partnership Is Not Premature, It Is Overdue," *Izvestia*, March 11, translated in *Current Digest of the Post-Soviet Press* 46(10).

(1995), "Partnership or Cold Peace?" *Foreign Policy* 99: 3–14.

Kramer, Mark (2002), "NATO, The Baltic States and Russia: A Framework for Sustainable Enlargement," *International Affairs* 78(4): 731–56.

Kratochwil, Friedrich V. (1989), *Rules, Norms, and Decisions: On the Conditions of Practical and Legal Reasoning in International Relations and Domestic Affairs*. New York: Cambridge University Press.

(2000), "Constructing a New Orthodoxy? Wendt's 'Social Theory of International Politics' and the Constructivist Challenge," *Millennium: Journal of International Studies* 29(1): 73–101.

(2007), "Of False Promises and Good Bets: A Plea for a Pragmatic Approach to Theory Building (The Tartu Lecture)," *Journal of International Relations and Development* 10(1): 215–47.

Kujat, Harald (2002), "Combating Terrorism: A Key Objective," *Kraznaya Zvezda*, reprinted and translated by NATO (www.nato.int/docu/articles/2002/a021225a.htm, accessed January 22, 2004).

Kupchan, Charles A. (1994), "Expand NATO – And Split Europe," *New York Times*, November 27.

Kvale, Steinar (1996), *InterViews: An Introduction to Qualitative Research Interviewing*. Thousand Oaks, CA: Sage.

Lakatos, Imre (1970), "Falsification and the Methodology of Scientific Research Programmes," in Imre Lakatos and Alan Musgrave, eds., *Criticism and the Growth of Knowledge*, 91–196. New York: Cambridge University Press.

Leander, Anna (2001), "Pierre Bourdieu on Economics," *Review of International Political Economy* 8(2): 344–53.

(2008) "Thinking Tools," in Audie Klotz and Deepa Prakash, eds., *Qualitative Methods of International Relations: A Pluralist Guide*, 11–27. New York: Palgrave Macmillan.

Lebow, Richard Ned (2008), *A Cultural Theory of International Relations*. New York: Cambridge University Press.

Legvold, Robert (2007), "Introduction," in Robert Legvold, ed., *Russian Foreign Policy in the Twenty-First Century and the Shadow of the Past*, 3–34. New York: Columbia University Press.

Lévesque, Jacques (1995), *1989 – La fin d'un empire. L'URSS et la liberation de l'Europe de l'Est* (1989 – The End of an Empire: USSR and the Liberation of Eastern Europe). Paris: Presses de Sciences Po.

Levitin, Oleg (2000), "Inside Moscow's Kosovo Muddle," *Survival* 42(1): 130–40.

Levy, Clifford J. (2008), "Russia Adopts Blustery Tone Set by Envoy," *New York Times*, August 28.

Lo, Bobo (2002), *Russian Foreign Policy in the Post-Soviet Era: Reality, Illusion and Mythmaking*. New York: Palgrave Macmillan.

Lukyanov, Fyodor (2004), "Final Act," *Vremya Novostei*, July 9, translated in *Current Digest of the Post-Soviet Press* 56(27).

Lynch, Michael (1997), "Theorizing Practice," *Human Studies* 20(3): 335–44.

MacFarlane, S. Neil (2008), "Russia, NATO Enlargement and the Strengthening of Democracy in the European Space," in Aurel Braun, ed., *NATO–Russia Relations in the Twenty-First Century*, 39–52. New York: Routledge.

Madsen, Mikael Rask (2007), "From Cold War Instrument to Supreme European Court: The European Court of Human Rights at the Crossroads of International and National Law and Politics," *Law and Social Inquiry* 32(1): 137–59.

March, James G. and Johan P. Olsen (1989), *Rediscovering Institutions: The Organizational Basis of Politics*. New York: Free Press.

(1998), "The Institutional Dynamics of International Political Orders," *International Organization* 52(4): 943–69.

Marti, Eduardo (1996), "Mechanisms of Internalisation and Externalisation of Knowledge in Piaget's and Vygotsky's Theories," in Anastasia Tryphon and Jacques Vonèche, eds., *Piaget-Vygotsky: The Social Genesis of Thought*, 57–83. Hove, UK: Psychology Press.

Mattern, Janice Bially (2001), "The Power Politics of Identity," *European Journal of International Relations* 7(3): 349–97.

(2005), *Ordering International Politics: Identity, Crisis, and Representational Force*. New York: Routledge.

McDonald, David (2007), "Domestic Conjunctures, the Russian State, and the World Outside, 1700–2006," in Robert Legvold, ed., *Russian Foreign Policy in the Twenty-First Century and the Shadow of the Past*, 145–203. New York: Columbia University Press.

MccGwire, Michael (1998), "NATO Expansion: 'A Policy Error of Historic Importance,'" *Review of International Studies* 24(1): 23–42.

Mearsheimer, John J. (2001), *The Tragedy of Great Power Politics.* New York: W. W. Norton and Company.

Mérand, Frédéric (2008), *European Defense Policy: Beyond the Nation State.* New York: Oxford University Press.

Mérand, Frédéric and Vincent Pouliot (2008), "Le monde de Pierre Bourdieu: Éléments pour une théorie sociale des Relations internationales" (Pierre Bourdieu's World: Elements for a Social Theory of International Relations), *Canadian Journal of Political Science* 41(3): 603–25.

Mercer, Jonathan (1995), "Anarchy and Identity," *International Organization* 49(2): 229–52.

Migranyan, Andranik (1994), "Russia's Foreign Policy: Disastrous Results of Three Years," *Nezavisimaya Gazeta*, December 10, translated in *Current Digest of the Post-Soviet Press* 46(50).

— (1997), "A Mistake or Not? Boris Yeltsin Will Sign Russia-NATO Treaty in Paris Today," *Nezavisimaya Gazeta*, May 27, translated in *Current Digest of the Post-Soviet Press* 49(22).

Milliken, Jennifer (1999), "The Study of Discourse in International Relations: A Critique of Research and Methods," *European Journal of International Relations* 5(2): 225–54.

Ministry of Foreign Affairs of the Russian Federation (2001), "Speech by President Putin of Russia before the Representatives of the American Public and US Political Figures," Washington, November 13 (www.ln.mid.ru/bl.nsf/900b2c3ac91734634325698f002d9dcf/0472a5da92607d0543256b050031fe41?OpenDocument, accessed June 3, 2009).

— (2007a), "The Foreign Policy Sovereignty of Russia – An Absolute Imperative, article by Sergey Lavrov," January 18 (www.ln.mid.ru/brp_4.nsf/e78a48070f128a7b43256999005bcbb3/4a94acbef393c22, accessed June 3, 2007).

— (2007b), "Transcript of Remarks and Replies to Media Questions by Russian Minister of Foreign Affairs, Sergey Lavrov Following Ministerial Meeting of Russia–NATO Council," Oslo, April 26 (www.nato-russia-council.info/htm/EN/statements26apr07_3.shtml, accessed June 3, 2009).

Mitzen, Jennifer (2006), "Ontological Security in World Politics: State Identity and the Security Dilemma," *European Journal of International Relations* 12(3): 341–70.

Morozov, Viatcheslav (2002), "Resisting Entropy, Discarding Human Rights: Romantic Realism and Securitization of Identity in Russia," *Cooperation and Conflict* 37(4): 409–29.

Moskovskiye Novosti (1996), "Primakov Starts with the CIS," *Moskovskiye Novosti*, January 14, translated in *Current Digest of the Post-Soviet Press* 48(2).

Mukhin, Vladimir (1998), "Warning by Russian Defense Ministry,"
   Nezavisimaya Gazeta, June 23, translated in *Current Digest of the
   Post-Soviet Press* 50(25).
Myers, Steven Lee (2008), "Bush Supports Ukraine's Bid to Join NATO,"
   New York Times, April 2.
NATO (1990), "Declaration on a Transformed North Atlantic Alliance
   Issued by the Heads of State and Government Participating in
   the Meeting of the North Atlantic Council," London, July 6
   (www.nato.int/docu/basictxt/b900706a.htm, accessed November 6,
   2004).
   (1994a), "Declaration of the Heads of State and Government Participating
   in the Meeting of the North Atlantic Council ('The Brussels Summit
   Declaration')," Brussels, January 11 (www.nato.int/docu/basictxt/
   b940111a.htm, accessed November 6, 2004).
   (1994b), "Final Communiqué," press communiqué M-NAC-1(94)46,
   Istanbul, June 9 (www.nato.int/docu/comm/49-95/c940609b.htm,
   accessed October 12, 2007).
   (1994c), "Final Communiqué," communiqué M-NAC-2(94)116,
   Brussels, December 1 (www.nato.int/docu/comm/49-95/c941201a.
   htm, accessed October 11, 2007).
   (1995), "Study on NATO Enlargement," September (www.nato.int/
   docu/basictxt/enl-9501.htm, accessed March 10, 2006).
   (1997), "Founding Act on Mutual Relations, Cooperation and Security
   between NATO and the Russian Federation," Paris, May 27
   (www.nato.int/docu/basictxt/fndact-a.htm, accessed June 11, 2004).
   (2001a), "Press Statement, Meeting in Extraordinary Session of the
   NATO-Russia Permanent Joint Council at Ambassadorial Level,"
   Brussels, September 13 (www.nato.int/docu/pr/2001/p010913e.htm,
   accessed October 18, 2007).
   (2001b), "NATO–Russia: Sit Down and Discuss Where Our Interests
   Meet," speech by Lord Robertson, NATO Secretary-General at the
   Moscow State Institute of Foreign Relations (MGIMO), February 21
   (www.nato.int/docu/speech/2001/s010221a.htm, accessed December
   2, 2007).
   (2001c), "Press Conference with NATO Secretary-General, Lord
   Robertson," Moscow, November 22 (www.nato.int/docu/speech/2001/
   s011122b.htm, accessed December 1, 2007).
   (2002), "NATO–Russia Relations: A New Quality," Rome, May 28
   (www.nato.int/docu/basictxt/b020528e.htm, accessed June 3, 2009).
   (2004a), "Joint NATO–Russia position on Ukraine," December 9
   (www.nato.int/docu/update/2004/12-december/e1209d.htm, accessed
   October 21, 2005).

(2004b), "The Istanbul Declaration: Our Security in a New Era," Press release 2004(097), June 28 (www.nato.int/docu/pr/2004/p04–097e.htm, accessed January 24, 2005).

(2006), "NATO-Russia News 2/06," NATO Public Diplomacy Division.

(2007), "NATO-Russia: A Pragmatic Partnership," NATO Public Diplomacy Division.

(2008a), "Bucharest Summit Declaration," Bucharest, April 3 (www.nato.int/docu/pr/2208/p08-049e.html, accessed June 3, 2008).

(2008b), "Statement at the Meeting of the North Atlantic Council at the Level of Foreign Ministers held at NATO Headquarters, Brussels, on 19 August 2008," press release (2008) 104 (www.nato.int/docu/pr/2008/p08-104e.html, accessed August 19, 2008).

Neufeld, Mark (1993), "Interpretation and the 'Science' of International Relations," *Review of International Studies* 19(1): 39–61.

Neumann Iver B. (1996), "Self and Other in International Relations," *European Journal of International Relations* 2(2): 139–74.

(1999), *Uses of the Other: "The East" in European Identity Formation.* Minneapolis: University of Minnesota Press.

(2002), "Returning Practice to the Linguistic Turn: The Case of Diplomacy," *Millennium: Journal of International Studies* 31(3): 627–51.

(2004), "Beware of Organicism: The Narrative Self of the State," *Review of International Studies* 30(2): 259–67.

(2005a), "To Be a Diplomat," *International Studies Perspective* 6(1): 72–93.

(2005b), "Russia as a Great Power," in Jakob Hedenskog, Vilhelm Konnander, Bertil Nygren, Ingmar Oldberg and Christer Pursiainen, eds., *Russia as a Great Power: Dimensions of Security under Putin*, 13–28. New York: Routledge.

(2007), "A Speech That the Entire Ministry May Stand for," or: Why Diplomats Never Produce Anything New," *International Political Sociology* 1(2): 183–200.

(2008a) "Discourse Analysis," in Audie Klotz and Deepa Prakash, eds., *Qualitative Methods of International Relations: A Pluralist Guide*, 61–77. New York: Palgrave Macmillan.

(2008b), "Russia as a Great Power, 1815–2007," *Journal of International Relations and Development* 11(2): 128–51.

New York Times (1994), "Include Russia, Too," *New York Times*, January 9.

(1997), "Former Enemies Speak of Peace," *New York Times*, May 28.

(2001), "Bush's Vision: 'We Will Not Trade Away the Fate of Free European Peoples," *New York Times*, June 16.

Nexon, Daniel H. (2009), *The Struggle for Power in Early Modern Europe: Religious Conflict, Dynastic Empires and International Change*. Princeton, NJ: Princeton University Press.

Nezavisimaya Gazeta (1994), "Yeltsin on Partnership in NATO," *Nezavisimaya Gazeta*, April 7, translated in *Current Digest of the Post-Soviet Press* 46(14).

Nicolson, Harold (1963 [1939]), *Diplomacy*, 3rd edition. New York: Oxford University Press.

Norris, John (2005), *Collision Course: NATO, Russia, and Kosovo*. Westport, CN: Praeger.

O'Neill, Barry (1999), *Honor, Symbols, and War*. Ann Arbor, MI: University of Michigan Press.

Onuf, Nicholas (1998), "Constructivism: A User's Manual," in Vendulka Kubalkova, Nicholas Onuf and Paul Kowert, eds., *International Relations in a Constructed World*, 58–98. Armonk, NY: M. E. Sharpe.

Parkhomenko, Sergei (1993), "Russia Gives Poland Leave to Join NATO," *Sevodnya*, August 27, translated in *Current Digest of the Post-Soviet Press* 45(34).

Paul, T. V. (2005), "Soft Balancing in the Age of U.S. Primacy," *International Security* 30(1): 46–71.

Pierson, Paul (2004), *Politics in Time: History, Institutions, and Social Analysis*. Princeton, NJ: Princeton University Press.

PIPA (2002), *Worldview 2002: American and European Public Opinion and Foreign Policy*, The Chicago Council on Foreign Relations, (www.ccfr.org/globalviews2004/sub/pdf/2002_Comparative.pdf, accessed January 24, 2004).

Polanyi, Michael (1983), *The Tacit Dimension*. Gloucester, MA: Peter Smith.

Poleshchuk, Andrei (1993), "Is an Expansion of NATO Justified?" *Nezavisimaya Gazeta*, November 26, translated in *Current Digest of the Post-Soviet Press* 45(47).

Polkinghorne, Donald E. (1988), *Narrative Knowing and the Human Sciences*. Albany, NY: State University of New York Press.

Ponsard, Lionel (2007), *Russia, NATO and Cooperative Security: Bridging the Gap*. New York: Routledge.

Pop, Liliana (2007), "Time and Crisis: Framing Success and Failure in Romania's Post-communist Transformations," *Review of International Studies* 33(3): 395–413.

Pouliot, Vincent (2003), "La Russie et la communauté atlantique. Vers une culture commune de sécurité" (Russia and the Atlantic Community: Toward a Common Security Culture?), *Études internationales* 34(1): 25–51.

(2004), "The Essence of Constructivism," *Journal of International Relations and Development* 7(3): 319–36.

(2006), "The Alive and Well Transatlantic Security Community: A Theoretical Reply to Michael Cox," *European Journal of International Relations and Development* 12(1): 119–27.

(2007), "Pacification Without Collective Identification: Russia and the Transatlantic Security Community in the Post-Cold War Era," *Journal of Peace Research* 44(5): 603–20.

(2008), "Reflexive Mirror: Everything Takes Place As If Threats Were Going Global," in Markus Kornprobst, Vincent Pouliot, Nisha Shah and Ruben Zaiotti, eds., *Metaphors of Globalization: Mirrors, Magicians, and Mutinies*, 34–49. New York: Palgrave Macmillan.

(n.d.), "The Materials of Practice: Nuclear Warheads, Rhetorical Commonplaces and Committee Meetings in NATO-Russia Diplomacy," paper presented at the annual meeting of the American Political Science Association, Boston, August 2008.

Pouliot, Vincent and Niels Lachmann (2004), "Les communautés de sécurité, vecteurs d'ordre régional et international" (Security Communities as Vehicles of Regional and International Order), *Revue internationale et stratégique* 54: 131–40.

President of Russia (2001), "Annual Address to the Federal Assembly of the Russian Federation," Moscow, April 3 (www.kremlin.ru/eng/text/speeches/2001/04/03/0000_type70029type82912_70660.shtml, accessed June 5, 2007).

(2007), "Speech and the Following Discussion at the Munich Conference on Security Policy," Munich, February 10 (www.president.kremlin.ru/eng/text/speeches/2007/02/10/0138, accessed April 4, 2007).

(2008), "Speech at the Meeting with Russian Ambassadors and Permanent Representatives to International Organisations," Moscow, July 15 (http://kremlin.ru/eng/text/speeches/2008/07/15/1121_type82912type84779_204155.shtml, accessed July 16, 2008).

Price, Richard and Christian Reus-Smit (1998), "Dangerous Liaisons? Critical International Theory and Constructivism," *European Journal of International Relations* 4(3): 259–94.

Primakov, Yevgeny (2004), *Russian Crossroads: Toward the New Millennium.* New Haven, CT: Yale University Press.

(2006), "Russia and the U.S. in Need of Trust and Cooperation," *Russia in Global Affairs*, February 8 (eng.globalaffairs.ru/number/14/1005. html, accessed April 5, 2006).

Pushkov, Aleksei (1999), "The Chernomyrdin Syndrome," *Nezavisimaya Gazeta*, June 11, translated in *Current Digest of the Post-Soviet Press* 51(23).

(2004), "The Aim Is Not to Divide Ukraine, But to Break It Away from Russia," *Trud*, December 1, translated in *Current Digest of the Post-Soviet Press* 56(48).

Reber, Arthur S. (1993), *Implicit Learning and Tacit Knowledge: An Essay on the Cognitive Unconscious*. New York: Oxford University Press.

Reus-Smit, Christian (1997), *The Moral Purpose of the State: Culture, Social Identity, and Institutional Rationality in International Relations*. Princeton, NJ: Princeton University Press.

Ricoeur, Paul (1977 [1973]), "The Model of the Text: Meaningful Action Considered as a Text," in Fred R. Dallmayr and Thomas A. McCarthy, eds., *Understanding and Social Inquiry*, 316–34. Notre Dame, IN: University of Notre Dame Press.

Ringmar, Erik (1996), *Identity, Interest and Action: A Cultural Explanation of Sweden's Intervention in the Thirty Years War*. New York: Cambridge University Press.

Risse, Thomas (2000), "'Let's Argue!': Communicative Action in World Politics," *International Organization* 54(1): 1–39.

Rodin, Ivan (1994), "NATO's Program Is Not Entirely to the Liking of the State Duma," *Nezavisimaya Gazeta*, March 18, translated in *Current Digest of the Post-Soviet Press* 46(11).

Rodionov, Igor (1996), "What Sort of Defense Does Russia Need?" *Nezavisimoye Voyennoye Obozreniye*, November 28, translated in *Current Digest of the Post-Soviet Press* 48(50).

Rossiiskaya Gazeta (1996), "Let's Leave Nuclear Ambitions to the History Books," *Rossiiskaya Gazeta*, September 26, translated in *Current Digest of the Post-Soviet Press* 48(39).

(1997), "Cooperation Instead of Confrontation," *Rossiiskaya Gazeta*, March 18, translated in *Current Digest of the Post-Soviet Press* 49(11).

(1999), "NATO Seeks to Enter 21st Century Wearing the Uniform of World Policeman," *Rossiiskaya Gazeta*, March 26, translated in *Current Digest of the Post-Soviet Press* 51(12).

Rossiiskiye Vesti (1995), "Abandon Reflexive Resort to Force in Favor of Considered Approach," *Rossiiskiye Vesti*, September 8, translated in *Current Digest of the Post-Soviet Press* 47(36).

Rubin, Herbert J. and Irene S. Rubin (1995), *Qualitative Interviewing: The Art of Hearing Data.* Thousand Oaks, CA: Sage.

Rudolph, Susan Hoeber (2004), "Toward Convergence," in Ian Shapiro, Rogers M. Smith, and Tarek E. Masoud, eds., *Problems and Methods in the Study of Politics*, 385–88. New York: Cambridge University Press.

Ruggie, John G. (1998), *Constructing the World Polity: Essays on International Institutionalization.* New York: Routledge.

Ryle, Gilbert (1984), *The Concept of Mind.* Chicago: University of Chicago Press.

Satow, Ernest Mason (1979), *Satow's Guide to Diplomatic Practice*, 5th edition. London: Longman.

Schatz, Edward (2009a), "Ethnographic Immersion and the Study of Politics," in Edward Schatz, ed., *Political Ethnography: What Immersion Contributes to the Study of Power*, 1–22. Chicago: University of Chicago Press.

  (2009b), "What Kind(s) of Ethnography Does Political Science Need," in Edward Schatz, ed., *Political Ethnography: What Immersion Contributes to the Study of Power*, 303–18. Chicago: University of Chicago Press.

Schatzki, Theodore R. (2005), "Practices and Actions: A Wittgensteinian Critique of Bourdieu and Giddens," in Derek Robbins, ed., *Pierre Bourdieu 2*, 167–191. Thousand Oaks, CA: Sage.

Schatzki, Theodore R., Karin Knorr Cetina and Eike von Savigny, eds. (2001), *The Practice Turn in Contemporary Theory.* New York: Routledge.

Schelling, Thomas C. (1980 [1960]), *The Strategy of Conflict.* Cambridge, MA: Harvard University Press.

Schimmelfennig, Frank (2001), "The Community Trap: Liberal Norms, Rhetorical Action, and the Eastern Enlargement of the European Union," *International Organization* 55(1): 47–80.

  (2003), *The EU, NATO and the Integration of Europe: Rules and Rhetoric.* New York: Cambridge University Press.

Schmidt, William E. (1994), "Russia Clarifies Hopes for a Link with NATO," *New York Times*, May 26.

Scott, James C. (1998), *Seeing Like a State: How Certain Schemes to Improve the Human Condition Have Failed.* New Haven, CT: Yale University Press.

Searle, John R (1995), *The Construction of Social Reality.* New York: Free Press.

  (1998), *Mind, Language and Society: Philosophy in the Real World.* New York: Basic Books.

Sending, Ole Jacob (2002), "Constitution, Choice and Change: Problems with the 'Logic of Appropriateness' and Its Use in Constructivist Theory," *European Journal of International Relations* 8(4): 443–70.

Shannon, Vaughn P. (2000), "Norms Are What States Make of Them: The Political Psychology of Norm Violation," *International Studies Quarterly* 44(2): 293–316.

Sharp, Paul and Geoffrey Wiseman, eds. (2007), *The Diplomatic Corps as an Institution of International Society*. New York: Palgrave Macmillan.

Shegedin, Aleksandr and Mikhail Zygar (2006), "Estonia Turns Its Defense Side to Russia," *Kommersant*, December 7, translated in *Current Digest of the Post-Soviet Press* 58(49).

Shevtsov, Leontiy P. (1997), "Russian-NATO Military Cooperation in Bosnia: A Basis for the Future?" *NATO Review* 45(2): 17–21.

Smirnov, Aleksei (2002), "Russia Is Given a Place in a Dying Alliance," *Noviye Izvestia*, May 16, translated in *Current Digest of the Post-Soviet Press* 54(20).

Solovyov, Vladimir and Sidorov, Dmitry (2006), "Sanction Master," *Kommersant*, October 4, translated in *Current Digest of the Post-Soviet Press* 58(40).

Stankevich, Sergei (1992), "Russia Has Already Made an Anti-imperial Choice," *Nezavisimaya Gazeta*, November 6, translated in *Current Digest of the Post-Soviet Press* 44(45).

Stanovich, Keith E. and Richard F. West (2000), "Individual Differences in Reasoning: Implications for the Rationality Debate?" *Behavioral and Brain Sciences* 23(5): 645–726.

Sterling-Folker, Jennifer (2002), "Realism and the Constructivist Challenge: Rejecting, Reconstructing, or Rereading," *International Studies Review* 4(1): 73–97.

Straus, Ira (2003), "NATO: The Only West That Russia Has?" *Demokratizatsiya* 11(2): 229–69.

Sysoyev, Gennady (1998), "Russian Assault Force Lands in Albania," *Kommersant*, August 18, translated in *Current Digest of the Post-Soviet Press* 50(33).

(2004), "Minister Gets Job Done at Highest Level," *Kommersant*, June 30, translated in *Current Digest of the Post-Soviet Press* 56(26).

Swidler, Ann (2001), "What Anchors Cultural Practices," in Theodore R. Schatzki, Karin Knorr Cetina and Eike von Savigny, eds., *The Practice Turn in Contemporary Theory*, 74–92. New York: Routledge.

Talbott, Strobe (1995), "Why NATO Should Grow," *New York Review of Books*, August 10: 27.

(2002), *The Russia Hand: A Memoir of Presidential Diplomacy*. New York: Random House.

Taylor, Charles (1993 [1981]), "To Follow a Rule ..." in Craig Calhoun, Edward LiPuma and Moishe Postone, eds., *Bourdieu: Critical Perspectives*, 45–59. Cambridge: Polity Press.

Thomas, Daniel C. (2001), *The Helsinki Effect: International Norms, Human Rights, and the Demise of Communism*. Princeton, NJ: Princeton University Press.

Tilly, Charles (1985), "War Making and State Making as Organized Crime," in Peter B. Evans, Dietrich Rueschemeyer and Theda Skocpol, eds., *Bringing the State Back In*, 169–91. New York: Cambridge University Press.

Toulmin, Stephen (2001), *Return to Reason*. Cambridge, MA: Harvard University Press.

Trachtenberg, Marc (2006), *The Craft of International History: A Guide to Method*. Princeton, NJ: Princeton University Press.

Traynor, Ian (2002), "Russia and Nato Reach Historic Deal," *Guardian*, May 15.

Trenin, Dmitri (2000), "Russia's Security Relations with the West after Kosovo and Chechnya," *Notes de l'IFRI 19*.

(2005), "Russia's Security Integration with America and Europe," in Alexander J. Motyl, Blair A. Ruble and Lilia Shevtsova, eds., *Russia's Engagement with the West: Transformation and Integration in the Twenty-first Century*, 281–94. Armonk, NY: M. E. Sharpe.

Tsebelis, George (1990), *Nested Games: Rational Choice in Comparative Politics*. Berkeley, CA: University of California Press.

Tsygankov, Andrei P. (2001), "The Final Triumph of the Pax Americana? Western Intervention in Yugoslavia and Russia's Debate on the Post-Cold War Order," *Communist and Post-Communist Studies* 34(2): 133–56.

(2003), "Mastering Space in Eurasia: Russia's Geopolitical Thinking after the Soviet Break-up," *Communist and Post-Communist Studies* 36(1): 101–27.

(2004), *Whose World Order? Russia's Perception of American Ideas after the Cold War*. Notre Dame, IN: University of Notre Dame Press.

(2005), "Vladimir Putin's Vision of Russia as a Normal Great Power," *Post-Soviet Affairs* 21(2): 132–58.

Turner, Stephen (1994), *The Social Theory of Practices: Tradition, Tacit Knowledge, and Presuppositions*. Chicago: University of Chicago Press.

UN Security Council (1993), "Resolution 836," S/RES/836(1993), June 4.

(1998a), "Resolution 1199 (1998)," S/RES/1199, September 23.

(1998b), "3937th Meeting, Saturday, 24 October 1998, 4.15 p.m, New York," S/PV.3937.

US Department of State (2004), "The NATO–Russia Council: A Vital Partnership in the War on Terror," remarks by R. Nicholas Burns, Moscow, November 8 (www.state.gov/p/eur/rls/rm/38244.htm, accessed April 2, 2007).

(2006), "Discussion on Russia/G8 issues," Washington, April 19 (www.state.gov/p/eur/rls/rm/65206.htm, accessed September 26, 2006).

Vaughn, Diane (2008), "Bourdieu and Organizations: The Empirical Challenge," *Theory and Society* 37(1): 65–81.

Villumsen, Trine (2008), "Theory as Practice and Capital: NATO in a Bourdieusian Field of Security in Europe: Toward a Sociological Approach to IR." PhD dissertation, Department of Political Science, University of Copenhagen.

Wacquant, Loïc J. D. (1992), "Toward a Social Praxeology: The Structure and Logic of Bourdieu's Sociology," in Pierre Bourdieu and Loïc J. D.Wacquant, *An Invitation to Reflexive Sociology*, 1–59. Chicago: University of Chicago Press.

(1995), "The Pugilistic Point of View: How Boxers Think and Feel about Their Trade," *Theory and Society* 24(4): 489–535.

Wæver, Ole (1998), "Insecurity, Security, and Asecurity in the West European Non-War Community," in Emanuel Adler and Michael Barnett, eds., *Security Communities*, 69–118. New York: Cambridge University Press.

Waltz, Kenneth N. (1979), *Theory of International Politics*. New York: McGraw-Hill.

Watkins, Susan Cotts and Ann Swidler (2006), "Hearsay Ethnography: Capturing Collective Life," CCPR-007–06, University of California, Los Angeles.

Watson, Adam (1991), *Diplomacy: The Dialogue Between States*. New York: Routledge.

Welch, David A. (2005), *Painful Choices: A Theory of Foreign Policy Change*. Princeton, NJ: Princeton University Press.

Welch Larson, Deborah and Alexei Shevchenko (2003), "Shortcut to Greatness: The New Thinking and the Revolution in Soviet Foreign Policy," *International Organization* 57(1): 77–109.

Weldes, Jutta (1999), *Constructing National Interests: The United States and the Cuban Missile Crisis*. Minneapolis: University of Minnesota Press.

Wendt, Alexander (1998), "On Constitution and Causation in International Relations," *Review of International Studies* 24 (special issue): 101–17.

(1999), *Social Theory of International Politics.* New York: Cambridge University Press.

(2004), "The State as Person in International Theory," *Review of International Studies* 30(2): 289–316.

(2006), "Social Theory as Cartesian Science: An Auto-Critique from a Quantum Perspective," in Stefano Guzzini and Anna Leander, eds., *Constructivism and International Relations: Alexander Wendt and His Critics*, 181–219. New York: Routledge.

Wenger, Etienne (1998), *Communities of Practice: Learning, Meaning, and Identity.* New York: Cambridge University Press.

White, Stephen (2006), "Russia and 'Europe': The Public Dimension," in Roy Allison, Margot Light and Stephen White, *Putin's Russia and the Enlarged Europe*, 130–59. Oxford: Blackwell.

White, Stephen, Julia Korosteleva and Roy Allison (2006), "NATO: The View from the East," *European Security* 15(2): 165–90.

White, Stephen, Margot Light and Ian McAllister (2005), "Russia and the West: Is There a Values Gap?" *International Politics* 42(3): 314–33.

Williams, Michael C. (2001), "The Discipline of the Democratic Peace: Kant, Liberalism, and the Social Construction of Security Communities," *European Journal of International Relations* 7(4): 525–53.

(2007), *Culture and Security: Symbolic Power and the Politics of International Security.* New York: Routledge.

Williams, Michael C. and Iver B. Neumann (2000), "From Alliance to Security Community: NATO, Russia, and the Power of Identity," *Millennium: Journal of International Studies* 29(2): 357–87.

Williams, Peter (2005), "NATO-Russia Military Cooperation: From Dialogue to Interoperability?" *RUSI Journal* 150(5): 44–7.

Wittgenstein, Ludwig (1958), *Philosophical Investigations.* Oxford: Blackwell.

Wohlforth, William C. (2009), "Unipolarity, Status Competition, and Great Power War," *World Politics* 61(1): 28–57.

Wörner, Manfred (1991), "The Atlantic Alliance in a New Era," *NATO Review* 39(1): 3–8.

Yost, David (1998), "The New NATO and Collective Security," *Survival* 40(2): 135–60.

Yusin, Maksim (1993), "On Eve of Dec. 12 Elections, NATO Gives Yeltsin Unpleasant Surprise," *Izvestia*, December 10, translated in *Current Digest of the Post-Soviet Press* 45(49).

(2001), "Havel Takes Zyuganov's Path," *Izvestia*, November 29, translated in *Current Digest of the Post-Soviet Press* 53(48).

Zehfuss, Maja (2002), *Constructivism in International Relations: The Politics of Reality*. New York: Cambridge University Press.

Zerubavel, Eviatar (1997), *Social Mindscapes: An Invitation to Cognitive Sociology*. Cambridge, MA: Harvard University Press.

Zimmerman, William (2002), *The Russian People and Foreign Policy: Russian Elite and Mass Perspectives, 1993–2000*. Princeton, NJ: Princeton University Press.

Index

Cambridge Studies in International Relations